IN A TAXI NU1 TO SE12

PAUL>> Both those cunts spilt fucking black coffee on my red and grey Air Max 95

JON>> Has anyone ever put together a book on trainers?

PAUL>> That would be a fucking great idea

ELL>> Innit!

JON>> It's a Fucking serious idea

PAUL>> Like a Booth-Clibborn type of thing

JON>> It would be wicked if it was actually like a book which had perforations,
you could rip pages out, and if it had a shoe box, you could actually tear out little . pictures

PAUL>> Develop that idea

JON>> Can you think of how many people are into trainers? Let's do it

ELL>> Yeah

PAUL>> And let's do photographs

ELL>> OK

PAUL>> Yeah, that would rule. Do a mock-up book

ELL>> Yeah with laces

PAUL>> Let's do it

JON>> All you gotta do is put an advert in one of the papers saying
"Would you like your trainers immortalised?"

Published © 1998 by
Booth-Clibborn Editions
12 Percy Street
London
W1P 9FB

Copyright © 1998 Booth-Clibborn Editions
Concept and Art Direction by 'Milk Projects'
Edited by Liz Farrelly, with thanks to Vicky Hayward

ISBN 1 86154 167 8

Distributed world-wide and by direct mail through:
Internos Books
12 Percy Street
London W1P 9FB

First published in paperback 2000

info@booth-clibborn.com
www.booth-clibborn.com

Printed in Hong Kong

www.milkprojects.net

THIS BOOK IS MORE THAN SIMPLY A FOOT FETISHIST'S WET DREAM, BUT I ADMIT TO HAVING HAD MY SUSPICIONS WHEN WE FIRST STARTED OUT. THESE PAGES CONTAIN OPINIONS, LIFESTYLES, CREATIVE ENDEAVOURS, HOPES AND FEARS FROM DISPARATE CORNERS OF THE WORLD. AND ALL BECAUSE FIVE MILK MEN PUT A FEW SEEMINGLY INNOCENT QUESTIONS TO A HIT LIST OF HEROES, PEERS, FRIENDS AND STRANGERS. THOSE RESPONSIBLE FOR THIS COLLECTION OF ANECDOTES, EPHEMERA AND SERIOUS THOUGHTS ARE MILK. ONE DAY WHILE SHARING A TAXI THEY HAD A BIT OF A REVELATION (SEE PREVIOUS PAGE) GAVE ME A CALL AND WE KNOCKED AN IDEA INTO SHAPE BEFORE TESTING IT ON EDWARD BOOTH-CLIBBORN; "A BOOK ON PLIMSOLLS, WELL IF YOU SAY SO."

PUTTING THIS BOOK TOGETHER HAS BEEN A SERIOUS COMMITMENT. IT'S LITERALLY TAKEN A MONTH OF SUNDAYS, AND SATURDAYS, DUE TO DEMANDING DAY JOBS ALL ROUND....AND IT'S MOST DEFINITELY BEEN AN EDUCATION. IF YOU READ THIS BOOK, AND I MEAN REALLY READ THIS BOOK, DON'T JUST LOOK AT THE PICTURES. YOU WILL DISCOVER MUCH MORE THAN YOU BARGAINED FOR. HERE'S HOW PAUL PUT IT TO SNOOP DOGGY DOG, DURING THE FIRST OF HIS MANY INTERVIEWS...

A MONTH OF SUNDAYS

FROM POSING TYPICAL QUESTIONS - SUCH AS "DO YOU REMEMBER THE FIRST PAIR OF TRAINERS YOU EVER WORE?" - WERE TOLD ABOUT SPONSORSHIP DEALS, MARKETING POLICIES, THE COLLECTORS' SCENE, HOW TO TIE YOUR LACES, WHERE TO SHOW-OFF YOUR PRIDES AND JOYS, AND, ABOUT THE LIVES OF THOSE WHO ACTUALLY MAKE THE THINGS.

THE FACT IS TRAINERS/SNEAKERS/KICKS/BASKETS, WHATEVER YOU CALL THEM, FUNCTION AS MUCH MORE THAN MERE PERFORMANCE-ORIENTED COVERINGS FOR YOUR FEET. THE ACT OF CHOOSING A MASS-PRODUCED OBJECT TO WEAR IS EFFECTED BY A COMPLEX SET OF CODES RELATING TO NOTIONS OF INDIVIDUALITY AND EXCLUSIVITY, FITNESS, FASHION AND ANTI-FASHION, PEER-GROUP PRESSURE, WHATEVER. AND AMID THIS MILKY CONSUMERIST SOUP TRAINERS HAVE TAKEN ON MORE MEANINGS THAN SLICED BREAD. THEY'VE BECOME A KIND OF "BLANK" ONTO WHICH MANY, MANY PEOPLE PROJECT ATTITUDES AND IDEAS. IN ALL THE INTERVIEWS MILK DID FOR THIS BOOK, PEOPLE TALKED SO PASSIONATELY ABOUT THEIR "WHATEVERS" THAT WE FELT WE SHOULDN'T STRAIGHT-JACKET THEIR WORDS...SO WE LEFT THEIR ENGLISH AS THEIR ENGLISH. CONSEQUENTLY, THIS IS A BOOK OF MANY DIFFERENT VOICES.

BY THE WAY, NOT EVERYONE IN THIS BOOK WOULD SELL THEIR GRANNY FOR THAT CERTAIN PAIR OF AIR MAX. GREG TATE, A WRITER FROM NEW YORK, PUT IT SO SUCCINCTLY WHEN HE SPOTTED THE COUP..."YOU CAN'T JUST HAVE ONE PAIR, YOU'VE GOT TO BE THE EMELDA MARCOS OF KICKS". READ ON FOR THE STORY GETS DARKER...FROM THE OFFICIAL LINE, AND THOSE PERSONALITIES WHO MAKE TRAINERS OH SO COOL, TO CRAZY OBSESSIONS AND STARK REALITIES.

"WE'RE DOING THIS BOOK WHICH IS A CELEBRATION OF SNEAKER CULTURE AND WE'RE SPEAKING TO PEOPLE FROM SPORT, MUSIC, ART, AND WE'VE GOT ARTISTS AND PHOTOGRAPHERS CONTRIBUTING AND INTELLECTUALS WRITING. THE BOOK IS AN AMALGAMATION FROM ALL AROUND THE WORLD, AND IT'S NOT JUST A HIP HOP THING, CAUSE YOU'VE GOT YOUR SKATERS AND INDIE KIDS, ALTERNATIVE KIDS, THEY WEAR DIFFERENT TYPES OF SHOES....EVEN IN LONDON, IN DIFFERENT PARTS OF LONDON YOU'VE GOT PEOPLE WHO WEAR DIFFERENT SHOES, AND YOU CAN TELL A LOT ABOUT SOMEONE BY THE SHOES THEY WEAR...AND WE'RE JUST TRYING TO CAPTURE THAT AND CELEBRATE IT."

AND SINCE WE BEGAN THIS PROJECT SOME OF THE BIGGEST PLAYERS HAVE BEEN FORCED TO WAKE UP TO THE STARKEST OF REALITIES...WITH THE US MARKET SATURATED AND ONCE EAGER CONSUMERS IN THE FAR EAST FEELING THE PINCH OF RECESSION, SALES ARE DOWN AND JOBS ON THE LINE. EVEN AT THE COMPANY WHICH UNTIL RECENTLY REVELLED IN 150 PER CENT ANNUAL GROWTH, ALLEGEDLY...

"IS THIS BOOK GONNA BE IN THE STATES?" ASKED SNOOP.
"YEAH - WORLD-WIDE."
"IT WILL BE MAJOR."

JUST IN CASE YOU'RE A BIT CONFUSED... THERE ARE CHAPTERS, HONEST!

TRIBAL	=	THE BRANDS
SWEAT	=	SPORT, BECAUSE SUPPOSEDLY TRAINERS ARE FOR SPORT()
TUNES	=	THE INFLUENCE OF MUSICIANS IN THE TRAINER GAME
CANDY	=	PRETTY PICTURES AND LOOKING PRETTY, MEANING FASHION AND ART
ILL	=	ALL THOSE MAD COLLECTORS
REAL	=	SOME OF THE REAL-LIFE CONSEQUENCES OF THE TRAINER INDUSTRY

...THE END

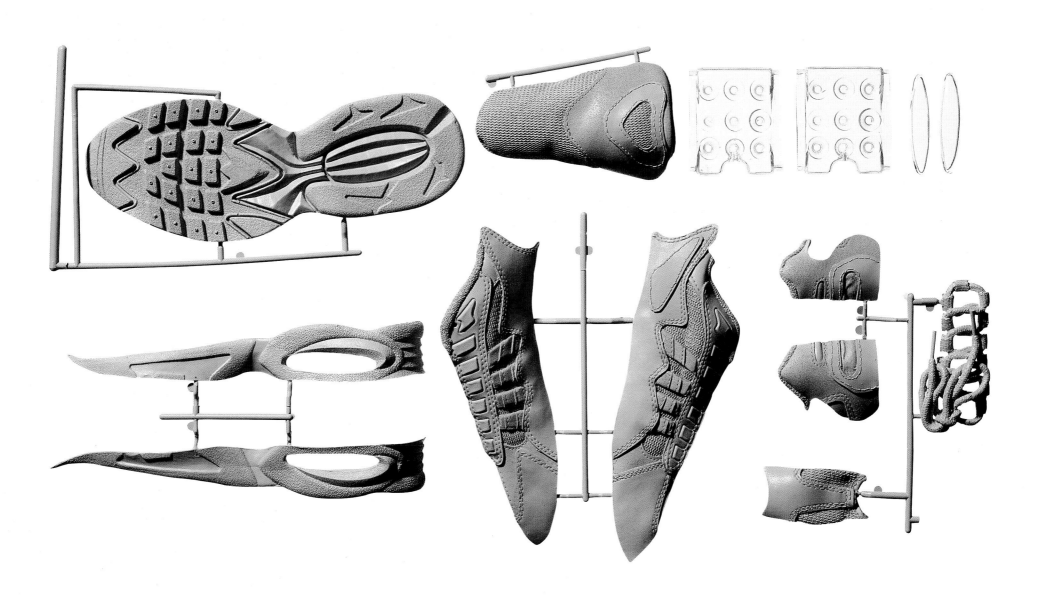

>> YOUR DESIRED SHOE

18:58   ::: . vision@cyberiacafe.net
Welcome to "Speaking in Tongues"...
a live internet chat on you and your
sneakers, trainers, whatever you call
them.

30/01/97
03:52   Joe Perrotto. United States.
Zo1Heat1@aol.com
i love nike

31/01/97
23:35   Hardy, usa
hi is anybody there?

03/02/97
22:48   steve. london. stevenw2@virgin.net
reeboks are top, especially when they
fall to bits.

06/02/97
05:48   tim, usa, tshea23191@aol.com
hey all

11/02/97   12:08
18:20   has anyone checked out the free nike cd
with this month's FHM magazine?

12/02/97   20:31
00:50   uk. sunday@express.co.uk
Date: 10 Feb 97 14:43:58 -0800
From:sunday@express.co.uk
Organization: Express Newspapers
Hello there, We would like to speak
to some trainer enthusiasts about
their love of footwear.
Lucy Miller

10:25   John Hassay, uk
galaxy 2 any comments? nike rip off
or dassler innovation??

10:30   massimo
myself I prefer the ones intended for
woman, the blue and green (cyan and
lime?) and I've already seen a bloke
sporting them.

---

vince. london
BORN IN KOREA DIED IN CALIFORNIA
I did own a pair of weird white and
black Adidas. they were a strange
hybrid of shell-toe and moulded
French mountain rescue snow boot. In
the comfort stakes they wore well. but
as for design longevity...well...the
snow white three striped toe went a
piss yellow hue after only two months
of careful puddle dodging ownership
and the inSOUL's edge pinched the
base of my heel like a witch's crack. I
bought them from Home in London.
they were imported and I knew not
their age. My shoes died in a freak
road incident when Sorren (Silverlake
dweller) drove the offside wheel of his
sky blue Nissan over my right foot, as I
stood kerbside bidding him farewell. I
attempted rescue from beneath the
rubber and in doing so caught the
right side on his blue rusty hull.
Smiling and looking south he put his
foot down and ripped the upper of my
shoe right to the SOUL! identical twins
born in Korea one slain in Silverlake.

hi vince Sneaker-Fucker, Switzerland,
Printnetgmbh@access.ch

The problem is that I have no concept
of male sneaker fashion. I have
NewBalance for jogging, and every
thing else is non-descript for working
around the house. So what
I am asking for is someone to recom
mend some brand names and styles.

Naomi. England.
scun2@central.susx.ac.uk
Just to add to the debate of those
Galaxy things...From a female perspec
tive great we have a sneaker that is
creating a response from men...still I
don't see them very highly..too low to
the ground...need more lift...I tried a
pair and they weren't doing it for my
feet. I need a spring in my step not a
reminder of the days when I did PE
classes in a crap pair of black
Woolworths plimsolls! Might look cool
for the summer...but it would be nice if
Adidas could get more technical and
while they are at it maybe visit a
colour therapist too! Men's trainers are
far better than women's ones...I don't
want to wear pastel shades or aerobic

16/02/97
16:58   did anyone see that program on
Nike the other night on BBC2?

21:42   What about the Converse Chuck
Taylor Allstar. It has been the
canvas high-top since 1917 and
part of American history
since the 1950s.

17/02/97
13:39   glyn kempster, england,
i don't know what the fuck's
going on. i need a reply. ok, ok,
i got the hang of this
now...can't talk long but i've got
some information which may
interest some of you. i presume
everyone's aware of the fall 95
air max (black to grey fade,
screaming green bubbles) for all
of you that didn't catch them first
time round you'll be able to
trundle to your nearest foot lock
er (well in europe at least) and
snap up a sparkling new pair...i
kid you not. oh, and another
thing...especially to naomi, who
complains that women get the
raw deal when it comes to train
er colourways....you'd be sur
prised how many guys out there
are wearing the ladies' colour
ways (probably not realising what
they bought until they got home and looked at
the box). examples? how about the recent
natural/mid blue triax II (very popular with
the fellas)...air max totals. all the
ladies colours selling equally well to the
guys...the cyan/slime galaxy II's...various
colours of GTS...new ladies
triax III (rad blue/emerald)...honestly
the list goes on and on. thing is, people
always seem to think the grass is
greener...no matter what size/gender/age
you're always jealous of other peoples'
trainers...i, however, have no qualms about this
i'll wear any shoes that i can. all phat and
dumpy. galaxy II any comments? hmm. funky
colours maketh not a shoe (although they help).
i'm just still waiting for visible adiprene!)
which apparently is coming soon...wow i
can't wait.

18/02/97
04:50   Adam tait, USA, blesarad

07:43   OoE ChEwY. North America. OoE ChEwY

17:56   ALFREDO. South China, Sir!.
al@fredo.aol.com
looyyyyyyyyyyyyyyyyyyvp8
erxu6zeeeeezzzztalatq47ry
dnfeiu7lrfdu65ehd57rmhrku
cxo76c976l67i75eaAAAAHTS
LY.8OTIUTLTIU/IU'8/IY.D
g. u.k.
oh and by the way, i got my original
air jordan vs (obviously the best jor
dans) off one of my friend's sisters
(yeah, sister!!). i was talking shoes,
when she came to visit (i know, sad)
telling her my dream shoes were the
jordans, but my chances of getting a
pair were slim, and she was like
'are they the ones with the big
reflective tongue?'...yeah why..."i've got
some...bought them in a sale years
ago, then didn't like them, so i never
wore them. i think they're under my
bed...why do you want them?'. how
much? 'no, no money. (she was
offended ha, ha!)) you can have them'
WOOOOOOOH!!! a week later they
arrived. NEVER BEEN WORN (the clear sole a
little yellowed due to age but at least
it shows they're originals). it was fate.
thats all i can say. i was MEANT to own
a pair, they're a little small, but that's
good 'cause it means i don't get tempt
ed to wear them all the time.... jealous?
you should be! HAHAHAHAHAHAHAHA

19:25

21/02/97
04:50   futuratwothousand, U.S., futura@dti.net
Stan Smith 82 velcro Adidas w/bleu
stripes Paris Rue de Louvre. As Darth
would/has and will say...IMPRESSIVE.
Being a NETnerd doesn't guarantee
any live experience????? Is this
LIVE? what'ev's....this site gets book
marked...NO DOUBT...back to
subject matter......the high top blue
suede PUMAs. I buy by the dozen.
have never played me out. headz are
still des. for those...when did you get
those old school jammies ?!?!?!?!?!?!
those are the shit. HINT: buy more.
and be happy...because they discontinue
any popular styles.
http://home.dti.net/futura/index.htm

23:21   bola. UK/london. bam@dircon.co.uk
hi there peeps.

24/02/97
11:45   Carmen Pryce. England.
pryce.carmen@mtvne.com
Elliott. can you get me a free pair of
trainers. I prefer Diadora.

.26/02/97
15:36   g.. uk.. fil3ssc@LEEDS.ac.uk
1. airmax (autumn '96) 2. airmax 1
(white leather) 3. airmax uptempo
(b/w) 4. airmax cw (white/blue) 5. air
max triax extra 6. air zoom flight 1 7.
air zoom turf (red/black) 8. air jordan
V's (black) 9. air jordan XIs (black) 10.
air marauder 11. air terra tor 12. air
darwin canvas 13. air darwin canvas
(b/w) 14. nike cortez II 15. nike bruin
16. nike gts 17. air pegasus (1989) 18.
adidas superstar (w/w) 19. adidas
super star b/w 20. adidas proshell
(b/w) 21. adidas campus (b/w) 22. adi
das campus (brn/wht) 23. adidas stan
smith (blu/wht) 24. adidas campus
(blu/wht) 24. puma clyde (b/b)
25. airwalk 19oz. 26. air force V
(knackered)...my trainers.

11:37   has anyone checked out the new puma
skatestyle shoe? shouldn't trainer compa
nies who say they only make shoes for
athletes steer clear of the fashion band
wagon and stick to what they know? the
day that new balance and saucony come
out with a pony skateshoe imitation I'll eat my
cat (leave it to those who know. DCs, etnies and
VANS.
so puma, nike, travel fox get off!!!!!

28/02/97
15:19   g. blighty
i agree. brands really should
stick to what they know. stay in their
own field of expertise. perfect
that before they move on-(and
NOBODY has made the perfect shoe
yet). but wait...didn't airwalk make
high-tech looking high tops for skating.
now they make sorry looking retro
shoes (yes, i do own a pair). aren't they
jumping on the skateshoe bandwagon
as much as anybody else? and why
loose one of the best logos i've ever
seen (remember the airwalk man?) it's
all about credibility, nike make shoes.
they don't make coats. ok, they do. but
badly which is exactly my point. so i
buy nike shoes...and i buy coats from
north face. helly hansen or carhartt.
they make coats. it pisses me off to see
big companies prostituting their hard-
won respect as a leading sports com
pany, so they can sell cheap crap
clothing to the local scallies.

02/03/97
19:40   James Collett. UK.
berniecollett@msn.com
If anyone cares, my top trainers to
date are my shells and my old mark 3
red, black and white Jordans which
don't fit me anymore. ps - nice site, say
hi to Hayley

04/03/97
12:41   E.B.. primal@dds.nl
Ever tried swimming or showering with
sneakers? I often swim with my new
Nike air Max 97. It's great! Please send
comment!

06/03/97
08:08 =.   uk. vision@cyberiacafe.net
never tried it...why do you do it? To
clean them at the same time or for
that squidgy underfoot feeling?

15:29   shoefreak1. usa. gkzg73a
wassup

12/03/97
23:41   Russ B.. USA. russb@harris-pub.com
Is there anybody out there?
Okay, I've got a pair of Nike Air
Revolutions in size 8, never worn,
that I don't have any use for. I'd be
willing to trade for another interesting
pair of Nike b-ball shoes in a 9 1/2
(Jordans?) or sell to anyone who
makes a reasonable offer. Any takers?

I got the constant-reloading.grammar
-reorganizing blues. Someone asked the most
I've paid for a pair of Air Jordans, and fortu
-nately, it's only been $150, for the new
ones and the black-on-black patent leather
ones. My 'vintage' red-black-and-white origi
nals were $5 at a good will who didn't realize
what they had. Of course, this was a few years
ago, before everything got so crazy. How much
WOULD I pay is another story. For the right pair
(baby blue and white or black and red originals:
white on white IIs (hi or lo), or the red gray and
white IIIs in the right size (9.5) in the right con
dition (I'd like the box, but 9.5) don't have to be
unworn), well. I'd be willing to take a pretty big
hit. I'm still on the lookout for a pair of
blue/black/white Air Revolutions, as well as a
pair of those green/black/grey Air Max's (who
isn't?). Funny. how I seem to gravitate towards
Nike. I mean, I wouldn't turn down a pair of
original Puma Clydes, or Converse Docs (Pro
Leather), or Adidas Superstars with the blue
and red stripes, or even those Adidas Ewing
high-tops (where will I EVER find those???).
Nike remains the shit.

24/03/97
14:11   Aaron Scott. U.S.A. ascott12@aol.com

25/03/97
13:23   Dot, U.K., ff.a@aol.com
How come NIKE is so popular in
AMERICA? I agree size isn't everything.

13:36   Holly Wrenbeck, England, ff.a@.com
You guys are pathetic!

13:37   Dot, U.K., ff.a@.com
No! We just like sneakers

15:55   George W Graves, USA.
rdrunner@capital.net

21:20   rachel, norway, rogert@online.no
which sneaker store is the best in london?

13/04/97
01:18   From:Roger Tangen rogert@online.no
hello where do I find the best sneaker
store in london?

01:23   depends what you're after. For skating
try Home, Bond, Slam City Skates.
Insane, Low Pressure. for sports
models. JD Sports, Lillywhites. Cobra.
Offspring, Frontiers. For Rare stuff try Simon
Gunning (you'll find him on our links page), or
for very new school try Kokon to zai (Greek
Street W1) latest Japenese imports. Duffer of St
George. For second hand Colin Hope in
Camden Market. Good Luck!

14/04/97

02:20 Bob, U.S.A, btai@uiuc.edu

04:04 Bert Moshier, USA,
sneakers@os2rus.com
Visit alt.clothing.sneakers and discuss
your sneakers. Also the Sneaker G/PG
FAQ (Frequently Asked Questions) list
http://www.os2rus.com

22:36 simon gunning, england,
101462.366@compuserve.com
i would love to have a sneakers want
ed flashing next to my name "SNEAK
ERS WANTED" FLASH FLASH ETC

15/04/97

07:49 greggie, USA, greggie@onramp.net
anyone here?

15:43 Jack, UK, guinpub1@itl.net
Any collectors out there?
Seeking avid private collectors for big
publishing project. Please e-mail as
soon as possible. Thanks.

17/04/97

21:07
Subject: I'm looking for......Date: Thu,17 Apr
1997 17:21:33 +0900
From: =?iso-2022-
jp?B?GyRCPj5CPBsoSg==?= VJ6J-
MTMR@asahi-net.or.jp
To: vision@cyberiacafe.net
Hello. I'm Japanese. I have wanted
"Adidas Master" or "Stan Smith (red)"
for a long time. But I have never seen
them. I will be happy if you give me
good news. Masahiro Matsumura

19/04/97

07:23 Charlie, USA,webmaster@sneakers.pair.com
I think the rest of the world must be in
bed -- dreaming of sneakers?

18:50 John Wallace III, USA,
jhwiii@engin.umich.edu
I would just like to say hi and ask
everyone to come and visit John's
Swoosh Page.

18:53
Anyone there? into sneakers/trainers,
Especially Modern stuff.

18:55 John Wallace III, USA,
jhwiii@engin.umich.edu
I recently got this message and
thought that this would be a good
place to get the answer. Please
respond to my address and I will write
back to the owners. Or just post it
here. Anyway here is the message: In
1984, my wife and I got a pair of
Nike running shoes from a friend that
worked for Nike at that time. These
shoes look like running shoes, and
they may be called "aloha". I can't tell
from the shoe, and we no longer have
the boxes. What I can tell you, is my
pair has bright red heel and toe,
suede leather with a bright yellow
Nike swoosh. The balance of the
uppers are nylon canvas with a distinct
Hawaiian print of flowers in multiple
colors. My friend told us the shoes
were part of a limited edition run of
5,000 shoes that were made for a
Nike sponsored Hawaii Ironman con
test. Thanks!

19.:46 Liz @paulshouse, large,UK
Funny you should say that. I was just flick
ing my boon, page 77, vol 2, while Elliott
picked the fleas off Adidas, and spotted
said florid spats. I can't believe my eyes, I
thought, so groovy. My surfing friend Jon
would really like those! Do we have a simi
lar taste in sneakers do you think?

20/04/97

Charlie, USA. webmaster@sneakers.pair.com
I think of myself as a Converse fan
(although I have been accused by certain com
petitors of being on the Nike payroll).
Converse does have the advantage that they
keep their shoes in stock for more than one
shipment. By the time you find out that a given
Nike is any good, they've discontinued it. I real
ly can't believe that the folks in Beaverton push
back the walls of technical improvement so
rapidly that they have to introduce a new line
four times a year. Of course, it does keep "THE
KIDS" buying. (Or does it?)
The latest news out on the wire is that FOOT
STAR thinks the market is slowing down.)
Another question about Nike: What do you
expect will happen when the Rudy (NIKE AIR)
patent expires later this year? Will we see
everybody else go with airbags or will they stick
with their respective technologies? But, I do
think Nike are taking the piss with prices...

00:56
BLACK LOOKS BEST. HATE WHITE
SHOES....

00:59 Charlie, USA, webmaster@sneakers.pair.com
Although it gets too repetitive at times: I
can remember a few years ago when
everything was black. Now, there's a lot
fewer all-black shoes out there.

01:20
How do you keep them fresh

01:25 Charlie, USA, webmaster@sneakers.pair.com
I had a friend who thought the best
thing for any pair of sneakers was a
trip through the washing machine. He
had some of the weirdest looking
leather Nikes I've seen...
My particular technique is "good sweat
[illegible] and a good airing." My floor is
[illegible] with airing out sneakers.

01:57 [illegible] parslowc@cadvision.com
[illegible] Chuck Taylor fans out

02:02
[illegible] (new joints) Get with
the program

02:05 Bob Tai, U.S.A. btai@uiuc.edu

08:36 [illegible] bittner@purdue.edu
hello

13:06 simon wilden, uk, simon.wilden@jwt.co.uk
Where can I get hold of some early-80s
Diadora Borg Gold (new, NOT used)

13:15 simon wilden, uk, simon.wilden@jwt.co.uk
We must act now to ban forever the evil
influence of the football trainer (horrible
black astro-turf numbers) and also any
product from North Wave. Definitly the British
Knights of the late-90s

13:38 Frank, usa, tesser@earthlink.net
Hey! What's this place?

19:04 Charlie, USA,
On the other hand, as long as there are
teenage musicians there will be a
demand for black high-top Chucks.

22:02 g., blighty
wow...doesn't charlie know an awful lot about
converse! but why? lets face it, converse were,
without a doubt one of the main players in the
athletic shoe industry...but unfortunately NOT
any more. sorry charlie, their new stuff is crap.
it is quite plainly a futile attempt to claw back
some of their once huge share of the athletic
shoe market. ok, so why do 80% of players in
the NBA wear nike shoes (when only around
20% of that huge majority, are directly spon
sered by nike?), because of the superior cush
ioning, stability and responsiveness? well, yes
of course, but the main reason is they are far
cooler shoes...period. the only reason converse
became a market leader is because they were
there first, and the only reason they're still here
is because there's people like charlie about.
nothing personal of course. remember the
original hi-top dr.j (pref.wht/red), gorgeous
shoes, absolute beauties, and have you seen
what they've done to them...........

21/04/97

01:52 Charlie, USA, webmaster@sneakers.pair.com
Well, even the Dr. J 2000 isn't as much
of a monstrosity as some of the Nikes.
Remember the Nikes with the big "AIR" on the
side? Oh, I'd rather forget....As to cushioning,
what will Nike do when the Rudy (AIR) patent
expires this year?

04:41 jbakator, canada, jbakator@cyberus.ca
Is anyone out there???

06:04 Bertram Moshier, USA,
I'm here!

08:51 Anders Blomgren, Sweden, espan
drillo@hotmail.com
ella ella espandrillos

20:02 Dave, Mongolia, davew@tinet.ie
Greetings from the gobi

11:12 sean, ireland, leesidejames@tinet.ie
huh?

14:28 g., blighty
charlie, when the patent for air cushioning runs
out (a nike rep told me it already has, but that's
beside the point) converse will probably
copy it. if they've got any guts and wish to
maintain any respect, they'll either stick with
that crap react juice, or preferably find a new
technology (all of their own). the air more
uptempo (the one with the big "air"on the side)
was simply an air uptempo II, restyled for
Scottie Pippen for maximum exposure on
court in the olympics. it was air in your face on
tv. it sold a lot of shoes, even at £120 a throw.
aggressive marketing is nike's strong point.
the shoe was simply a means to an end. it's
going out on a limb to do different things that
keeps nike at the top of the market
(and converse near the bottom) converse's idea
of aggressive marketing is larry johnson in a
dress! sorry, didn't work for me. i want to see
some more collections displayed for public
inspection (ridicule?). add to my list: leather
cortez (b/w), air increment (wlk/gry), air mad
max (original colours) and i'm waiting for nike
to send me some air skarn (grn/blu)...should be
any day now! i buy trainers, not to be fashion
able but 'cause i like them, simple as that. if i
wanted to be "fashion able" i'd buy reebok clas
sics or triax. if i wanted to be "trendy" i'd be buy
ing vintage shelltoes or hunting down the last
stocks of footscapes (even though i think
they're shit). get my point. i'd just like to take a
moment to say something which really frus
trates me...the finite lifespan of a shoe. why do
shoes have to wear out? why can't they last for
ever? why can't i be buried in my beloved jor
dans all shiny and new. it's just not fair.
you know that every time you pull on a
pair of kicks it's another day nearer the
bin. and can you replace them? no.

30/04/97

13:04 cg evans, england,
cge23@orlando.umds.ac.uk
nike air slant rock in my book. any of you fred
dy hubbards out there? actually I have a ques
tion, one of our supporters has a serious prob
lem with foot odour. is there a medical condition
which may be the cause?

14:25 vince, uk
it's all about soap between the toes, towel dried
feet, talc, in-souls(!), off days and quality shoes.
and if you've got the cash (puffy has!) a pedi
cure

02/05/97

07:25 =
Hi vince, what are you doing up so
early?

04/05/97

14:25 vince
chef are you in the space.
anyone check out Blair's Filas?

10/05/97

18:23 g. blighty
what's going on? i spend time and effort,
pressurising my superiors at foot locker
to meet with adidas requesting previ
ously unreleased (apart from their origi
nal release) shoes we've all been wait
ing for. this could well happen....foot locker has
a huge amount of clout when it comes to manu
facturers, so c'mon fuckin' well help me out.
WHAT DO YOU WANNA SEE AGAIN? i've gotta
hand in a report on monday, so far it's just
shoes i want. i want YOUR opinions....quickly
now.

16:10 hayley
my favourite trainers right now are those adi
das that alistair's got, the xtrs in orange, but
you can't get them in ladies! out of the ones I've
got, well it's my green airmax, the ones that
everyone wants. I bought them about a year and
a half ago from JD and they cost £59.99 and
how much are they charging in camden mar
ket? how much? £160!!! laters, I'm rolling with
the collick!!!
ààààààààà

16:11 vince
hayley, why do you like them? do people eye
your feet with envy?

16:12 hayley
I just like 'em! and they're rare!

16:30 aj hill, UK, ah6342@bris.ac.uk
I just started a business (HILL
BROS. UK) which imports and exports
US and 'vintage'

18:33 mike c meredith, usa, kwords@aol.com
good sneakas are just so hard to throw
away. my ex-wife made it seem so easy -
maybe that explains why she is my ex.

15/05/97

14:40 jonc, pal@online.rednet.co.uk
aj post up what you're selling or planning to!

15:37 =, uk, vision@cyberiacafe.net
CLASSIC QUOTE. Anyone else out
there had any split ups with girlfriends/
boyfriends over their sneakers?

15:59 MATT KISS, USA, KISS@ONLINE.EMICH.EDU
My first pair of nikes I got when I was three and
I've had them ever since. I'm nine years old. My
friends think I'm obsessed......
cause I got nike skates and lots of nike shoes,
shirts, hats and my friends say I've never seen
you not wear nikes clothes or shoes.

16:44 GAGI, USA Newark BRICK CITY,
gugaro@conductor.com

17.45 g. blighty
I hate FILA kicks and don't like REEBOK. NIKE
are phat...DKNY kicks too. But NIKE are no
doubt tight and always will be...Shell Toe
Adidas...got a pair of them i still rock. they've
been discontinued for a long time. unlike futura
2000 i can't afford to buy trainers in bulk. i
have a quick question for all you skaters out
there. a few years back (probably around
1990), vision did an amazing shoe i think it was
called the DV8...a mid top, black leather with a
white panel round the ankle with a massive red
"V" on either side of the ankle. really dumpy,
phat looking boot. are they still available? i
would absolutely kill for a new pair (uk.8/8.5)...i
think they may have had lace protectors
(remember those!). i've got a question for all
you guys across the pond. in an old nike cata
logue i was drooling over some baseball shoes
called cornerstones. real simple (they come in
blu, blk, wht, red etc.) nice swoosh, and one of
those little fold over tongue lace-protectors.
what do they retail at? the only turf shoes we
get in the good old u of k. are the turf maxs,
turf raiders, but NO actual baseball shoes. if i
could get a pair into this country they'd be vir
tually unique. if you can get access to a copy of
the current u.s. nike footwear catalogue, just
photocopy the relevant baseball page(s) and
send them to me. then i can see what's avail
able. and when my mate goes to the
states he can pick me up a pair. you know
i'd do the same for you...cheers.

23/05/97

01:10 Does anybody remember a really cheap
make of trainers (Winfield?) that Marks &
Spencer (I think) used to sell in England
that were supposed to look like the super
cool Adidas trainers back in the 70s?
I used to get those from my mum all the
time 'cos they had a similar 3 stripe theme,
but were a fraction of the price.
Unfortunately they wouldn't last very long
either as they were very "plasticy". I won
der if anyone out there has kept a pair for
old time's sake - a sad thought but
it's possible!

01:13 Subject: Re: Sneakers
From: Photo4u@aol.com
To: vision@cyberiacafe.net
I have a wee thatched cottage in Ireland where I
spend my summers...other than them referring
to sneakers as basketball boots I have no other
information...In Belize there is a place called
Orange Walk Town a small town filled mostly
with cocaine dealers...the shops carry nothing
but boom boxes and sneakers...it would most
certainly merit a photograph...I was in the
Adidas factory in Taiwan photographing sneak
er production...they have since moved to
lower wage scales in Vietnam and
Thailand...perhaps I should do a story for
National Geographic on sneakers around the
world!!!

18:07 JGH, USA, FECK666@aol.com
The only pair of sneakers I own
are Adidas Superstars....27 pairs
to be exact

24/05/97

02:02 I am very glad to see you're covering the child
labor issue with regard to manufacturing...Nike
pays 20 cents to laborers then pays Tiger
Woods 70 million to wear them!!!!!

03:27 michelle, usa
Hello.... I just have to say that my Asics Gel
Deuces never fail to get noticed whenever I
wear them. They are like Lamborghinis for the
feet - very tough! Best in the black/white/
reflective blue low-top incarnation, skip the
green high-tops. And an added bonus - they're
really comfortable. the gel really does work.
Great for walking/stair-climbing.

15:38 g.. blighty.
ok, ok, it's taken me a while to pluck
up the courage, i'm coming.........
out of the closet....i admit that i have the rather
sad habit of padding my shoes out severely
with rolled up socks...................ok, if i
designed shoes (which most of you who come
to this site would love to do) then they would be
fatter (phatter?). nike try to do this by simply
making the laces cover more of the shoe. shell
toes, campus, stan smiths, all have that open
toe kinda design, which means you can make
them really over the top phat, if you so desire. it
started with certain shoes (things like chris
webbers or uptempos, 'cause they've got elas
tic straps across them which i didn't have the
heart to cut off (a brand new £109.99 shoe, are
you surprised?), took me a couple of days of
constantly stretching the straps before they
were loose enough, but i've got them on now
and they look fucking wicked. the habit gradu
ally spread to all my shoes and they look so
much better. i challenge anyone to put one of
my artificially enhanced shoes next to an exact,
yet tightly laced shoe, and to honestly tell me
the strangled shoe looks better......and if you did
i know you'd be lying. anybody out there in the
phat trainer camp, we should pull together and
destroy all these puny skinny shoes...almost
blasphemy. stylish trainers aren't so much
WHAT you wear, as HOW you wear it.

28/05/97

04:33 Jesredstar, usa, jesredstar@aol.com
I have a pair of Adidas running shoes.
They are the most awesome pair of shoes I
have ever owned, regretfully though, they dis
continued the model and I have to treat them
very carefully. They get compliments wherever I
go. Adidas always discontinues the good
sneakers..they need to stop.

23:05 Russ Bengtson, USA, russb@harris- pub.com
Air Jordan. Air Jordan. AIR Jordan. Is
it the shoe? Of course it is. All the Jordans ever
made stack up against any other shoe – in
comfort, style, and just plain badassedness.
It's either the Jordan 1s or 3s. Don't know if
I'm totally down with the new ones, they did
some ankle damage (a li'l tight), but worse
comes to worse I'll just leave 'em in the future
generation like I did with the black-on-black
patent leather and the grey-on-white low-tops.
Still in the box? I've got the aforementioned
Jordans, the Jordan 2 reissues, a pair of gold-
on-white Adidas Superstar high-tops, a pair of
blue-and-red-on-white Nike Air Force pumps,
a pair of red-and-black-on-white Nike Air
Revolutions (size 8, that I'd like to unload), and
a pair of olive-and-black Air Jordan 10s. The
new hype stuff? The Iversons, the black-and-
silver Uptempos, the red-on-black Jordans....

19:09 g., u.k.

ah yeah...respect to russ b. now there's a man who knows a nice pair of shoes when he sees it. one thing i will say is, i think the jordans went through a bit of a slump (mk 8,9,10) but i think they've picked up. the patent ones were the turning point. and the grey and white low tops. they were NICE, although them not being released in the uk was a bit of a pain in the arse. russ, at least you could have bought a pair if you'd have wanted, spare a thought for us poor folks across the pond who only get to buy what someone thinks we might want to buy. p.s. anyone got a pair of olive/blk air raids they wanna sell?

14/06/97

21:21 J Mega, usa
hello?

16/06/97

14:34 =, uk, sneaker@pemail.net
i suggest all you sneaker lovers check out the BOYCOTT NIKE SITE. Think you know everything about sneakers? What about how they are made and the conditions of the workers. Forced overtime, corporal punishment, sexual abuse, etc. find it all at http:www.saigon.com~nike

14:55
hey, did anyone go down to that launch for the air zoom in battersea power station?
wick wick wack
not a lot more I can say really.

17/06/97

02:46 puma-dood, usa, numantin@creative.net

18/06/97

17:31 Alexandra, England/Greece.

19/06/97

09:07
I have met a person who has a trainer fetish and who has been arrested for it on several occasions! At that point in time, I was way into the old school Pumas. Both pairs (white leather, black stripe) (blue suede, white stripe) wore out and got tossed long ago. I haven't really had any favorites since. Collecting? I don't really collect per sé. I just have a cool set of tennies though I'll probably add to it once I've money again. Hasta la rasta. Puma Dood. What I am most into is girls who wear those tennis shoes. Bike messengers, skaters, graff-writers. what my friend likes to call "militant tomboys".

10:15
We are threesome, my left shoes, my right shoe and me. I remember where we first met, my Air Max 95s. and I, it was on a wet February day in a Department Store. I know the girl that introduced us was aware of the glint in my eye. I don't know if it was just the occasion, but I left a small part of my heart with that girl. I hope she still has it, hasn't given it away free with £30 worth of Umbro equipment. I was sagging behind my mother who was buying two grey tops when something hooked the corner of my eye. then gripped my heart and pulled me across the ground floor. I weaved past the pretty perfumes, ran along the racks of shirts and arrived at the grotto of the sports section. Just below the Adidas Sambas and above those anaemic looking Hi-Tec Shadows sat, majestically, what had caused my heart to beat so fast. I picked them up in my own fair hands and the clouds outside seemed to clear, letting a soft golden ray of sun settle on the Green and Grey Nike Shoe. They had come all the way from Oregon, USA, home of the goddess of victory, to rest under the neon lights of the sports department. An assistant appeared and spake thus "We only have one pair of size nines left in those, my love." Then I knew I was the chosen one for I am size nine. I paid my #110 and left the shop. Then I went back in again when I remembered my mother. Since that day we have parted company only briefly, we go everywhere together. we look after each other. We do get looks sometimes but it is one in which I can see that same glint in the eye. People wonder from whence they come, they want to touch but don't know if they should. want to stare but are sometimes too overcome. And yesterday the first pilgrim arrived at my door.

24/06/97

16:15 richard, UK, maaf45@dial.pipex.com
Any other guyz in London into sneaker fucking ?

25/06/97

01:47 Chuck, usa, ces2@eos.net
I just purchased a pair of Nike's Zoom Air...Now all I need is someone to share them with...

11:02
have you ever had any drawbacks from fucking your sneaks? Like laces getting caught under the rim or catching athletes cock from your dirty insoles?

27/06/97

11:18 Julia, UK, jaf@ic.ac.uk
As far as fucking them goes - I couldn't comment, I've never tried it!

13:07 Lily, England, jojo@easynet.co.uk
Fucking your trainers, that's so sad. Trainers can be cared for, groomed and bragged about but not shagged. Why don't sneaker manufacturers put Odour Eaters in their shoes as standard!?

19:03 John Wallace III. USA.
jhwiii@engin.umich.edu
I'm looking for old pictures, stories, memories of the first Nike shoes and even the original one if someone remembers them. Please email me what you have. Does anyone know how to get a pair of old NIKE Air Pegasus Racers? Those were/are my all-time favorite shoes and I ran PRs in the mile and 2 mile runs with them. If you have a new/almost new pair please email me and I will send my address. I'll even pay $$ for them. Hope to hear from some sneaker store, sneaker museum, sneaker owner or someone!!! My first Nike were those waffle numbers in blue/lt blue

21:28 Achim, Germany, Sven@aol.com
Yeah watz up?

22:32 UK
Ola amigos, do ya'll like movies with gladiators in them? Has anyone heard of the serial sneaker? Well apparently there is this person who breaks into people's homes and steals the innersoles of their sneakers and puts them down his black pvc pants - strange ! But I just love the feel of them.

23:59 Charlie, USA, webmaster@sneakers.pair.com
Black PVC pants or sneaker innersoles?

31/06/97

01/07/97

18:20 tuff enuff, u.k,mchu5jo1@fs2.ee.umist.ac.uk
I love garage and hip hop, Long live Todd Terry and Wu Tang Clan! I've lost my love for Nike. I seem to have the craving for white leather Reeboks with "ICE" clear soles.

18:32 Jr. Vas'Qez, Manchester,UK, msrx5ka1@fs1.ec.man.ac.uk
YO! ARE THERE ANY WOMEN OUT THERE WHO WANT TO TALK ABOUT SNEAKERS, OR ANY OTHER STUFF? HEY TALK TO ME !!!!!!!!!!

18:34 Tuff Enuff, England, mchu5jo1@fs2.ee.umist.ac.uk
I find women in white leather Reeboks quite a turn on! Especially at garage raves. What sneakers do u wear Mr.Jr Vas'Qez? What sneakers do u wear Derrick?

02/07/97

02:08 From: Victoirepr@aol.com
To: vision@cyberiacafe.net
i love all baskets but i prefere really the jordan shoes. i have maybe 25 baskets and special one: compessed basket: so long life and i hope see your book: bye

02:09 fructuoso@arrakis.es
HI, We're GAM, a guide for alternative cultural events and trends in Madrid. We've become aware of UP COLLECTIVE through the magazine MILES AHEAD; and MDB, UK with whom we have contacts. We're specially interested in the book you're about to publish on cult trainers. The trainers trend is not so developed here due to availability problems but it is starting to develop and we're thinking of doing a piece for our July issue. (We have a trainer freak in our midst). Waiting for your answer ASAP. We'll try and contact some of these folk and what we could do is give your web site as reference in our piece so they can get in direct contact with you. We'll probably update on progress in each month's issue if that's cool with you guys. Is it possible for you to send images'n'stuff by normal post as well? Keep on truckin'. GAM

08/07/97

19:46 Eric Filardo, USA, a0320@aol.com

10/07/97

04:56 Doug, Ontario
Hi all

18:36 duifje, holland, duifje@duifje.demon.nl
ik snap er niks van?

22:11 Eric. USA, A0320@aol.com
Does anyone know where I can find some old style high tops (1991). I am looking for the Nike Air 180 Pumps, and The original Reebok Pumps? Drop me an e-mail for any suggestions. Also the Chris Weber Nike Air Max 1994.

11/07/97

23:12 Malissa, France, malissa@easynet

13/07/97

09:55 James Clarke, jameclar@dk-uk.com

15/07/97

7:38 muir., Hong Kong, tamuir@asiaonline.net

10:06 vincent uk
I've got to tell you guys that I've been told by a couple of people about other books in production right now and they too are about sneakers!!!! If I'm not mistaken you tools were the originators....nothing's sacred least of all an idea!!! good luck to you and a note to all browsers 'accept no imitation'!!!

JUST AFTER WW1: HERZOGENAURACH, GERMANY: ADOLF DASSLER STARTS MAKING SHOES IN HIS BACKYARD. 1926: FATHER, CHRISTOLF AND BROTHER, RUDOLF LEAVE THE LOCAL SHOE FACTORY TO JOIN HIM. FIRST PAIR OF FOOTBALL BOOTS WITH NAILED-ON CLEATS. 1936: BERLIN OLYMPICS: US ATHLETE JESSE OWENS WINS FOUR GOLD MEDALS, BREAKS TWO WORLD RECORDS AND ONE OLYMPIC RECORD, WEARING DASSLERS. 1948: RUDOLF AND ADOLF SPLIT. RUDOLF STARTS RUDA, LATER CHANGED TO PUMA. ADOLF CHANGES NAME TO ADIDAS AND THE TWO SUPPORTING STRIPES BECOME THREE. 1954: WORLD CUP: VERY MUDDY FINAL. GERMAN UNDERDOGS BEAT HUNGARY WITH INCREASED TRACTION BY SWOPPING ADIDAS REPLACEABLE CLEATS AT HALF TIME. 1956: MELBOURNE OLYMPICS: ADI'S SON HORST GIVES NEW FOUR-SPIKE TRACK SHOES TO BEST ATHLETES. 1960: ROME OLYMPICS: RUDI PAYS ARIMIN HARRY TO SWITCH TO PUMA AND WINS A GOLD. PRECEDENT IS SET. 1968: ADI AND RUDI SUE EACH OTHER LOADS. 1970: ADIDAS HAS 16 FACTORIES, 6 SALES COMPANIES, PRODUCE 22,000 PAIRS OF SHOES DAILY, IN OVER 140 MODELS. 275 WORLD TRACK AND FIELD RECORDS HAVE BEEN BROKEN IN ADIDAS. 1970: THE SUPERSTAR IS LAUNCHED, ADIDAS'S FIRST BASKETBALL SHOE DESTINED FOR AMERICAN MARKET, ALONG WITH THE PROMODEL, THE HIGH TOP VERSION. 1971: MADISON SQUARE GARDEN, NEW YORK: "THE FIGHT OF THE CENTURY" BETWEEN MOHAMMED ALI AND JOE FRAZIER. INSCRIBED BOOTS FROM BOTH FRAZIER (WINNER) AND ALI, WERE SENT TO DASSLER'S PERSONAL MUSEUM. 1972: MUNICH OLYMPICS: FRANK SHORTER WINS MARATHON IN ADIDAS. JOGGING BOOMS IN AMERICA. 1975: ADIDAS PRODUCTION UP TO 130,000 PAIRS OF SHOES DAILY. WARY OF RIP-OFFS, THE TREFOIL AND ROUNDED TYPEFACE ARE COMBINED INTO A NEW TRADEMARK. 1978: ADI IS INDUCTED IN THE US SPORTING GOODS MANUFACTURERS ASSOCIATION HALL OF FAME. SEPTEMBER 9, ADI DIED, AGED 77. 1979: TOP TEN BASKETBALL MODEL LAUNCHED. LOOKED WEIRD. PROVED TOO RADICAL FOR ALL BUT HARDCORE. INCREASINGLY ADIDAS PRODUCTS ARE DIFFICULT TO FIND, EXPENSIVE AND THE US-MADE PRODUCTS SUFFER FROM BAD WORKMANSHIP. 1984: MICHAEL JORDAN BEGS TO BE SIGNED TO ADIDAS, BUT THEY GIVE NO SPECIAL INCENTIVE AND HE RELUCTANTLY TAKES NIKE'S BETTER DEAL. 1986: RUN DMC TOP THE CHARTS WITH "MY ADIDAS". 1987: APRIL 9, HORST'S UNTIMELY DEATH. THE FAMILY DECIDE TO SELL. A FRENCH INVESTMENT BANKER AND MINISTER OF URBAN AFFAIRS, BERNARD TAPIE, BUYS 80% OF SHARES FOR $305.9 MILLION. ROB STRASSER AND PETER MOORE, EX-NIKE MARKETING GURUS, START SPORTS, INC. AND CONSULT FOR ADIDAS. THEY LAUNCH THE EQUIPMENT LINE, FEATURING THE BEST OF ADIDAS. 1993: ADIDAS FLOURISHING IN US. DISTRIBUTION CENTRE IN SPARTANBURG, SOUTH CAROLINA WINS AN INDUSTRY AWARD. SPORTS, INC. BOUGHT OUT BY ADIDAS. IT BECOMES ADIDAS AMERICA, WITH STRASSER AS PRESIDENT. CREDIT LYONNAIS BUYS TAPIE'S SHARE OF ADIDAS AG AND ROBERT LOUIS-DREYFUS, EX-SAATCHI AND SAATCHI TAKES OVER AS CHAIRMAN. ROB STRASSER DIES ON OCTOBER 30. 1994: ADIDAS RISEN FROM NUMBER 8 TO NUMBER 3 RANKING IN US MARKET. 1995: MADONNA WEARS OLD SCHOOL TO MTV MUSIC AWARDS. AND THE REST IS HISTORY!!

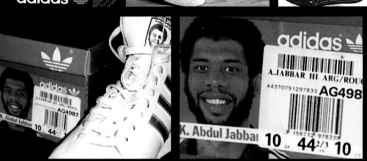

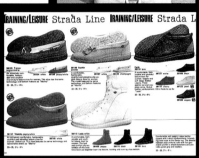

PHILIP H. KNIGHT FOUNDED BLUE RIBBON SPORTS IN 1971, IMPORTING THE ONITSUKA TIGER SHOE FROM JAPAN. RENAMED NIKE IN THE LATE 70S, AFTER THE GREEK GODDESS OF VICTORY, KNIGHT PAID A PORTLAND GRAPHIC DESIGNER $35 FOR THE SWOOSH LOGO

WORTH IT

CASH REGISTER, AND ILLICIT NOTES TAKEN FROM
SUMMER 98 CATALOGUE IN NIKETOWN

DERICK PROCOPE
DP: NIKETOWN IS JUST PURE SPORT. LIKE TO GO TO THE GYM. NEED A PAIR OF SNEAKERS? IT'S AN UPPER WEST SIDE SPORTS STORE.

=: WHAT I FOUND, WHICH WAS QUITE FUNNY, WAS THAT WHEN I PICKED UP A SHOE TO LOOK AT IT, THE ASSISTANTS WERE ASKING
"WHAT ARE YOU GOING TO DO, ARE YOU GOING TO JOG IN IT?" I SAID, "NO, I JUST WANT TO WEAR IT, THAT'S IT". LEAVE ME ALONE
BUT I LIKE THE WAY THEY DISPLAY THINGS. IT'S ALMOST LIKE AN ART INSTALLATION. I THOUGHT THAT WAS MIND BLOWING. BUT,
IN TERMS OF THEIR SELECTION OF SNEAKERS, IT'S BETTER IN BROOKLYN...

NIKETOWN TOUR, NEW YORK, 97

Welcome...We opened this sports super store on November 1, here in Manhattan on 57th between 5th and Madison. The concept of the store is a ship in a bottle. We built an old Manhattan school gymnasium, the bottle, and inside we built a brand new Niketown store. You can see the old gym floor and the tiled walls. The thinking behind the store is "sports heritage meets Nike's product innovation", and each of the floors has been designated a sporting value; teamwork, honour, courage, victory.

We're building a limited number of Niketown stores, and are looking for sites in Europe, the Asian Pacific and Canada. These are where we can show off what Nike's all about - a passion for sport. You may wear the Air Max, or have seen Michael Jordan in action, or Cantona, but this is our way of really welcoming people into what Nike's all about.

The store mixes lots of elements; an archive of sports memorabilia [eight of Carl Lewis' gold medals are here], with multi-media extravaganzas, a big show takes place about every thirty minutes when a forty-foot video screen descends, the store darkens and one of five different Nike films is shown. The store is constantly changing, with new archival memorabilia coming in. We now have a golf area with some of Tiger Woods' signed paraphernalia. He is our newest athlete. And there are Michael Johnson's gold running shoes from his 200 and 400 metre gold medal victories at the Atlanta Olympics.

Within the old gymnasium concept we actually came up with a team that may have played here in the 1930s, called the Knights and you can see the bleachers at the back, and the helmets with their logos. We even laid out a regulation-size high school basketball court and then figured out where the bleachers and the baskets would be. Another really fun display is the Air Jordan Radio. It looks like an old radio, but you spin the ball and it takes you to a great moment in Michael's career, and links with the footwear he was wearing at the time.

I'd like to point out this display which means a lot to those of us who work for Nike. It's "Bowerman's garage". Bill Bowerman, was one of the people who helped Phil Knight start Nike. He was very much a tinkerer. He was the guy who, one day when his wife had gone to church, poured some hot tyre rubber into her waffle iron and came up with the idea of the waffle sole, which started Nike back in 1972, when we came out with our waffle trainer. This is an ode to him, his garage really looked like that and he's still tinkering to this day, trying to come up with new products to help athletes perform better.

One of the new technologies that we've introduced in Niketown New York City is what we call NGAGE, which is the first digital sizing system for footwear. It uses infrared light to measure the heat off your foot and it's able to come within a millimetre of accuracy in telling your size, both the width and the length. It prints out a card which you give to the sales assistant, which helps us to get the size right first time. The assistant keys it into the computer and someone in the basement stock room will grab the shoes, put them on the shoe tube, which zips up here and hopefully it's your size. Up on the fifth floor we're entering the rafters of the old gymnasium, and you can see the trusses supporting the old ceiling and the staining from years of rainwater seeping in, and the flag hanging from the rafters, which you'd see in just about any old school gymnasium...as well as old shoes which somebody's thrown over the rafters.

When we first open a store, we are targeting the local population and our hope is that New Yorkers will really find it fun, a place where they can find out about sports. Likewise we expect to see lots of visitors come through Niketown. Over a quarter of a million people have been in the New York Niketown since it opened. We expect from 7,000 to 14,000 daily. The average is about 10,000.

We opened our first Niketown in Portland, Oregon in 1991 and we really wanted to see if we could bring something new to retail. We looked at how fast the world was changing and felt that retail hadn't come along the same way, and we also felt that our product was something that we'd spent a great deal of time designing and that it wasn't being displayed in a way that was very exciting to consumers. We wanted to bring Nike excitement and innovation to retail by creating showcase stores. Every time we open a store we know the concept is going to be copied, and that's fine! So we know we have to do something different, raise the bar and take it to a new level. The next one will be very different. That's the challenge to us and that's really what makes Nike what it is!

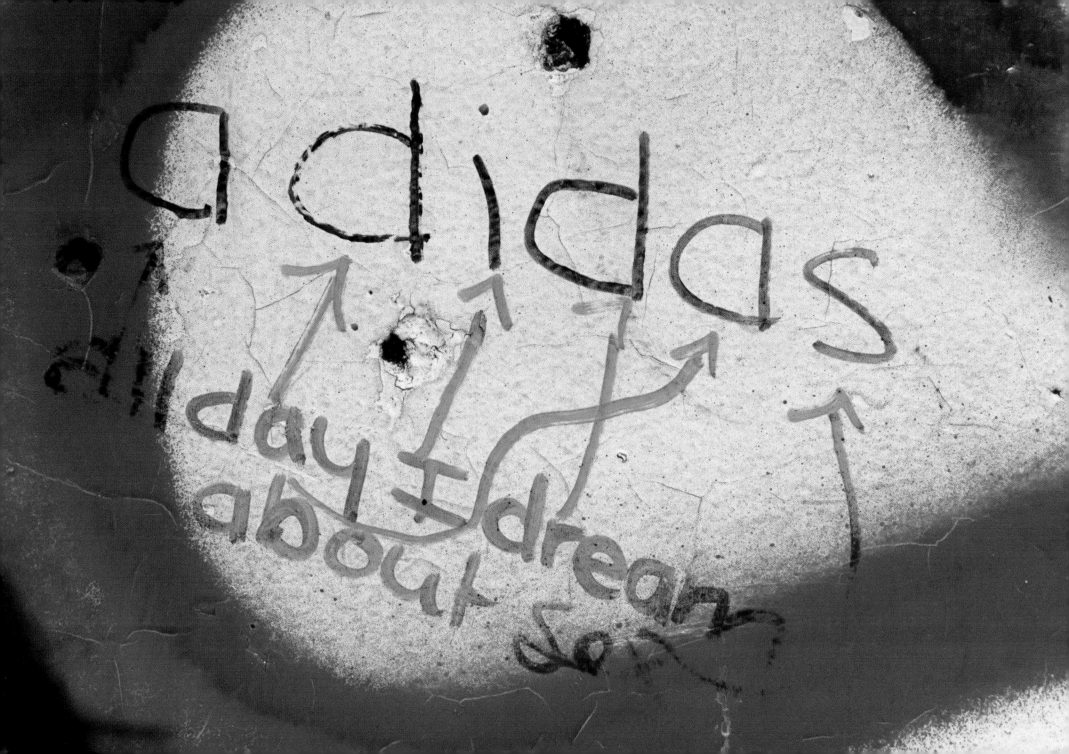

The grunge phenomenon has many shrines in Seattle, from venues like The Vogue to Kurt Cobain's old home. Even the St Vincent de Paul chain of thrift stores advertise themselves as "your first choice for grunge wear". But when it comes to the Mecca for grunge-star trainers - the ubiquitous Converse tennis shoe - there is only one place anyone would go.

That, of course, is Chubby & Tubby's, a three-site Seattle institution. The prime spot for trainer fans is the store on Aurora Ave. After picking one's way through lawn furniture, bedding plants, drill bits, chain saws, fishing tackle, flannel shirts, kitchenware, Swiss army knives, scented candles, sets of Star Wars Pez and bedroom lamps that come on when you clap your hands, one is confronted with a wall of Converse sneakers. There are low-tops, high-tops, Jack Purcells, one-stars and all-leather models - surrounded by every other trainer known to man. Star sales person Terry runs this mad arena. She says, "We have everything, but what we sell out is Converse. Always Converse". The shoe sells to kids, stars, grannies, tourists, Microsoft executives and - Courtney Love.

In the late 90s, the Converse fad is peaking, and Terry worries about her supply of stock. "We've already drained our two other stores and there's no sign things are slowing down. We heard they're gonna stop making one-stars. So we just tell customers to write to the company." Of course, she still has models in purple, red, maroon, pine, yellow ["only one low-top, size four, and half a pair of high -tops"], candy pink, chino ["that's creamy brown, chocolate and umber are separate colours, but we're out of em"], light chino, burnt orange ["that's Mark Arm's favourite, the guy from Mudhoney"], bright blue, aqua and two kinds of white.

"There's unbleached white and optical white which is really hard to keep cheap. But when we run out of a colour I sell em unbleached white and a packet of Rit." Rit, a fabric dye, is another in-store staple. Terry claims it will duplicate any Converse colour. "Some of those guys in the bands paint the soles with Vaseline - they cover all the rubber, to make the paint jobs cleaner." But Terry stresses they needn't bother. "Rit is so easy you just paint it on, where you want."

At Chubby & Tubby's, such advice is part of the history. The stores were openned by a pair of poker buddies: Woody Ague and Irving Freese. After World War II, Freese [once a potato-chip salesman] went to work in his family's petrol station. He let Woody sell army surplus gear from a Quonset hut on the premises. When the pair went into business as retailers, they used their nicknames: Chubby and Tubby. Irving, who died in 97, was Chubby: Woody who passed away before grunge hit, was known as Tubby. Terry thinks, though, that Woody would have liked grunge. "They were old-time salesmen, in the truest sense. Grunge was great for us, it made this department."

Chubby and Tubby's on Aurora Ave is between Dave's Transmission and Sports Rack Vehicle Outfitters. Open 8am to 9pm, Monday to Friday, 9am to 7pm on Sundays. Converse shoppers are advised to come early, "...by early I mean 8am!"

BY CYNTHIA ROSE

insta pump

PAUL LITCHFIELD -REEBOK CONCEPT DESIGNER

IT'S BEEN A DIFFICULT JOB TO GET HOLD OF YOU, I'VE BEEN TALKING TO JULIE OVER THE LAST COUPLE OF WEEKS...
Yeah, I apologise, I'm a tad elusive, but I think Reebok make it that way. They don't really talk to the public very often.

COULD YOU TELL ME WHAT YOUR JOB IS, IN A NUTSHELL?
Crisis, crisis, crisis...well, I'm managing director of the "advanced products group" at Reebok, and what we do is make products that addresses consumer benefits in a non-typical way.

DO YOU THINK SNEAKER DESIGN HAS REACHED A PLATEAU?
Absolutely not. There's a couple of different opportunities, one is styling which is fairly limitless because you deal with colours, patterns and new materials all the time, and the other aspect is, the functional components. So, how they're styled and combined creates new looks. We're exploring a whole lot of new production and manufacturing techniques that will give us a load of new opportunities.

SO, IS THE DESIGN DICTATED BY THE AVAILABLE MATERIALS AND TECHNOLOGY?
It's like the chicken and egg. Certainly the design will be led by functional components and the manufacturing techniques, but then again, new designs can create brain teasers for manufacturing folk. So there's a ying and yang...the way you make shoes defines the design but the design can also help define the manufacturing process.

I WAS READING ABOUT A SMART SHOE WHICH LEARNS TERRAIN. IS THAT POSSIBLE?
Absolutely, and it's viable. You're essentially talking about a shoe which can be customised to the user, based on the user's performance, are they walking or running, is the terrain smooth or rough. With chip and sensor technology where it's at now.... One of the things we do is look outside the footwear business, and there is a whole world of opportunity out there, to make both sophisticated and very elegantly simple products. When you're exploring different production disciplines sometimes you think, hey, what if I could do this or that, and it ends up never coming out as you expected.

BUT DO YOU THINK THE PUBLIC HAS PROBLEMS ASSIMILATING NEW CONCEPTS AND TECHNOLOGY SO THAT SNEAKER DESIGN CAN DEVELOP AT THE RATE IT'S CAPABLE OF?
Without a doubt, because it's not only the public, but it's the retailer who you've got to sell your product to, before the public sees it. But it's more of a challenge, because you can make the future meet the present. You do it in a series of steps. If the steps are too small, someone else is going to take your lead, so it's a balance, and sometimes you take a risk. It's a constant discussion, that balance between being normal or typical and being so aggressive that you disturb people.

AT THE MOMENT, HOW FAR ADVANCED ARE THE CONCEPTS YOU'RE WORKING ON, IN COMPARISON TO WHAT IS IN THE SHOPS?
I need to speak in generalities because I can give away trade specifics. Within the advanced products group we continually critically evaluate, hopefully more harshly than anyone else, in order to improve our technologies. Then, everything we work on is addressing a consumer need. When you go into a shoe store Jon, what do you tolerate? Do you say, ok, I'll buy these, even though the shoe is too hot or doesn't fit? There are ways for us to address these problems, so we're working on a whole host of levels.

Remember, I'm manager of the advanced products group, I'm not an industrial designer, but we work hand in hand with our industrial designers, and the conversation in the evolution of a product is a synergistic one between design, development and engineering. You can't have them work independently because you'd end up with a bunch of interpretations.

OK, SO HOW FIERCE IS THE COMPETITION BETWEEN COMPANIES?
I think this is the greatest thing. The competition is enormously fierce, even within our company, within our group, but certainly with out competitors. You want to tin, that's why we're doing this, but I hold no animosity towards them. They've got some great product, and that keeps you hungry, keeps you going. What are we trying to do? What do we stand for?

WHICH DO YOU CONSIDER TO BE THE MOST SUCCESSFUL SNEAKER, TAKING INTO ACCOUNT THE TECHNOLOGY AVAILABLE AT THE TIME?
For Reebok?

YEAH!
There have been a couple which have been benchmark successful. The first was in the early 80s, the Freestyle aerobics shoe. That actually helped define Reebok as a major competitor in the athletic footwear industry, because it addressed consumer needs and benefits, in aerobic shoes at the time.

Then we did quite well with our original Pump shoe. That was one of my projects.

STRANGELY ENOUGH, I PICKED UP A PAIR OF ALL BLACK INSTAPUMPS TODAY...
Do you like them?

I PARTICULARLY LIKE THE ONES WITH PURPLE IN THE HEEL, BUT I LIKE THE WHOLE CONCEPT.
That shoe does a couple of things, one of which is pretty apparent, that you can customise a fit without using a lace, but the other thing it did was help us define and streamline our manufacturing process, because rather than cutting out and stitching all those layers of fabric together, we made that pump bladder which is the backbone of the shoe upper, and we redefined the closure system...

...DESIGNERS MUST BE TIRED OF LACES...
One of the problems with laces is that they're so damn elegant and they work well, but they're also tired. The trick is, how do we close a shoe up with something as simple and elegant as laces but not as constrictive in design terms. And when you get that answer, Jon, give me a call!

I THINK THE DESIGN OF THE PUMP WAS ACTUALLY OUTSIDE PEOPLE'S CRITERIA OF TRAINER AESTHETICS, BUT A LOT OF PEOPLE LOVE THAT SHOE.
Thank you. There were a couple of folk here, particularly Steven Smith, who's with Fila now, who worked together for years, and that shoe was too advanced for a lot of people. Half the bottom's gone, most of the upper, no laces...what the hell am I buying the shoe for? But when people put it on they were like, hey, it's pretty good. I think you'll see the Pump come back for Reebok. And the company didn't want to do the shoe in our colours, but we said no, it's so controversial. If you put up a mundane colorway people might buy it, but less people would talk about it.

DO YOU THINK THAT PEOPLE'S CRITERIA FOR JUDGING A SNEAKER HAS CHANGED OVER THE LAST DECADE?
Absolutely, the consumer is much more sophisticated than we sometimes give them credit for. But they also want to spend less time thinking about why they're buying what they're buying. One of the things we've worked on, since 1994, is the DMX....

YEAH, I WAS LOOKING AT THEM THE OTHER DAY AND I COULDN'T BELIEVE HOW THE SOLE FELT. TO BE HONEST I WAS TOTALLY THROWN BY IT. I REALLY LIKED IT. I TRIED ON THE AUTUMN COLOUR WAY, THE PURPLE WITH THE BROWN SOLE AND I LOVED THE COLOUR, VERY ORGANIC AND I COULDN'T BELIEVE THE WAY THE AIR MOVED.
Oh thanks man, I appreciate it.

IT'S A KIND OF MASSAGE EFFECT, REALLY ALIVE. MORE AND MORE YOU CAN HAVE DIFFERENT SNEAKERS WITH DIFFERENT CHARACTERS.
Absolutely. I think that's one of our strengths at Reebok, we have at least four distinct technologies which we work on daily.

WHAT ABOUT YOURSELF, HAVE YOU GOT A HUGE COLLECTION OF SNEAKERS?
I'm a US size nine which happens to be the sample size and I've been working in development since 1985, there's my answer.

SAYS IT ALL...OK, THANKS PAUL, I THINK WE'RE DONE.
Ok Jon, but hey could I just ask you one question...what's this book about?

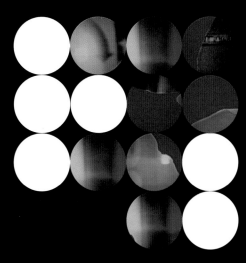

There have been a couple which have been benchmark successful. The first was in the early 80s, the Freestyle aerobics shoe. That actually helped define Reebok as a major competitor in the athletic footwear industry, because it addressed consumer needs and benefits, in aerobic shoes at the time. Then we did quite well with our original Pump shoe. That was one of my projects.

STRANGELY ENOUGH, I PICKED UP A PAIR OF ALL BLACK INSTAPUMPS TODAY...
Do you like them?

I PARTICULARLY LIKE THE ONES WITH PURPLE IN THE HEEL, BUT I LIKE THE WHOLE CONCEPT.
That shoe does a couple of things, one of which is pretty apparent, that you can customise a fit without using a lace, but the other thing it did was help us define and streamline our manufacturing process, because rather than cutting out and stitching all those layers of fabric together, we made that pump bladder which is the backbone of the shoe upper, and we redefined the closure system...

...DESIGNERS MUST BE TIRED OF LACES...
One of the problems with laces is that they're so damn elegant and they work well, but they're also tired. The trick is, how do we close a shoe up with something as simple and elegant as laces but not as constrictive in design terms. And when you get that answer, give me a call!

I THINK THE DESIGN OF THE PUMP WAS ACTUALLY OUTSIDE PEOPLE'S CRITERIA OF TRAINER AESTHETICS, BUT A LOT OF PEOPLE LOVE THAT SHOE.
Thank you. There were a couple of folk here, particularly Steven Smith, who's with Fila now, who worked together on that shoe for years. And that shoe was too advanced for a lot of people. Half the bottom's gone, most of the upper, no laces...what the hell am I buying the shoe for? But when people put it on they were like, hey, it's pretty good. I think you'll see the Pump come back for Reebok. And the company didn't want to do the shoe in our colours, but we said no, it's so controversial, if you put up a mundane color-ways people might buy it, but less people would talk about it.

DO YOU THINK THAT PEOPLE'S CRITERIA FOR JUDGING A SNEAKER HAS CHANGED OVER THE LAST DECADE?
Absolutely, the consumer is much more sophisticated than we sometimes give them credit for. But they also want to spend less time thinking about why they're buying what they're buying. One of the things we've worked on, since 1994, is the DMX....

YEAH, I WAS LOOKING AT THEM THE OTHER DAY AND I COULDN'T BELIEVE HOW THE SOLE FELT. TO BE HONEST I WAS TOTALLY THROWN BY IT. I REALLY LIKED IT. I TRIED ON THE AUTUMN COLOUR WAY, THE PURPLE WITH THE BROWN SOLE AND I LOVED THE COLOUR, VERY ORGANIC AND I COULDN'T BELIEVE THE WAY THE AIR MOVED.
Oh thanks man, I appreciate it.

IT'S A KIND OF MASSAGE EFFECT, REALLY ALIVE. MORE AND MORE YOU CAN HAVE DIFFERENT SNEAKERS WITH DIFFERENT CHARACTERS.
Absolutely. I think that's one of our strengths at Reebok, we have at least four distinct technologies which we work on daily.

WHAT ABOUT YOURSELF, HAVE YOU GOT A HUGE COLLECTION OF SNEAKERS?
I'm a US size nine which happens to be the sample size and I've been working in development since 1985, there's my answer.

SAYS IT ALL...OK, THANKS PAUL, I THINK WE'RE DONE.
Ok, but hey could I just ask you one question...what's this book about?

Instapump...was way ahead of its time...they're in me collection and people want them now, they're redoing them now. It took a few good retailers who basically just thought, fuck it, we like them - Duffer of St George, Offspring - who pushed it forward and it came back round, because they bought all the bulk stock. If it wasn't for them it wouldn't have happened. JUSTIN DEAKIN @ STRIDE

CAINE GAYLE

SUCCESS IS A MIND GAME.

DC SHOE CO

MIKE CARROLL

DISCARD YESTERDAY LIKE AN OLD PAIR OF SHOES.

DC SHOE CO

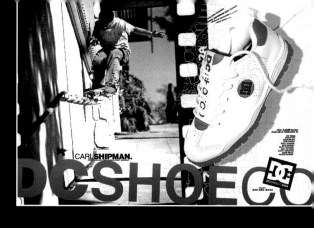

CARL SHIPMAN.

DC SHOE CO

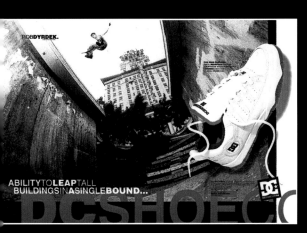

ROB DYRDEK.

ABILITY TO LEAP TALL BUILDINGS IN A SINGLE BOUND...

DC SHOE CO

RICK HOWARD

THE DIFFERENCE BETWEEN INNOVATION AND IMITATION...

DC SHOE CO

DANNY WAY

STOP

AIRCRAFT OPERATING AREA

N6025W

IF YOU NEVER TRY, YOU WILL NEVER SUCCEED.

DC SHOE CO

MOSES ITKONEN.

"COUNTDOWN TO TAKEOVER."

DC SHOE CO

RUDY JOHNSON.

DC SHOE CO

CARL SHIPMAN

FOR THOSE INTERESTED IN RIDING A SKATEBOARD, NOT A BANDWAGON.

DC SHOE CO

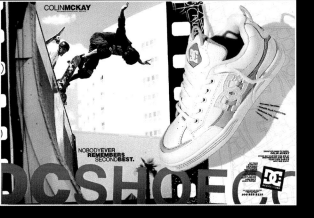

FORTHOSEINTERESTEDIN
RIDINGA**SKATEBOARD,**
NOTA**BANDWAGON.**

ROB, DC SPONSORED SKATER, PHONE INTERVIEW

HOW DO SAY TRAINERS IN YOUR MOTHER TONGUE?

KICKS

WHY DO YOU LIKE TRAINERS?

BECAUSE MY FEET ARE SENSITIVE

WHAT'S THE WEIRDEST THING THAT HAPPENED BETWEEN YOU AND YOUR TRAINERS?

I GOT DRUNK ONE NIGHT AND FUCKED A PAIR

WHAT'S THE RAREST PAIR OF TRAINERS YOU OWN?

ALL WHITE DC BOXERS WITH CLEAR SOLE

DO YOU WEAR LACES?

SKINNY, FAT, ROUND, SQUARE, ALWAYS

HOW DO YOU CLEAN YOUR TRAINERS?

BY THROWING THEM AWAY

WHAT'S THE CRAZIEST THING YOU'VE DONE FOR A PAIR OF TRAINERS?

TOOK THEM AND SHOWED THEM TO THE WHOLE WORLD

WHAT TRAINERS CAN'T YOU STAND?

REEBOK ANYTHING REEBOK

HAVE YOU EVER CUSTOMISED YOUR TRAINERS?

I USED TO CUT DOWN CABS, YOU KNOW BEFORE HALF-CABS

IF A TOP BRAND COULD MAKE YOU A SHOE WHAT WOULD IT BE?

DC DYRDEK, CHECK THE CRAZE

DO YOU EVER SAVE UP TO BUY TRAINERS?

I IMPULSE BUY EVERY HALF-WAY-DECENT SHOE. I IMPULSE-BOUGHT SOME CRAZY NIKES BUT CAN'T GET MYSELF TO WEAR THEM

WHEN DID YOU BUY YOUR FIRST PAIR?

JORDANS IN 86, BECAUSE THEY WERE JORDANS

DO YOU KNOW ANY INTERESTING FACTS ABOUT A BRAND?

REEBOK IS A GIRL'S AEROBIC SHOE COMPANY PULLING THE WOOL OVER YOUR EYES

DO YOU CHANGE YOUR TRAINERS DURING THE DAY?

SOME FOR LUNCH, SOME TO SKATE, SOME TO PARTY

DO YOU CONSIDER YOUR TRAINERS TO BE MORE THAN SHOES?

A REFLECTION OF MY FOOTWEAR FANTASY

WHICH COUNTRY MAKES THE BEST

COME ON, ONLY THE BEST COME FROM THE USA

DO YOU THINK TRAINERS ARE GOOD FOR YOUR FEET?

OH YEAH BABY

DO YOU SWOP TRAINERS WITH FRIENDS?

NEVER STAND IN THEIR STINKY FEET

HOW DO YOU FIND OUT WHAT ARE THE LATEST RELEASES?

I STEAL CATALOGUES

WOULD YOU BE BURIED WITH YOUR TRAINERS, AND WHICH WOULD YOU BE SEEN DEAD IN?

WITHOUT A DOUBT, I AM MY SHOES LIKE MY SHOES ARE ME. DC

DO YOU THINK ALIENS WEAR TRAINERS?

NOPE DOPE, KICKS ARE STRICTLY FOR THE MATERIAL WORLD
SHOE I SEE. I IMPULSE-BOUGHT SOME CRAZY NIKES BUT CAN'T GET MYSELF TO WEAR THEM.

WE WANT TO ASK YOU A FEW QUESTIONS ABOUT SNEAKERS AND HOW YOU SEE DCS. SO, THE OBVIOUS QUESTION.ARE YOU INTO SNEAKERS?

I ALWAYS HAVE BEEN. OUR COMPANY ORIGINATED AS A BASIC T-SHIRT COMPANY BACK IN 91 BECAUSE I LOVE TO DO GRAPHICS. PLUS MY BUSINESS PARTNER AND I WANTED TO MAKE CLOTHES. WE BEGAN MAKING SHOES BECAUSE WE THOUGHT THERE WAS A GAP IN THE INDUSTRY, AND WE HAD A GENERAL INTEREST IN SHOES. AS FOR SNEAKERS AND ALL THAT STUFF, I'VE ALWAYS WORN THEM, BUY THEM ALL - ABOUT TWO PAIRS A MONTH.

DO YOU DESIGN THE SNEAKERS YOURSELF?

I DESIGN FIFTY PER CENT OF THEM, AND ON THE REST I COLLABORATE WITH FIVE PROFESSIONAL SKATEBOARDERS SO AS TO DESIGN THEIR OWN SIGNATURE SHOES. THESE FIVE GUYS HAVE REALLY GOOD IDEAS BECAUSE THEY ARE ALL REALLY FASHION CONSCIOUS. THEY ALSO SKATEBOARD EVERYDAY, SO NOT ONLY DO THEY KNOW WHAT LOOK THEY WANT, BUT THEY ALSO KNOW THE FUNCTIONS THEY WANT FROM THEIR GEAR. WE BASE EVERYTHING AROUND THOSE DESIGNS.

DO YOU THINK THE AESTHETIC OR THE STYLE OF SNEAKERS IS DICTATED BY TECHNOLOGY AS WELL AS FASHION?

YES, I THINK SO. THE GUYS THAT WE'VE WORKED WITH FROM THE BEGINNING - DANNY (WAY), COLIN (MCKAY), ROB (DYRDEK) AND RUDY (JOHNSON) - THEY'RE VERY INDIVIDUAL. THEY LOOK AT THEMSELVES AS BEING SOME OF THE BEST PEOPLE IN THE WORLD AT WHAT THEY DO IN SKATEBOARDING. EACH RIDER CONSIDERS BOTH STYLE AND FUNCTION SO AS TO MAKE THEIR PRODUCT WORK WELL FOR SKATEBOARDING. WHEN THEY'RE OUT SKATEBOARDING, THEY WANT THEIR SIGNATURE SHOE TO REPRESENT THEM AS BEST AS POSSIBLE FROM BOTH PERSPECTIVES. WHEN WE STARTED, SKATEBOARDING SHOES ALL LOOKED PRETTY MUCH THE SAME, SO WE WANTED TO CREATE SOMETHING THAT WAS VERY INDIVIDUALISTIC FOR EACH ONE OF THOSE GUYS. WE BEGAN TO RESEARCH THE TECHNOLOGY AND THE AESTHETICS THAT COULD BE PUT INTO THESE SHOES, BUT MADE A POINT TO KEEP THEM LOOKING GOOD. THERE IS TECHNOLOGY THAT CAN BE PUT INTO SHOES THAT DOESN'T NECESSARILY LOOK GOOD. WE FOUND THAT RESEARCHING STUFF OURSELVES HELPS US TO UNDERSTAND WHICH MATERIALS CAN WORK FOR SKATEBOARDING. WE'RE LEARNING ALL THE TIME.

DO YOU THINK THAT THE DESIGN OF SKATEBOARD SNEAKERS HAS REACHED A PLATEAU?

IF YOU HAD SAID THAT TO ME TEN YEARS AGO, THEN I WOULD HAVE SAID YES, YOU KNOW? BUT IT'S RELATED TO WHAT'S GOING ON AT THE TIME, BECAUSE TRENDS ARE ALWAYS CHANGING. I DON'T THINK THAT THINGS WILL EVER COMPLETELY LEVEL OFF. THERE MAY BE CERTAIN LIMITATIONS AS TO THE MATERIALS ONE CAN USE, BUT THINGS ARE ALWAYS CHANGING, AND STYLES ARE ALWAYS CHANGING, AND PEOPLE WILL ALWAYS GET BORED OF ONE STYLE OR ANOTHER. THERE WILL ALWAYS BE THE CHUCK TAYLORS. THEY'RE PRETTY MUCH A SET STYLE, AND WILL BE AROUND FOR A REALLY LONG TIME. BUT ON TOP OF THAT, 99 % OF ALL OTHER STYLES OF SHOES WILL HAVE TO CHANGE CONSTANTLY, BECAUSE PEOPLE GET BORED. THAT'S WHAT WE BASE EVERYTHING ON. WE HAVE A WIDE SPECTRUM OF SHOES. WE CHANGE STYLES CONSTANTLY AND TRY TO UPDATE STUFF WITH NEW AND FRESH IDEAS.

KEN BLOCK, HEAD OF DC SHOES,
INTERVIEWED BY FAX AND PHONE

I SUPPOSE THAT BECAUSE YOU'VE GOT A BACKGROUND IN GRAPHIC DESIGN, YOU CAN TRANSLATE THOSE IDEAS INTO SHOE DESIGNS.

I LOOK AT MYSELF AS BEING A REALIST, IN THAT AS AN ARTIST AND A SKATEBOARDER I CAN STEP BACK AND SEE WHAT THE AVERAGE PERSON WOULD ALSO LIKE. I'M JUST A CONSUMER YOU CAN DO GRAPHICS REMEMBER, WE COME FROM AN INDUSTRY - SKATE-BOARDING- THAT REALLY SETS TRENDS IN YOUTH CULTURE.

THAT'S TRUE, ESPECIALLY IN AMERICA, BUT ALSO IN ENGLAND, A LOT OF PEOPLE HAVE ADOPTED THAT SKATEBOARDER-HIP HOP LOOK. IN LONDON YOU CAN'T TELL REAL SKATEBOARDERS FROM THE IMPERSONATORS BECAUSE THE STYLE HAS CROSSED OVER. BESIDES SKATEBOARDING, I THINK THAT HIP HOP HAS HAD A SIMILAR INFLUENCE ON YOUTH CULTURE, NOT IN THE SAME DIRECTION, BUT THE TWO SCENES HAVE DEFINITELY MERGED OVER THE LAST COUPLE OF YEARS. AS SOME OF THE PRODUCTS HAVE CROSSED OVER, WE'VE SEEN ONE INDUSTRY COPYING ANOTHER INDUSTRY. SO THAT'S WHAT WE TRY AND KEEP IN TOUCH WITH WHEN WE DESIGN, WE KEEP IN MIND THOSE CONSUMERS. THE GOOD THING IS THAT IN OUR CREATIVE DEPARTMENTS, MOST OF US ARE THOSE CONSUMERS. ESSENTIALLY, WE'RE DESIGNING FOR OURSELVES AND CAN STEP BACK AND ASK, "WOULD WE WEAR THIS, AND WILL THIS SELL?"

DC SHOES REALLY DO STAND OUT. THEY DON'T LOOK LIKE TYPICAL SKATEBOARDING SHOES, LIKE VANS OR AIRWALK. JUST LOOKING AT THEM THEY LOOK LIKE A STURDY SHOE, BUILT FOR THE JOB. SINCE THE BEGINNING MYSELF AND MY PARTNER HAVE TRIED TO, AND SUCCEEDED IN MAINTAINING CONTROL OVER THE DESIGN, MARKETING, ADVERTISING, TEAM AND PROMOTIONS DEPARTMENTS. WE DO ALL OUR ADVERTISING IN-HOUSE, ALL OUR OWN MARKETING, EVERYTHING OURSELVES, SO WE CAN WORK REALLY QUICKLY PICKING UP NEW IDEAS AND NEW PERSPECTIVES. WE SEE WHAT'S HAPPENING AND IMMEDIATELY ADJUST OUR COMPANY ALONG WITH CHANGES IN TRENDS. WE HAVE SEVERAL DESIGNERS ON STAFF TO HELP US DEVELOP EVERY ASPECT OF THE LINES, BUT THE LINES DIRECTLY REPRESENT US. I THINK THAT ONE OF THE REASONS WE'RE SUCCESSFUL IS BECAUSE WE'RE NOT LIKE OTHER MAJOR MANUFACTURERS WHERE SOME OLDER, OUT OF TOUCH, PERSON RUNS THINGS, AND EVERY MONTH HIRES AND FIRES DIFFERENT KIDS WHO DESIGN THE STUFF. IT'S BEEN AN IMPORTANT ASPECT OF OUR COMPANY TO KEEP UP WITH THE TRENDS SO WE'VE DEVELOPED A FAST TURNOVER. WITH MOST COMPANIES A SAMPLE TURN-OUT IS THREE MONTHS. OURS IS FOUR WEEKS. SO, WHEREAS MOST COMPANIES ARE PLANNING NINE MONTHS TO A YEAR AHEAD, WE'RE PLANNING THREE TO FOUR MONTHS AHEAD FOR A COMPLETE LINE. IN MAY WE'LL HAVE FINISHED DESIGNING THE FALL LINE THAT WILL BE IN PRODUCTION IN AUGUST.

EXCELLENT! SO, WHERE ARE YOUR SHOES MANUFACTURED?

ALL OUR SHOES ARE MANUFACTURED IN KOREA. KOREANS ARE THE BEST MANUFACTURERS OF ATHLETIC SHOES. YOU CAN GO TO CHINA OR OTHER COUNTRIES AND MAKE A CHEAPER SHOE BUT THE QUALITY ISN'T AS HIGH.

HOW FAST AND FIERCE IS THE COMPETITION BETWEEN SHOE COMPANIES?

IN THE SKATEBOARDING MARKET, MOST SHOPS ARE VERY SMALL. IT'S ACTUALLY FAIRLY DIFFICULT TO BE SUCCESSFUL IN THIS MARKET BECAUSE A TYPICAL SKATEBOARDING SHOP ISN'T GOING TO CARRY TEN DIFFERENT LINES, FIVE MODELS DEEP - THEY JUST CAN'T AFFORD IT. SO THEIR MAIN SUPPLIERS OVER THE PAST FIVE TO EIGHT YEARS HAVE BEEN AIRWALK, VANS AND ETNIES. THEN, OVER THE LAST THREE YEARS THERE'S BEEN A BOOM IN SKATEBOARDING SHOES BECAUSE THEY'VE BECOME TRENDY AND YOU CAN MAKE JUST A COUPLE OF THOUSAND SHOES A MONTH AND BE SEMI-SUCCESSFUL. LOTS OF PEOPLE HAVE JUMPED ON THIS AND ONLY TIME WILL TELL WHO WILL BE SUCCESSFUL IN THE LONG RUN AND WHO WON'T.

TELL ME, HOW DO YOU FEEL ABOUT THE LARGER CORPORATIONS LIKE ADIDAS AND NIKE GETTING IN ON THE SKATEBOARDING MARKET BY STARTING TO MAKE SKATE SHOES? ARE THEY COMPETITION, ARE YOU WORRIED ABOUT THEM?

I'M NOT WORRIED BECAUSE THEY WILL NEVER BE ABLE TO DO THE JOB WE DO. THEY'LL NEVER BE AS CONNECTED TO OUR INDUSTRY AS WE ARE. I MEAN, IT ACTUALLY CONFUSES ME WHY THEY'RE DOING THAT. MAJOR BASKETBALL SHOE BRANDS HAVE POPULAR APPEAL TO PEOPLE INTO HIP HOP AND SKATEBOARDING BECAUSE THEY MAKE A GOOD SHOE FOR BASKETBALL, CROSS TRAINING, ETC. BUT WHEN THEY TRY AND GO AFTER A MARKET THEY KNOW NOTHING ABOUT IT MAKES THEM LOOK STUPID. I THINK IT TENDS TO HURT THEM. THE ONLY REASON WHY I CAN SEE THAT THEY'RE DOING THIS IS BECAUSE THEY GO TO A HIGH SCHOOL AND SEE FIFTY PER CENT OF THE KIDS WEARING SKATEBOARD SHOES, TRIGGERING A RESPONSE IN SOME OF THEIR MARKETING PERSONNEL WHO EXCLAIM, "HOLY SHIT, WE'RE LOSING ALL THIS BUSINESS BECAUSE WE DON'T HAVE THIS LOOK". BUT IT TAKES THE BIG COMPANIES A YEAR OF PLANNING AND TURN-AROUND TIME BEFORE THEY CAN MAKE MAJOR CHANGES. SO, BY THE TIME THEY REALIZE THEY'RE GOING IN THE WRONG DIRECTION, THEY'RE SCREWED. WE'RE A SKATEBOARDING SHOE COMPANY. WE'RE COMING FROM THE OPPOSITE DIRECTION THAN THEY ARE. WE'RE BUILDING UP FROM THE GRASSROOTS. THEY'RE COMING FROM ABOVE US AND TRYING TO MARKET DOWN.

HOW MANY SHOES DO YOU OWN NOW? I SUPPOSE YOU GET EVERY MODEL THAT COMES OUT?

NAH. I STILL BUY TWO OR THREE PAIRS OF SHOES A MONTH. BUT I ALWAYS BUY SHOES BECAUSE I LIKE THEM. BESIDES, I DON'T MIND ADMITTING THAT I CHECK OUT WHAT OTHER PEOPLE DO...I HAVE ABOUT THIRTY SHOES AT HOME THAT I WEAR ALL THE TIME. THE FUNNY THING ABOUT MAKING SHOES IS THAT I GET TO CHECK OUT ALL THE SAMPLES IN MY SIZE IN WHATEVER COLOR I WANT. I PROBABLY HAVE ABOUT TWENTY CUSTOMIZED SHOES IN MY CLOSET.

EXCELLENT, THAT'S WILD!

THAT'S MY FAVORITE PERK.

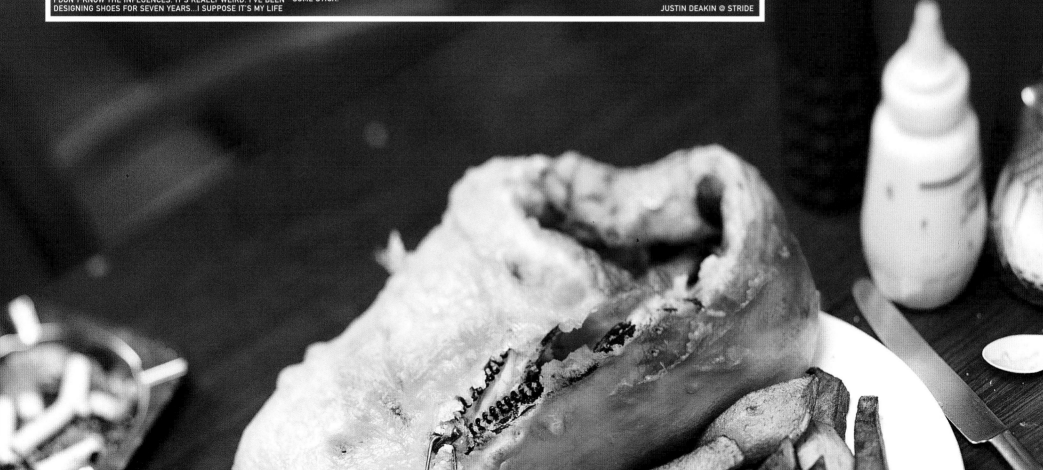

WHAT IS STRIDE ABOUT?

STRIDE IS FOOTWEAR MOVING FORWARDS. IT COMES IN THE SNEAKER BRACKET BECAUSE THAT'S WHERE MY WHOLE FASHION EXPERIENCE STARTED, WHEN I GOT INTO BRANDS FROM 10 YEARS OLD. SNEAKERS ARE THE FIRST DESIGNER OBJECT YOU GET AS A KID. I BEST MAMBOED IN MY FIRST PAIR OF BRANDED ITEMS, AND THEY WERE £12.99. I REMEMBER I BOUGHT THEM ON A SATURDAY MORNING. THEY'RE THE FIRST THINGS THAT I PLAYED ROUND IN...CHECKING OUT THE SNEAKERS. IF YOU FEEL GOOD YOU KNOW YOU LOOK GOOD, YOU KNOW YOU GIVE OFF AN AURA, AND THAT TO ME IS WHAT A LOOK IS ALL ABOUT. A LOT OF PEOPLE SAY, OLD SCHOOL SNEAKERS ARE THE BEST, OR WHATEVER. HALF OF THOSE PEOPLE WEREN'T EVEN WEARING THAT SHIT IN THE FIRST PLACE. I REMEMBER AS A KID, I'D SWAPPED SOME WITH ME MATES AT SCHOOL AND I HAD 14 PAIRS OF SNEAKERS UNDER MY BED.

AT THAT AGE, THAT'S A LITTLE BIT OBSCENE...

YEAH...STRIDE ISN'T GOING TO BE EVERYBODY'S CUP OF TEA AND IT NEVER WILL BE BECAUSE IT'S PERSONAL, IT'S NEW, BASICALLY. THE MORE I SEE, THE MORE PLACES I GO, THE MORE THINGS, THE MORE TECHNIQUES I LEARN, THE MORE IT MOVES ON. THESE FACTORS PROGRESS THE PRODUCT, NOT FOLLOWING A MARKET. I'M JUST DOING ME OWN THING FOR ME.

WHAT INFLUENCES THE DESIGNS?

I DON'T KNOW THE INFLUENCES. IT'S REALLY WEIRD. I'VE BEEN DESIGNING SHOES FOR SEVEN YEARS...I SUPPOSE IT'S MY LIFE AT THAT TIME. THE WORD IS PROGRESSIVE AND THAT IS WHAT I WANT TO GET OUT OF DESIGN, AND THE BONUS IS, PEOPLE LIKE EM, BRILLIANT. SNEAKERS ARE MADE ON TECHNOLOGY, IT'S DIFFERENT TO CLOTHING BECAUSE YOU CAN ONLY GO AS FAR AS THE MACHINERY. SOMETIMES YOU HAVE TO REWORK IDEAS WHEN IT COMES TO THE MANUFACTURING, BECAUSE IT'S JUST NOT POSSIBLE. BUT YOU KEEP TRYING AND YOU GET THAT LITTLE BIT FURTHER. I THINK THE TECHNOLOGY OF FABRICS WILL ADVANCE. OUR SNEAKERS ARE MADE WITH INJECTION EDA, OR INJECTION POLYURETHANE WITH TPR OR LIGHT-WEIGHT RUBBER SOLES.

MY FIRST COLLECTION WAS PLAYING AROUND WITH VELCRO, AND I AIN'T GOT BORED WITH IT YET, AND I WON'T BECAUSE IT'S BEEN AROUND SINCE THE 60S BUT IT'S SO SIMPLE YET IT FEELS SO ADVANCED. WITH COLOUR, WE JUST DO WHAT WE LIKE AND WHAT MATCHES, AND IT'S NOT FOLLOWING WHAT'S GOING ON ANYWHERE ELSE, BECAUSE IF YOU START PLAYING THAT GAME THEN YOU'RE CHASING SOMETHING YOU WON'T FIND. IF IT BLOWS UP IN YOUR FACE YOU'LL BE SAT WITH A LOT OF SNEAKERS IN WRONG COLOURS. NOW WE'RE WORKING WITH MORE MAN-MADE FIBRES RATHER THAN LEATHER BECAUSE IT WIPES AND YOU CAN GET YOUR COLOURS BANG ON. THE SUEDE WE USE IS 30% WATERPROOF WHICH IS THE MAXIMUM WATERPROOF THAT YOU CAN GET FOR SUEDE. IF THERE WAS 100% WATERPROOF I'D HAVE IT. THEY HAVE TO BE ABLE TO TAKE SOME STICK.

WHAT IS THE MOST USELESS DESIGN FEATURE YOU'VE SEEN ON A SHOE?

THE ONE THAT SPRINGS TO MIND, THE PUMA CELLS, WITH THE STUPID GIZMO THAT JUST CLICKS ROUND AND DOESN'T DO FUCK ALL. THAT IS SUCH A WASTE BECAUSE TO PUT THAT MOULD DOWN WOULD HAVE COST A LOT OF MONEY AND IT DOESN'T TIGHTEN THE SHOE. THERE'S ONE COMPANY WHO HAS MADE A PROPER MECHANISM, CALLED OLIVIO. IT WORKS, IT LOOKS GOOD, IT HAS A FUNCTION.

YOU'RE WORKING WITH INFLATE (LONDON-BASED PRODUCT DESIGNERS)?

WE ARE. THE INFLATABLE SHOW IS A JOINT VENTURE, WE PATENTED IT. IT'S JUST SO SIMPLE...

...YOU CAN SEE IT BECOMING A CLASSIC...HOW FIERCE DO YOU THINK THE COMPETITION IS BETWEEN COMPANIES? I THINK THEY PLAY ALL SORTS OF SILLY GAMES WITH EACH OTHER AND I THINK BECAUSE FOOTWEAR IS AN EXPENSIVE PRODUCT TO MAKE I THINK THAT AT THE HIGHER END OF THE BUSINESS THERE'S A LOT OF JUST PLAIN BUSINESS MEN AND THEY LOOK AT IT LIKE SELLING TOMATOES OR ORANGES, THEY'RE NOT BOTHERED. IT'S JUST A JOB.

JUSTIN DEAKIN @ STRIDE

"NIKE AIR MAX IS TOO MUCH POPULAR. PRICE IS OVER US$400!! SO THERE OCCUR SEVERAL INCIDENTS, E.G. IN OSAKA CITY A FEW KIDS HAD THEIR AIR MAX STOLEN BY BAD GUYS WHEN WALKING IN THE STREETS!!!" FROM BOON MAGAZINE, ONE OF JAPAN'S BIBLES OF TRAINER COLLECTING

"A LOT OF PARENTS ARE UNDER A LOT OF PRESSURE TO BUY EXPENSIVE TRAINERS, ESPECIALLY WITH LITTLE GIRLS, BECAUSE ONE OF THE SPICE GIRLS WEARS AIR MAX, ALL THESE LITTLE GIRLS WON'T HAVE ANYTHING LESS THAN AIR MAX, WHICH IS ABOUT £65. WHEREAS YOU COULD GET A TRAINER FOR £35 NOW YOU HAVE TO SPEND OUT...NOW EVERYBODY AT SCHOOL HAS GOT TO HAVE AIR MAX."

THE PURE DESIGN OF THE 98 AIR MAX IS ALMOST THERE. THE FEATURE WHICH STOPS THIS SHOE FROM BEING 100% IS THE POSITION OF THE SWOOSH. WHAT MADE THE 95 AIR MAX PERFECTION, APART FROM ITS GREY & GREEN COLOUR, WAS THE MINIMAL BRANDING. THE SWOOSH WAS POSITIONED AT THE BACK FOLLOWING THE LINE OF THE SHOE. BRANDING CAN FUCK A SHOE UP. SAID A SAVANT ONCE.

IF YOU REALLY WANT TO KNOW ABOUT TRAINERS, WHO DO YOU TALK TO. YOU WANT THE HISTORY, THE FUTURE, THE STORIES, THE GREAT TRAINERS AND THE CARPET SLIPPERS. TALK TO THE MARKETING PEOPLE AND EITHER 1) THEY HAVE A VERY BIASED VIEW TOWARDS THIER OWN BRAND OR 2) THEIR HISTORY IS DUBIOUS. THEY WILL HAVE COME FROM AN FMCG BACKGROUND AND THE HISTORY OF THE MARS CONFECTIONARY LINE OVERTAKES THEIR ABILITY TO SPOT A PAIR OF ADIDAS SL 76 AT 100 PACES. NO, YOU HAVE TO SPEAK TO PURISTS. WHAT MAKES A TRAINER JUNKIE? THE JUNKIE CARES ABOUT TRAINERS TO THE POINT OF OBSESSION. SO I FOUND TWO OBSESSIVES. BOTH ARE RETAILERS OF TRAINERS AND INCREASINGLY IT IS THE RETAILERS WHO CONTROL THE DIALOGUE WITH THE CONSUMER. LONDON EFFECTIVELY CONTROLS EUORPEAN STREET FASHION AND TRAINERS LIE AT THE HEART OF STREET FASHION. NOT ONLY THAT BUT IT IS LONDON WHERE THE PURISTS FLOCK (READ JAPANESE) TO SEE AND PURCHASE THE LATEST AND GREATEST. BASICALLY LONDON, NEW YORK AND TOKYO RULE THE TRAINER WORLD. RICHARD WHARTON (AKA LORD TRAINER) RUNS OFFICE SHOES AND OFFSPRING, POSSIBLY LONDON'S MOST INFLUENTIAL RETAIL OUTLET FOR TRAINERS. PAUL FOX, IS HEAD OF SPECIAL DEVELOPMENT AT J-D SPORTS, BRITAIN'S BIGGEST AND MOST SUCCESSFUL SPORTS SHOE RETAILER. THE FOLLOWING IS A SELECTION OF OUT TAKES FROM DINNER WITH TWO OF ENGLANDS'S PREMIERE TRAINER JUNKIES. WE STARTED WITH A DIFFICULT ONE.

WHAT MAKES YOU A TRAINER JUNKIE?
RW: BASICALLY YOU HAVE TO CARE. IT PROBABLY COMES WITH A DESIRE TO LOOK DIFFERENT. STREET FASHION CYCLES ARE PRETTY QUICK BUT NOTHING COMPARED TO TRAINERS. WHETHER THEY'RE DONE RIGHT OR WRONG TRAINERS CHANGE EVERY THREE MONTHS, YEAR IN, YEAR OUT. WITH FOUR RANGES A YEAR, YOU CAN LOOK VERY DIFFERENT, MOST OF THE TIME.

PF: WELL, IN ONE WAY, I'VE PERSONALLY JUST PASSED THE 500 BARRIER FOR TRAINERS OWNED, SO THAT PROBABLY COUNTS. WHEN I WAS YOUNGER AND LIVING IN BIRMINGHAM, I USED TO CATCH THE TRAIN TO MANCHESTER, BUY UP THE NEW STUFF AND BE BACK ON THE TRAIN AT 10.15. I TOOK A SERIOUS CUT IN SALARY TO WORK AT J-D JUST SO I COULD GET THE STAFF DISCOUNT. WHAT DOES THAT MAKE ME?

WHAT ARE THE ALL-TIME LEGENDS?
RW: WELL, I'M A BIT OF A PURIST. FOR ME, RUN DMC SHELL-TOP SUPERSTARS. I'D PUT A PAIR OF CONVERSE ALL STARS UP THERE. RIPPED OFF BY EVERYONE FOR ETERNITY AND NEVER GOT THE RECOGNITION (CONVERSE) THAT THEY DESERVED. ALWAYS A CULT WITH SOMEONE, CURRENTLY THE JAPANESE. NIKE AIR MAX I LEMON/GREEN AND ALSO POTENTIALLY THE NEW SILVER REFLECTIVE AIR MAX FOR THE NEXT SEASON. FINALLY, AND IT'S A REEBOK, THE INSTAPUMP FURY. WHY? BECAUSE IT'S A DESIGN CLASSIC.

PF: WELL THAT SHOWS THE NORTH, SOUTH THING BUT ADIDAS WOULD TEND TO RULE IN THE NORTH. THE LA TRAINER, THE FIRST PEG SYSTEM SHOE. THE ADIDAS DALLAS WITH

THE WEBBING MID-SOLE. ADIDAS JEANS WHICH WAS A FORERUNNER TO THE GAZELLE. ADIDAS MADE THEM SPECIFICALLY TO GO WITH JEANS AND THEY WERE PALE BLUE SUEDE WITH NAVY SUEDE STRIPE. THE SL 82 OLYMPIC SHOE, NAVY NYLON WITH GOLD STRIPES AND THE 1988 ZX8000. AS FOR OTHERS, THE NIKE CORTEZ, THE NIKE INTERNATIONALIST, NIKE'S FIRST RUNNING SHOE. THE DIADORA GOLD ELITE BORG BECAUSE IT'S A BEAUTIFUL SHOE AND ONE OF THE FIRST TO USE KANGAROO AND THE REEBOK CLASSIC LEATHER.

HOW IMPORTANT IS LONDON?
RW: TAKE THE REJUVINATION OF ADIDAS. IT WAS FASHION PING PONG BETWEEN LONDON, NEW YORK AND TOKYO. ADIDAS SELL SHELL-TOP SUPERSTARS TO THE NEW YORK AUTHORITIES TO OFF-LOAD THEM. PRISONERS IN NYC WEAR ADIDAS SUPERSTARS, THIS IN TURN KICKS OFF THE RAPPERS WEARING SUPERSTARS. LONDON KIDS PICK UP ON THIS AND WE GET A SECOND WAVE. NOW YEARS DOWN THE LINE THE JAPANESE ARE WEARING SUPERSTARS AND ULTRASTARS AND WE HAVE A THIRD WAVE.

WHAT'S THE STORY BEHIND THE SUCCESS OF AN OTHERWISE VERY BLAND SHOE, THE REEBOK CLASSIC LEATHER?
RW: IT WAS A MISTAKE. REEBOK AT THAT TIME WERE FLOUNDERING. THERE WAS ONLY REALLY ADIDAS AND PUMA. NIKE WERE NOWHERE. THEY WERE LOOKING FOR A NEW SHOE AND THE TANNERY DELIVERED SOFT NAPPA LEATHER SHOES. I THINK PAUL BROWN WAS CREDITED WITH THE DESIGN. ANYWAY EVERYONE WAS MAKING AND USING BLACK PLASTICS SO THE NAPPA SHOE STOOD OUT. EVERYONE KNEW THAT A PAIR OF NAPPA SHOES WOULD BE BENT OUT OF SHAPE VERY QUICKLY BUT BOY WERE THEY COMFY.

PF: YEAH, APPARENTLY THEY WERE DESIGNED BY PAUL FIREMAN'S WIFE WHO WANTED A MORE COMFORTABLE SHOE. TODAY AND THEY ARE A TERRACE CLASSIC. WE AS A COMPANY GO TO THE MAJOR LEAGUE GAMES AND IF YOU COULD IDENTIFY WITH ONE LOOK IT WOULD BE STONE ISLAND (OR ANYTHING) JACKET, ARMANI JEANS AND CLASSIC LEATHERS BY REEBOK. MOST TRAINERS LOOK BEST WORN IN. THESE LOOK BEST RIGHT OUT OF THE BOX.

HOW IMPORTANT IS THE FOOTBALL FAN IN DEFINING TRAINER FASHION?
RW: YOU COULD ARGUE ADIDAS WAS BORN ON THE ANFIELD TERRACES. THEY WERE THE ONLY TEAM IN EUROPE AT THE TIME AND FANS SHOPLIFTED THE COOLEST SHOES FROM ALL OVER EUROPE PARIS, MILAN ETC. IT HASN'T CHANGED. LOOK AT YOUR INTELLECTUAL TOURING FOOTBALL FAN. HE KNOWS WHERE TO GET THE BEST, BEST OSTI, BEST ADIDAS, PUMA ETC. THEY KNOW WHICH SHOPS ANYWHERE IN EUROPE HAVE WHAT.

PF: CRITICAL. WE HAVE OVER 100 OUTLETS AND SO WE SEE THE REGIONAL VARIATIONS. OVERALL THE FOOTBALL FAN ALWAYS GOES FOR STYLE OVER DESIGN. THAT'S WHY MOST

PLACES OUTSIDE LONDON WILL ALWAYS GO FOR CLASSICS, WILHELM, CORTEZ, CLASSIC LEATHER. THEY MAY BE WEARING £600 WORTH OF KIT BUT THEY VERY RARELY SPEND MORE THAN £50 ON TRAINERS. LONDON IS MORE TRANSIENT AND GOES WITH PHENOMENA. IT PICKS STUFF UP AND DROPS IT QUICKLY. LONDON HAS PICKED UP THE ADIDAS WILHELM THIS YEAR. IT'S BEEN SELLING EVERYWHERE ELSE FOR YEARS. RETRO, OLD SCHOOL CLASSICS, ORIGINALS. ALL WE DO IS PIGEONHOLE GREAT DESIGN AND THAT WILL ALWAYS SELL AND THAT'S THE PREMISE OF THE FOOTBALL FAN.

WHAT'S THE FUTURE OF THE TRAINER?
RW: OVER THE NEXT TWO YEARS WE WILL SEE THE MARRIAGE OF THE TRADITIONAL OUTDOOR BOOT (RED WINGS, TIMBERLAND, ROCKPORT) WITH THE PERFORMANCE TRAINER LIKE NIKE ACG AND ADIDAS ADVENTURE. THE WHITE TRAINER WILL BECOME A THING OF THE PAST AND AS THEY DO THEY'LL BECOME A CULT AGAIN AND I'LL SELL THEM AGAIN. WE'LL ALSO SEE COMPANIES REALISE THE POWER OF STREET FASHION. STRIDE NOW HAVE GOLDIE DESIGNING A SHOE FOR THEM. LIAM AND NOEL SELL MORE ADIDAS THAN BORIS BECKER. THE ONLY WAY FORWARD FOR REEBOK IS FASHION. IT WILL TAKE THEM FOREVER TO DESIGN THEIR WAY OUT OF THIS NIGHTMARE BUT WHAT ABOUT STUSSY FOR REEBOK, GUCCI OR PRADA FOR REEBOK.

PF: SPORTS COMPANIES WILL ALWAYS HAVE TO JUSTIFY THEIR POSITION WITH A SPORTS BACKGROUND BUT COMPANIES LIKE ADIDAS NOW REALISE THE POWER OF THE STREET. ADIDAS NOW HAVE A "SPORTS STYLE" SECTION TO THEIR CATALOGUE WHICH IS NON-SPORTS SPECIFIC. BRENDON FOSTER RAN THE 1,000 METRES IN A GAZELLE BUT NOW THE GAZELLE IS THE PERFORMANCE DANCE SHOE FOR CLUBBERS BECAUSE IT SLIDES.

RW: AS FOR OVERALL PERFORMANCE LIKE ACG OR ADVENTURE, I CAN'T SEE THEM PROPERLY TAKING OFF - IT'S ALL AMERICAN BOLLOCKS. GO OUT IN THE WOODS, A SPOT OF KAYAKING - FUCK OFF. PERFORMANCE CLOTHING (NORTH FACE, NAPAPIJRI) HAS A PLACE BECAUSE IT PERFORMS, IT KEEPS OUT THE COLD, RAIN ETC. BUT FOOTWEAR WILL ALWAYS BE ABOUT STYLE, WHICH TAKES ME BACK TO THE CLASSICS, CORTEZ, SUPERSTARS, WILHELM.

VARIOUS BRANDS, NAPAPIJRI?
RW: BRILLIANT BRAND BUT FOR FOOTWEAR, THEY'RE NOT LISTENING.

MIZUNO?
RW: JAPANESE AND TECHNO DRIVEN. DO SOMETHING WITH IT, WAKE UP MIZUNO. IN TEN YEARS TIME, THEY WON'T BE TALKING ABOUT PINE DRESSERS ON THE ANTIQUES ROAD SHOW. A KID WILL BE ON THERE WITH A 1969 ADIDAS TRACKSUIT. PEOPLE HAVE TO UNDERSTAND THAT THE FIRST EVER PERFORMANCE OUTERWEAR HAS A PLACE IN OUR CULTURE. REEBOK INSTAPUMP WILL COST YOU £400 NOW, IN FOUR YEARS TIME £4,000. THESE THINGS APPRECIATE QUICKER THAN GOLD.

DEBBIE, LONDON

WHY DONNA KAREN TRAINERS?
I LIKE THE LOOK OF THEM MORE THAN ANYTHING ELSE, AND
THE DKNY ON THE SIDE DEFINITELY ADDS THAT FINAL TOUCH.
AND THEY'RE TINY, AND MY FEET ARE TINY AND THEY JUST
LOOK SO CUTE.

SO YOU DON'T LIKE NIKE OR ADIDAS...?
NO, ADIDAS ARE OK, BUT I DON'T LIKE NIKE.

WHY IS THAT?
NIKE ARE TOO COMMON, EVERYBODY HAS THEM AND THEY
ALL LOOK THE SAME, BUT THIS, THIS IS CLASS.

HOW MUCH DID YOU PAY FOR THEM?
£95. COME ON YOU'VE GOT TO SAY IT'S WORTH IT, GO ON IT'S
ON THE TAPE, YOU'VE GOT TO SAY YES!

YEAH, BUT THEY'RE MODELLED ON A NIKE SHOE,
THAT'S THE IRONIC THING ABOUT THEM.
THEY'RE NOT, THEY'RE NOTHING LIKE NIKE.

WELL, APART FROM THE DKNY LOGO.
EXACTLY, AND THE D ON THE BACK AND THE D ON THE TONGUE,
AND I'LL TELL YOU SOMETHING ELSE THEY'VE GOT. INSIDE THE
TONGUE THERE IS A BIT OF ELASTIC EITHER SIDE, SO THAT YOUR
TONGUE WON'T SLIDE DOWN YOUR FOOT....

DATE: FRI 4 APR 97 00:39:18 0100
FROM: AFROMORPH GLOBALNET.CO.UK (AKURE WALL)
MY BROKE COUSINS IN RURAL NIGERIA REJECT FAKE FILAS
FROM DALSTON MARKET (EAST LONDON). CAPITALISM GOT TO
THEM TOO.

THE CHEAPEST PAIR OF SNEAKERS I EVER BOUGHT WERE
THESE FAKE NIKE FROM MEXICO CALLED NIKI. THEY WERE $35.
MATHIEU KASSOVITZ

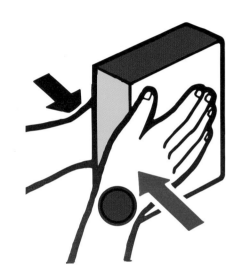 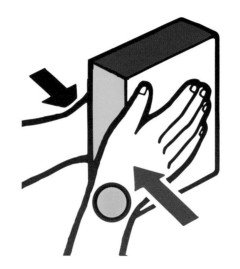 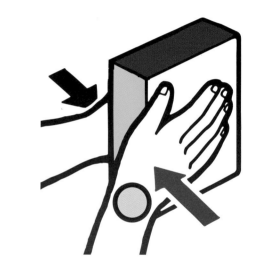

MEMBER I WAS WATCHING THE BLUES BROTHERS. AND THERE'S THAT SCENE.
I JOHN LEE HOOKER. AND ALL THESE KIDS DANCING ON THE STREETS WEARING
YS WITH LONG WHITE SOCKS. I THINK THAT, EVEN THOUGH THEY WERE CONSIDERED
UB-NIKES OR NIKE-IMITATIONS. LOTS OF PEOPLE MISSED THE POINT ABOUT PONY.

I THINK THE BASKETBALL SHOES WERE REALLY COOL. WELL SHAPED, BASIC...BUT YOU
KNOW. YOU ALWAYS GOT A BAD LOOK BECAUSE YOU WERE WEARING PONYS. IF YOU WEAR
PONY, THAT'S BECAUSE YOU'RE TOO POOR TO BUY NIKE! FUCK OFF! FOR ME, PONY RUNNING
SHOES FROM 1983-84 ARE AS COOL AS NIKE CORTEZ OR PUMA STATES.

I - MEXICO/REETOCK - TUNISIA/KIKE - MEXICO/PUERTO RICO/HABIBAS - ISRAEL/REEDOKTRAX - LONDON/DKNY - NEW YORK/POMA - PARIS - I

FOR US IN EUROPE. PONY WERE IMPORTED SNEAKERS FROM THE U.S.. AND ALL
THE GRAFFITI GUYS FROM THE BRONX WERE WEARING THEM. I WISH I HAD A PAIR
OF SILVER CITY LIMITS.

>>NIC AND MARK ON PONYS

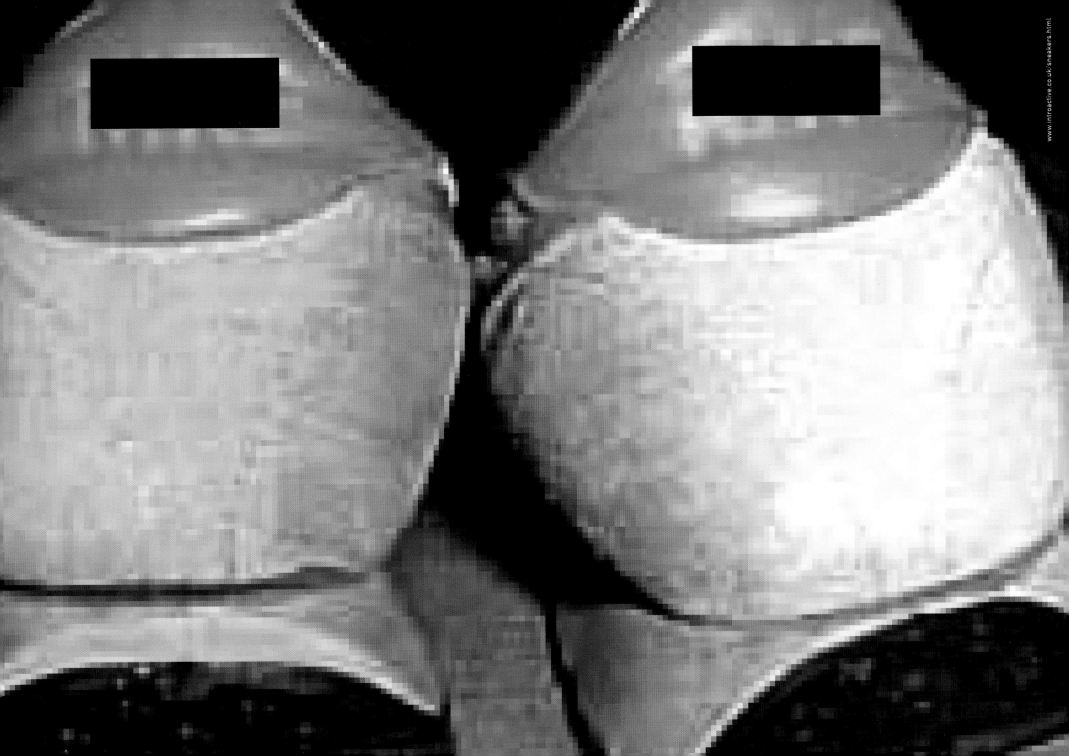

adidas

earn them

adidas®

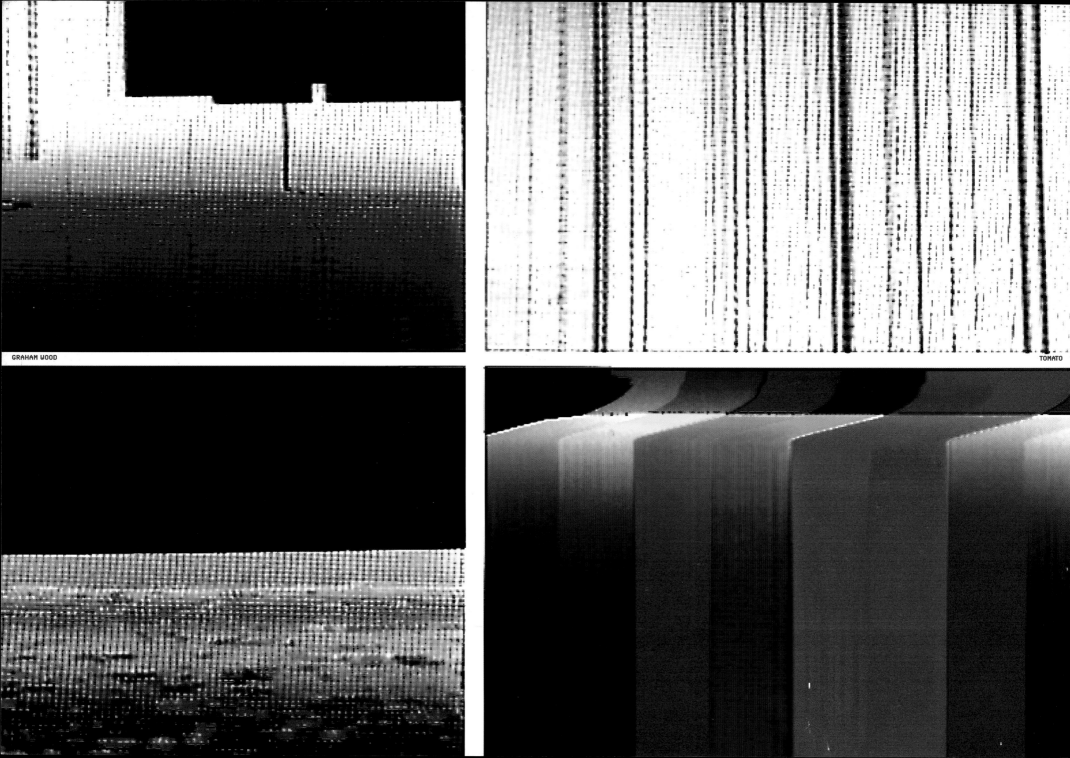

GRAHAM WOOD   TOMATO

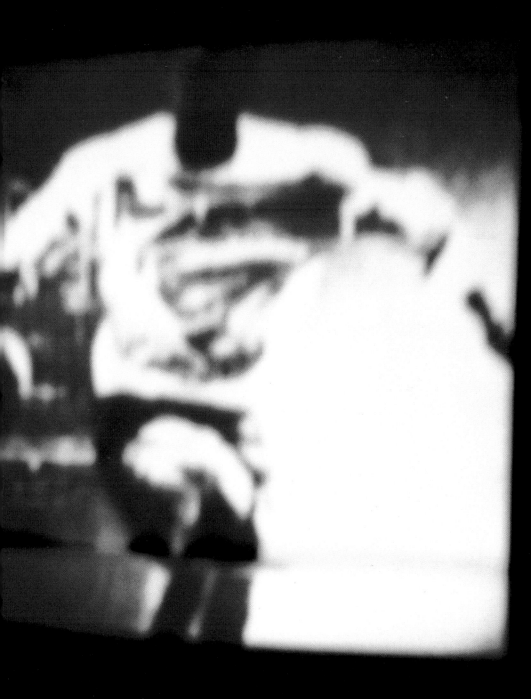

I was asked to do some press ads for Nike by Warren Eakins at the ad agency Wieden & Kennedy, just as they were about to set up in Amsterdam in 1992. Coincidentally, I'd taken my portfolio to Leagas Delaney who were working for Adidas. It was quite weird that Leagas Delaney offered me a job, and the first stuff we did was kinda good. I don't know if it ever got used.

THE DOUGLAS BROTHERS ADS?
Yeah, those ads turn up in design annuals and magazines, but I don't actually know if they'll ever get used. It was really interesting for me, cause I didn't know anything about advertising. I knew things should be more open and straightforward and honest, and how to "brand", which basically means giving a product a sense of its own life. I'm not talking in terms of sticking a logo on everything. What I mean is to imbue something with the emotion that comes out of it. With those Adidas ads it was an emotion of strong sports, not pretty, not street.

I always thought of Adidas, personally, as being the best, just cause I always wanted Gazelles. I was on a hunt for them two years before I started working for Leagas Delaney. They never fitted me anyway so it was always frustrating. One thing Adidas did that I thought was really good...they were going to invent this kinda "Shit City", and the only connection would be that in these photographs people would be wearing Adidas, and they would appear in magazines like Ray Gun. It sort of guts the whole style thing...Adidas have that sense of the individual.

The reason I left Leagas Delaney was to do some Michael Jordan TV ads with Warren Eakins for Nike. They had some stuff which wasn't working and were really up against it and had no money left. They trusted me and it worked because they had a really good track, which was a rap by Guru from Gangstar. There was no script but the track was all sorted. It sounds cliched but you always try and make sure it's as real as it can be. And to me it sounded real. I thought, OK, I'm not trying to do too much. I had access to all the Michael Jordan footage, and I was pleased with it. And then there was the Charles Barkley ad and then Scottie Pippen. Then I did "Freedom is a Movement" and the Brazilian soccer thing. We just got loads and loads of samba CDs and Jo Pittman shot the footage.

The reason I think the graphic approach is relevant for these ads is because so often the people aren't available. But there's a whole untapped side to it. I think Nike or Adidas should give their advertising money to a youth group here and a school there, and say, you make the films, or whatever, do an event, do something. That would be an innovation, a real change in the way advertising is approached. Advertising isn't like graphic design because it is a specific business, the application of something towards an end, whereas design is a purity. At the point at which someone is given a budget they should stop and say...we could do one sixty second ad with a top movie director, and with the rest of the money we'll do something a bit more human, involving people. There will always be good and bad ideas and that's all advertising will ever be if we don't widen it.

Nike could do so much. They could do a commercial that is just sixty seconds of silence and then the logo comes up. But most people do things that are so conservative, which they think will win them an award.

IT'S AMAZING THOUGH BECAUSE YOU GUYS AT TOMATO HAVE ADVERTISED ALMOST EVERY SHOE COMPANY....
Yeah. The funny thing is that now Warren Eakins is working with Leagas Delaney, and last summer I did the first Adidas press ads for America with him, the Feet You Wear campaign. They wanted it to be done in handwriting, so I made my handwriting into a typeface. I just wish clients would think more. With Nike, they chop and change people, so there's no consistency. They always want the latest trendy designer and it becomes a fashion thing.

BUT NIKE IS ALWAYS SAYING THEY'RE NOT A FASHION COMPANY. SO WHY MAKE SHOES IN DIFFERENT COLOUR-WAYS?
They should just relax about it.

DO YOU THINK ADVERTISING SIGNALS WHETHER A COMPANY IS FASHION LED OR NOT?
I honestly don't know what effect advertising has. I do know that if it is any good it contributes to the quality of a product. People are astute enough to see what's being forced on them and what isn't. If a shoe is for sport, then why do a new Shaquille O'Neal shoe every six months? There's something weird going on there because a sportsman needs consistency and a shoe which he is used to.

I think the most interesting thing to have happened with trainers in the last five years has been with Adidas. Because the old stuff still flies out of the shops but it was never backed up with an advertising campaign.

SUBCULTURES LATCH ONTO A CERTAIN SHOE BUT BY THE TIME THE COMPANIES REALISE, IT'S TOO LATE...
It just goes to show, because advertising is credited for pushing trainers over the edge in terms of popularity, but it's always the case that the ground work is laid by people thinking, hey that's great, that's really interesting. In the end that becomes the standard, and it's no longer about fashion. The good things remain good. Things that look all spacey and futuristic, they still work fifty years later because they're comfortable, or they reflect an aspect of someone's personality. It's what Vivienne Westwood says, if something is good, it will always be good. Do we get described by the things we wear? I suppose we do, because you make your choices don't you?

SCREEN SHOT FROM NIKE COMMERCIAL

sepance 4

		LUI Ouais... t'as raison. En plus, ça fait longtemps qu'on n'y a pas été. J'aime bien leur chou farci et leur saucisson est... **ELLE** Non, une viande, ça me tente bien. Tu boiras quoi, toi? Du pinard? **LUI** Non, pas d'alcool.	Fondu au noir (dernière phrase du dialogue : écran noir)	(arrêt musique)
6	13	Encore plus loin... ELLE s'arrête brusquement. **ELLE** Et un pakistanais?! Ca te dit un pakistanais?	Ouverture au noir Caméra fixe en plongée Le trottoir vide Les pieds d'ELLE envahissent l'écran en gros plan (face caméra).	Bruits de rue Dialogue (off)
6	14	**LUI** Ouais... Pourquoi pas?	Caméra fixe en plongée Gros plan Les pieds de LUI qui se retournent.	Idem pl.13
6	15	**ELLE** (reprenant sa marche) Offff... Puis non, c'est lourd après. Je le sens pas finalement. Ca m'saoûle.	Travelling arrière Plan moyen ELLE avance (en amorce, D cadre, la jambe droite de LUI apparaît) et le dépasse pour sortir à l'avant-plan G cadre (LUI reste à l'arrière-plan).	Bruits de rue Dialogue (off) Musique

Sepance 3

E = Elle SHE
L = Lui HE
P = Passant (people walks)

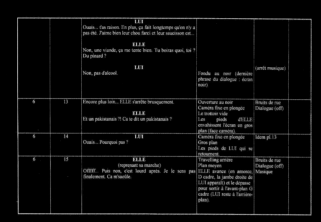

		ELLE Si, si... une bonne viande...		
5	8	**ELLE** Mais avec le truc de la vache folle...J'sais pas. Non?	Caméra fixe en plongée Gros plan Les pieds traversent le passage-piéton G cadre vers D cadre (de profil).	Idem pl. 7
5	9	**LUI** Attends, je rêve!... Mais ça fait quinze ans que t'as été contaminée, toi! Et quand on te regarde, c'est clair que ça attaque grave.	Caméra fixe Gros plan Elle et lui de 3/4 dos, qui s'éloignent vers l'arrière-plan et croisent un passant qui s'avance vers l'avant-plan et sort D cadre.	Idem pl. 7,8
5	10	**ELLE** (lui donnant un coup de pied) Arrête, espèce de tache! Toi non plus, ça t'a pas réussi, hein? Mon taureau... Non, attends, pas mon taureau, mon "boeu" ouais, mon p'tit "boeu".	Caméra fixe Raccord dans l'axe : gros plan sur les pieds.	Idem pl. 7,8,9
5	11	**LUI** Peut-être... Mais avec une paire de couilles comme ça.	Léger travelling arrière puis caméra fixe en légère plongée Leurs pieds (elle marche devant, lui arrive par derrière et se colle à elle).	Idem pl. 7,8,9,10
5	12	**LUI** Bon, une viande, ça te dit ou pas? **ELLE** OK. Alors on essaie notre vieux "Sabot Auvergnat"?	Travelling arrière Gros plan Leurs pieds	Idem pl. 7,8,9,10,11

FEET FOOD STORY-BOARD FOR FILM BY © CARMEN ATIAS, 97

How They Get There

FILM BY SPIKE JONZE

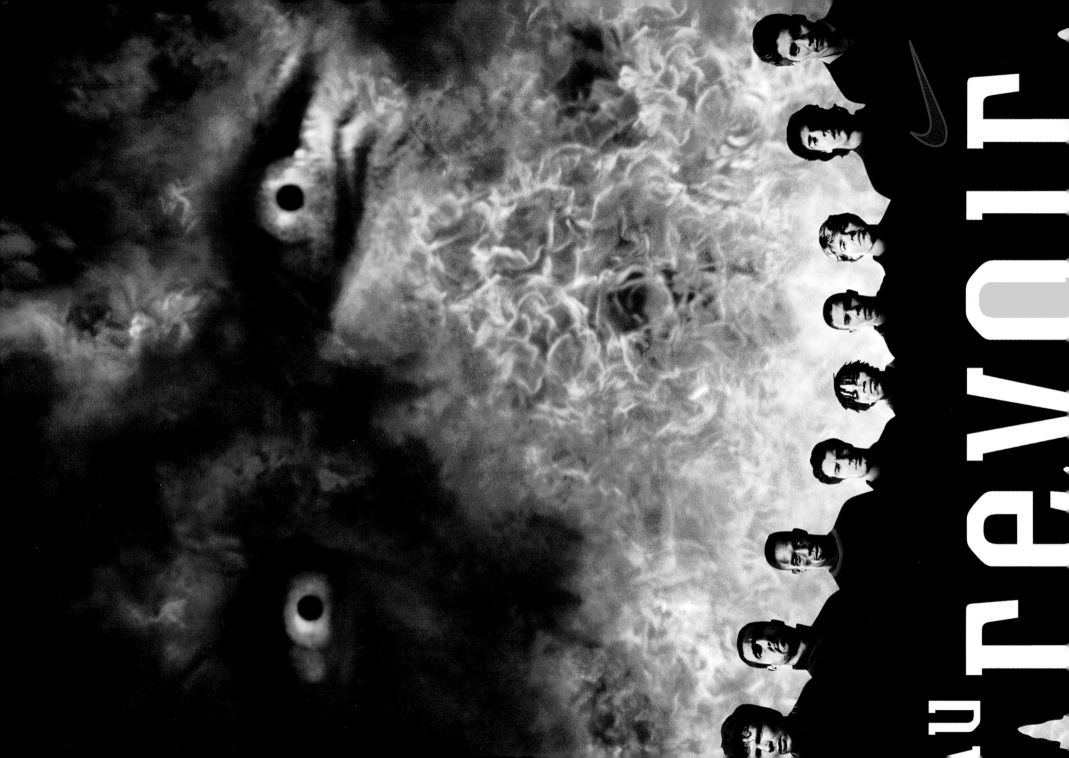

Sudden Death: what any team faces without Eric.

NIKE HAVE JUST BOUGHT ITALY AND BRAZIL. THEY'VE SPENT SOMETHING LIKE THREE HUNDRED MILLION DOLLARS TO GET BRAZIL. MY FRIEND, A PHOTOGRAPHER, WENT TO SHOOT THE BRAZILIAN NATIONAL TEAM. THAT'S THE ULTIMATE GIG. AND THE GUY AT NIKE SAID, "WE JUST WANNA OWN SOCCER. IT'S GONNA BE HUGE LIKE BASKETBALL. THREE-QUARTERS OF THE WORLD PLAYS SOCCER. TO TAKE OVER FROM ADIDAS AND PUMA WE JUST HAVE TO GET THE BEST..."

DERICK PROCOPE

NIKE'S DREAM TEAM BY TIM RICH

ON THE ONE HAND YOU HAVE A MULTI-NATIONAL MEGA-CORP THAT MASS PRODUCES OBJECTS WHICH SELL PRETTY MUCH WORLD-WIDE. ON THE OTHER YOU HAVE SOME OF THE MOST OPINIONATED, OUTSPOKEN, PEER GROUP-CONSCIOUS CONSUMERS AROUND, WHO DEMAND THAT A BRAND SAYS THE RIGHT THINGS IN THE RIGHT TONE OF VOICE AT ALL TIMES. HOW DOES THE FORMER MAKE THE LATTER WANT TO SHELL OUT SERIOUS CASH FOR ITS PRODUCTS? ENTER THAT STRANGE AMALGAM OF BUSINESSMEN, PSYCHOLOGISTS AND AESTHETICIANS - THE ADVERTISING AGENCY. THEIR FORM OF ALCHEMY TRANSLATES SALES-SPEAK INTO YOU-AND-ME-SPEAK AND MAY PERSUADE MILLIONS OF US TO PAY OVER THE ODDS FOR A PIECE OF FACTORY-MADE FOOTWEAR.

OF ALL THE EUROPEAN ADVERTISING CAMPAIGNS FOR SPORTS SHOES, NIKE'S HAS CONSISTENTLY BEEN THE MOST ADVENTUROUS. HOW MANY TIMES HAVE YOU BEEN SLUMPED IN FRONT OF A TV AD BREAK WHEN SOMETHING SO ODD, SO NEW AND YET SO RIGHT TAKES OVER THE SCREEN? YOU'RE TOO BUSY DEVOURING IT TO SECOND GUESS WHO IS ADVERTISING WHAT. IT'S ONLY AT THE END THAT YOU SEE THE SWOOSH. NOW THINK OF THE NUMBER OF TIMES YOU'VE BEEN SLUMPED IN FRONT OF AN AD BREAK WHEN SOMETHING KIND OF NIKE-LIKE COMES ON. YOU'RE THINKING, THIS AD IS OK, BUT IT'S NOT ONE OF THEIR BEST. THE MUSIC'S GOOD, THE EDITING'S GOOD, THE LIGHTING'S GOOD, THE WORDS ARE GOOD BUT IT NEVER GOES QUITE FAR ENOUGH. IT FEELS LIKE NIKE LITE. YOU GET TO THE END AND YOU DISCOVER IT'S FOR...WELL, SOMEONE ELSE.

UNLIKE MOST ADVERTISERS, NIKE DOESN'T FOLLOW THE RULES OF THEIR ADVERTISING GENRE. THE COMPANY AND ITS AD AGENCIES HAVE CREATED ITS OWN LANGUAGE AND ARE BUSY DEVELOPING NEW WORDS, PHRASES AND DIALECTS. EVERYONE ELSE IS RUNNING BEHIND, TRYING TO CREATE STORIES BUT GETTING ALL THEIR WORDS FROM THE NIKE DICTIONARY. THE MAIN AGENCY RESPONSIBLE FOR THE COMPANY'S EUROPEAN ADVERTISING IS WIEDEN & KENNEDY AMSTERDAM - THE EUROPEAN ARM OF THE MAIN US NIKE AGENCY, WIEDEN & KENNEDY IN PORTLAND, OREGON. ALTHOUGH THERE ARE NUMEROUS ROSTER AGENCIES SPREAD ACROSS THE CONTINENT, IT'S WIEDEN & KENNEDY AMSTERDAM THAT COMPILES THE EUROPEAN VERSION OF THE DICTIONARY.

EQUALLY THE AGENCY'S APPROACH TO EXPLAINING ITS WORK DOESN'T FOLLOW THE GABBY, LOOK-AT-ME STYLE OF OTHER AGENCIES. GETTING THEM TO AGREE TO AN INTERVIEW IS OK, CONFIRMING A TIME TO DO IT IS TRICKY, GETTING THEM TO TALK IN DETAIL ABOUT NIKE AND THEMSELVES IS LIKE TRYING TO GET A RABID POLECAT INTO A CRISP PACKET. IN TRUTH, THEY ARE POLITE AND HELPFUL, BUT DESPERATELY ELUSIVE.

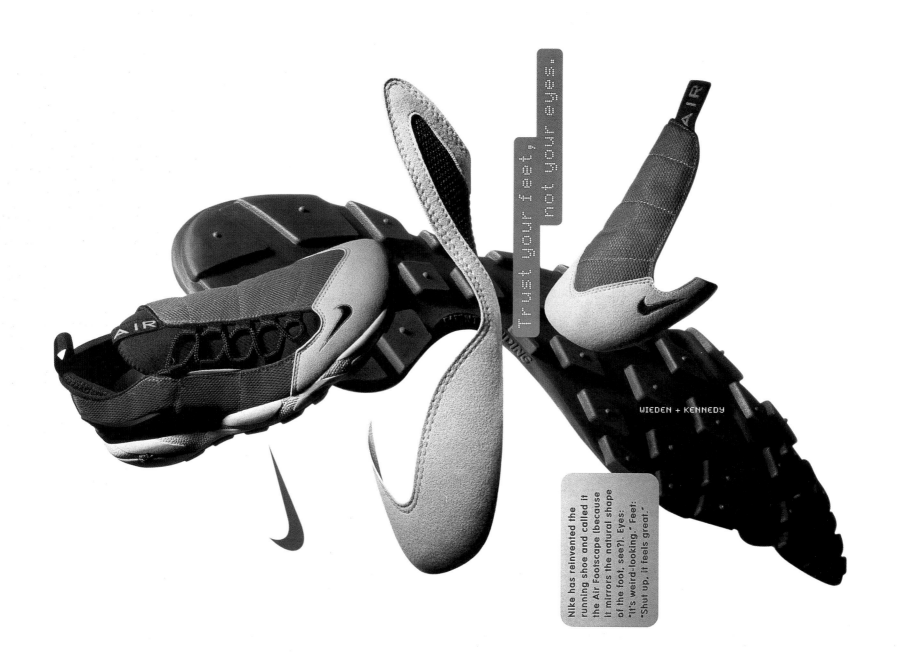

Trust your feet, not your eyes.

Nike has reinvented the running shoe and called it the Air Footscape (because it mirrors the natural shape of the foot, see?). Eyes: "It's weird-looking." Feet: "Shut up, it feels great."

WIEDEN + KENNEDY

Having seen their work for Nike and Coca-Cola - the two mega-clients which dominate their business - you might expect the agency to be housed in an airy and angular warehouse conversion or a post-modern glass and concrete confection. The reality is more prosaic. From the outside it looks like the office of a genteel solicitor, set within a generously proportioned terrace, in a pleasant, unremarkable street near the Vondelpark and about fifteen minutes walk from the centre of the city. The hush is punctuated every few minutes by the urgent mechanical clatter of a cyclist. Inside it's a different story. As I open the door seven or eight people are dotted around the reception area, and a be-denimed art director-type is galloping down the wide staircase with a large artwork folder and a deadline-heavy brow. A digital symphony of phones, faxes and modems blends with a babble of voices. Everyone is speaking English, but the accents are exotic. I appear to have stepped into the United Nations of advertising.

It turns out that the staff at the sharp-end don't stick around too long. Since its founding in 1992, the Amsterdam office has been under the creative directorship of Susan Hoffman (1992-1993), Bob Moore and Michael Prieve (1993-1996), David "Jelly" Helm and Chris Wall (1996), then Helm with Charlotte Moore (1996-1997), then Moore with Jon Matthews (1997) and - at the time of writing - Matthews on his own. There's a company joke that they're thinking about fitting a revolving door to the creative director's office.

Sometime before "Jelly" Helm left he did relax his guard a little and talk to me about how the agency operates. This tall, intense, Kentucky-born graduate of the design course at the University of Louisville worked as a graphic designer before going into advertising. "A lot of people told me that I might be cut out for advertising. I'm not sure why, I always wondered whether that was an insult or not," he says.

When he was sent out to Europe his brief was straightforward. "It was basically, 'don't fuck up'. The only thing Dan Wieden told me...nothing else...was 'have fun'. It sounds nice in the context of an interview, but it wasn't reassuring. I had never been a creative director before and I needed a bit more than 'have fun'. Now I see what he was saying. We all inherently know what our job involves in terms of keeping the standard of work high, but the idea of having fun is pretty easily forgotten, especially in this environment because there are more details over here.

"It's nice when you come up with an idea in America, you don't ever have to worry about adapting it to different cultures or whether cultural references are understood. Over here there's a lot more questioning. Markets are so different and the role of sports are so different. I grew up as a real basketball junkie, I still love basketball but it's just not part of people's background here. I didn't know anything about soccer when I came over, so all of a sudden I'm second guessing things that normally come to me naturally, intuitively."

When we spoke Helm was charged with ensuring that the Portland culture was brought into the agency, although he admitted that it is difficult to define what Wieden & Kennedy's culture is: "It's easier to say what isn't a Wieden & Kennedy ad, it's harder to say what is. It's weird talking about this theoretical stuff...."

Well, obviously the work is the best evidence, and the ads from Amsterdam are infused with attitude - tongue-in-cheek cockiness, powerful art direction and a willingness to take risks.

Boiled down to its essence, Wieden & Kennedy Amsterdam have taken an American brand with a huge personality - Nike - and presented it with a European sensibility. This blend of European and American cultures parallels the brand image of Nike - because it's obviously American but it feels strangely familiar and local to Europeans. Some of the Nike ads wouldn't look out of place in American magazines, while others - like the Me Company-designed Dutch soccer stars ads - employ the latest European graphic aesthetics and feature sports heroes whose reputations are strictly local. The logic behind the Nike work seems clear; immerse your thinking in the brand and create ideas for local audiences. This is different to the approaches of most multinational agencies, which tend to spray a multinational idea onto each market, or create servile campaigns that simply reflect the tastes, expectations and language of the local consumers. The result with Nike isfresh, confident ads that have a conversation with the audience.

Although Wieden & Kennedy Amsterdam produces ads for all Nike's markets, from basketball to running to tennis, its greatest challenge

is in building the brand in Europe's most passionately followed sport, football. This is where the vagueness of Nike's perceived geographical placement has paid dividends, for when it comes to talking football "American-ness" is just about the last quality footie fans want to buy into, despite the success of the 94 World Cup. So the agency has been entertaining European football fans with the same aggressive and informed language you can see in the Portland-generated work about basketball and athletics. Of course, brave creative ideas can go wrong and Nike work has balls-ed up here and there. Print work running pre- and during the 1996 European Football Championships saw a focus on players such as Eric Cantona and Ian Wright who didn't actually get to play in the tournament. Worse, Cantona's stiff-collared taunting of England looked lame when the French team fell far short of setting the competition on fire - football has a habit of making gobshites look stupid. For a couple of weeks Nike's one-leap-ahead reputation quivered, particularly as Reebok was bulk screening its excellent "celebs talk about football" commercial featuring the likes of Vic Reeves, Robbie Williams and Jarvis Cocker, and Adidas was continuing its use of rough, Tomato(ed) spots.

Even Umbro managed one or two half-decent print ads.

What saved Nike at that point was the stunning "Devil's Eleven" commercial featuring Europe's finest taking on the best Beelzebub could muster, a sort of Arsenal squad with horns (yeah right, Ed). Despite the fact that it too focused on the sidelined Cantona, the commercial pushed the language of footie-related sports shoe ads into yet another new, and shadow world. It looked doubly impressive when running in an ad break between two halves of a dull game - a new twist on the well-worn idea of advertising being more entertaining than the programme.

Another support to Nike's rep was a series of extraordinary ads that appeared during the build-up to the tournament. Art directed by Dutch duo Kessels Kramer (who now run their own agency) and crafted by the modish London 3D design team Me Company, the ads presented key Dutch-based players as protagonists in some aggressive cyber-war-game. Patrick Kluivert was moulded into a star-shaped space weapon, while Edgar Davids roared off the page as a warped cross between a mean road bike and a missile-laiden space cruiser.

This was sports shoe advertising moving into a new, electronically-lit realm more often used for music-related advertising. And why not? The links between the image-conscious sections of football fans and cutting-edge music have always been close.

That campaign illustrates three central points about the Wieden & Kennedy approach to Nike: it exemplifies the agency's ability to spot and bring in new wave designers to work with their creative teams. It demonstrates their desire to go well beyond the generic language of a product sector. Finally, it illustrates the unpredictable nature of their subject matter; for all their cartoony cyber-power, the Dutch team was roundly whooped on the field by Shearer and co.

It's highly unlikely that the zipped lips at Wieden & Kennedy Amsterdam will reveal anything about what's coming next before any ads (or direct mail shots, or sponsorship programmes, or TV stations, or theme parks) turn up near you. However, in the context of the way the product is moving and the nature of the sector, the agency's somewhat manic, organic, brave, dynamic and instinct-focused modus operandi means that it remains the agency most likely to be there, adding to the burgeoning Nike dictionary of advertising language. Of course, I can say that, and they couldn't possibly comment.

SOME OF THE MATERIAL USED IN THIS ARTICLE ORIGINALLY RAN IN PRINT MAGAZINE'S EUROPEAN SPECIAL ISSUE (APRIL 1997).

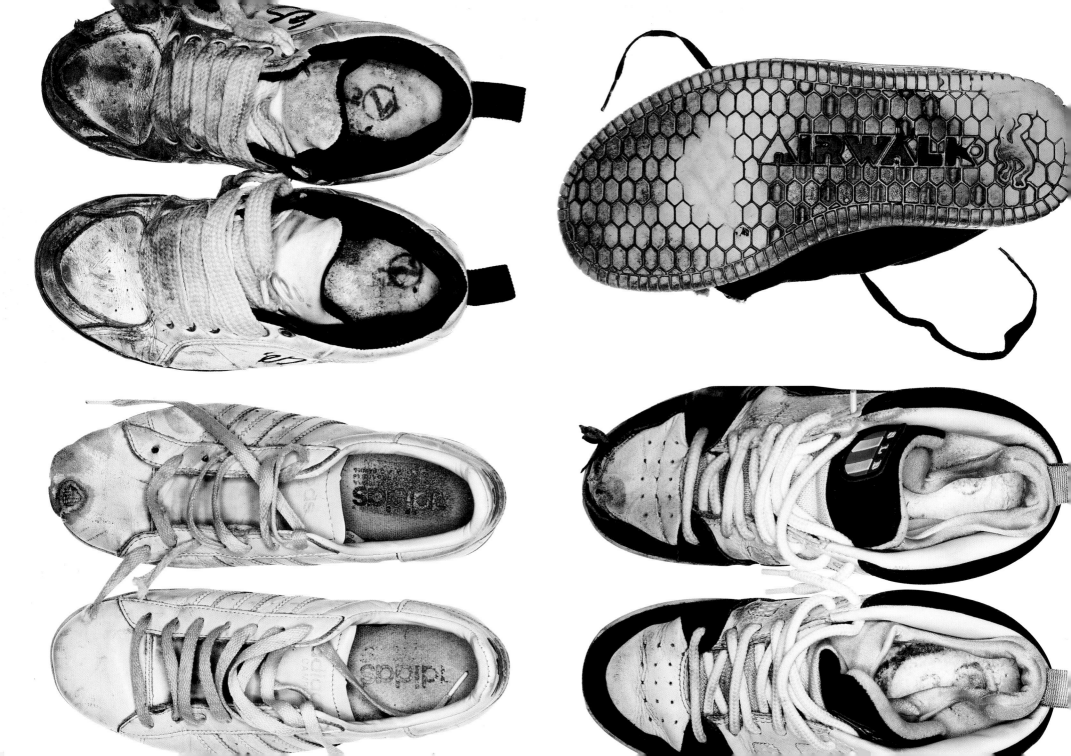

A black and white photograph of a hazy beach, shot at dawn. A man running in the middle distance. An asterisk by him links him to the word "FREE" in hand-written letters at the bottom of the page. Then in the corner, a small Adidas logo and the word "RUNNING".

Freedom is certainly intoxicating. The concept is also pretty big, bigger than a brand of trainers. Freedom, or the lack of it, has sparked revolutions, people live and die for it. Yet now it's linked to trainers. Of course that is what skilled advertising is all about, bringing two unrelated concepts together and enhancing the product by the association: nope, experiencing freedom's fine, but in order to enjoy it, you must be wearing trainers... and the right ones at that.

A shot of a peaceful river meandering through tree-lined hills. "HURRY" is written in large letters at the bottom of the photo, while dotted about in smaller type we see: "MULTI-STOREY CAR PARK, HIGH RISE FLATS, TRAIN STATION, FLYOVER, INDUSTRIAL ESTATE, SUPERMARKET, HIGH STREET DIY SUPERSTORE, SHOPPING MALL".

The oppositions and ironies in this, the second advert in the series, break down in several ways. Get out of the city, get into yourself, push yourself, don't be pushed. It's about personal choice. Yet just by being there these words remind us where we and our trainers come from. The warehouse on the industrial estate stores and distributes them, the shop sells them, we battle through traffic to the carpark, down the high street and dig deep into our purses to buy them (free?). Ironically the advert does not contain the word "factory", for this might make us pause to consider where trainers are made. It might conjure up images of the words "Just do it" on the wall of a factory. Out of sight and out of mind. How flimsy is this concept of freedom when linked to trainers?

Ironically, in the context of a history of footwear characterised by the restriction of movement and highlighting divisions in society, it is not hard to see how the trainer, which was initially cheap, unisex, proletarian, practical and comfortable, became equated with freedom and equality.

In the 90s, while trainers are deeply hip and the hold of the brands is so strong, it's considered rather crass to admit it. Supposedly trainers are chosen on quality and performance. But while consumers are seduced to varying degrees by their fashion appeal, manufacturers are repositioning their image firmly in the sports domain. There are now scores of adverts endorsed by sports stars, mostly men, who are our new popular heroes.

Essentially we have come full-circle since the medieval Poulaines worn with shorts reflected the gothic ideal of beauty, fixed on the male body and in particular the legs. The male body is once more an ideal of perfection, yet this time athleticism and dynamic movement are desirable, not the opposite. Trainers have gone hi-tech. It's all about support and stability for the foot: they're "engineered", with "kinetic wedges", "die-cut EVA midsoles" and that "Hexalite unit for extra cushioning". Some adverts show a cut-through section to reveal the trainer's inner workings, as if the shoe has been tested and perfected in a lab. Unfortunately, this is quite hard to reconcile with images of the sweatshops where they are actually made. Nonetheless most trainers are well-designed and do perform better, yet in order to differentiate themselves from the competition they need to communicate this, and so such qualities are highlighted with bold colours, distinctive detailing and lots of technical jargon.

Hi-tech reminds us of the city but often we yearn for something more than that, to rediscover "quality of life" and "personal fulfilment". Our desire for increased technology and, at the same time, greater freedom are two opposite poles, yet today the trainer companies advertise their product as inspired by, and consequently, an extension of the human body: the runner and trainer are one.

Recently a flood of women's "trainers" have appeared, with their own distinctive style. These are high-heeled, backless, silver or baby pink - some even have built-in purses. Tongue-in-cheek, they look refreshingly fun amongst so much macho hi-tech. Let's face it, whatever the trainer manufacturers maintain, we know that when it comes to people and sport, most of us just don't do it.

Like all good advertisers, the global trainer brands keep themselves appealing by embodying the most desirable qualities prevalent in our culture at any one time. Freedom never goes out of fashion, and what it means to be free is perpetually changing. People interpret adverts in a way that is meaningful to them. Yet for all the rhetoric about the West being free, we're not. Our reality is constructed around what money can buy and the global brands which control our "consuming" habit. After this work-out it's back to the office.

FREEDOM BY MONIKA FABTINGER

symmetry

19/5/97 01:12:03
FROM JANKWIG@PANIX.COM
SUBJECT: RE AD IN INTERVIEW +
QUEER SEX IN SHITE HIGH TOPS

...About half way into this issue of
Interview is an ad for Airwalks that
you'll love. Barefoot and kneeling
female, dressed in tight red is
carrying a pair of Airwalks on a red
heart. Very submissive pose.
Woman serving her sneaker-loving
guy's ultimate needs...

I'm saying that from the 80s...they started making shoes that crossed over...basketball and skate shoes you could wear on the street and we'd all go out and try and reproduce what we saw on video, the clothing, the shoes, the way the artists are holding themselves...like ads, those music videos had a great influence.

BOMA, SKATER, LONDON 03/97

BM: Another aspect of the non-sexual side of my website is, one of the people on my mailing list suggested a sneaker movie database and when we get enough submissions we'll publish the database. If you look, there are some movies where sneakers are highly visible, like "Grease", "Footloose" and "Voyage to the Bottom of the Sea".

IT'S FUNNY HOW A LOT OF THESE SHOE COMPANIES ARE TARGETING MOVIES. IN "BATMAN" HIS BOOTS WERE MADE BY NIKE...IN THE "ALIEN" FILMS SIGORNY WEAVER'S BOOTS WERE MADE BY REEBOK..."BACK TO THE FUTURE" HAD THE CHUCK TAYLOR ALL STARS AND HI-TECH NIKES...
In "Anaconda" a character was in Chuck Taylors for the entire movie. One of the things we do is find photographs from movies and post them. Some people like really grungy sneakers, really torn up, and others like pristine clean, and of course you can find sneakers in all conditions in the movies.

I READ IN A NEWSPAPER OVER HERE THAT REEBOK WERE TAKING THE PRODUCERS OF "JERRY MCGUIRE" TO COURT BECAUSE THEY SIGNED A DEAL THAT THEIR SHOES WERE TO BE FEATURED IN 70% OF THE MOVIE AND THEY WERE ONLY FEATURED IN ABOUT 10%. REEBOK WERE PRETTY PISSED. Then again I find it very interesting that Converse can get 100% exposure in "Anaconda" and end up not paying a cent.

YEAH, BUT IT'S ONE OF THESE THINGS WHERE THE CHARACTER PLAYED BY ICE CUBE WAS WEARING CONVERSE SHOES, PROBABLY BECAUSE HE'S ALWAYS WEARING CONVERSE... HE WAS PROBABLY PLAYING HIMSELF IN THAT FILM. He walked through the water from one boat to the other, and as he was walking down the stairs from the deck to the second level in the boat, his sneakers were still bone dry.

MARTY MCFLY'S (MICHAEL J FOX) SNEAKERS IN "BACK TO THE FUTURE PART 2" WERE DEVELOPED IN CONJUNCTION WITH NIKE. THE SHOE HAD SIX LACES INSTEAD OF ONE, WITH LOOPS THAT WENT THROUGH THE SOLE AND THROUGH THE GROUND. THAT GROUND WAS A RAISED PLATFORM UNDER WHICH THE SPECIAL FX PEOPLE PULLED THE LOOPS VERY TIGHT AS MICHAEL J FOX STEPPED INTO HIS SNEAKERS.

My first memory of trainers in films...a key one was "Beat Street", the hip hop film. It was the first time that hip hop culture, what was happening with the street was on the big screen - graffiti, great music, dancing, fashion - the whole political statement of black culture taking a new twist. It was a key film in understanding the development of urban culture. We can see trainers being part of that style and culture...the way they had their laces tied...the Adidas that RUN DMC used to wear. These represent statements that make you stand out from the crowd. One of the other crucial films for me was "She's got to have it". The Mars Blackman character was "The ultimate B-boy" circa 86. It's interesting to see how it developed, with the culmination of "Do the right thing"...the scene with Gian Carlo Esposito, when the white guy scuffs his sneakers with the bike. The idea that stepping on a man's shoe or trainer is a fate worse than death. When you went to a club like Bally High, you could die for that. It was something that black people could connect with...in the cinema everyone woke up at that scene. When I realised that Spike was doing a series of Nike ads...

THE SAME CHARACTER WAS USED IN THE NIKE AD...
...so it ends with the commodification of urban culture, how fashion, music and film have melted into one. I think Spike was very clever in bringing those three together in commercials. We tracked down the ad agency that produced them...

WIEDEN & KENNEDY. WHAT WAS THEIR RESPONSE WHEN YOU ASKED FOR ALL SPIKE'S ADS?
We got blanked. Maybe they didn't realise the cultural significance, and that was something we were trying to get across...the context of the trainers...we weren't into just showing films of sneakers. One of the spots shows racial warfare on the court, between black and white and the idea that it played out on a basketball court, equalised by sharing the same goals...by having Nike trainers. The idea might seem a bit trite but it's a clever device to use a brand as a means of creating peace. I think American youth are more susceptible. Europeans aren't. What does that tell you about Americans?
For advertisers, it's the power of music and fashion. Kids are far more conscious of what they look like. Funny how they're easily influenced by advertisers. It raises some worrying question... advertisers have responsibilities and so do shoe companies. They operate on a subliminal level.

WHAT ABOUT PRODUCT PLACEMENT IN FILMS? "DO THE RIGHT THING" WAS A WALKING NIKE AD...
Product placement's being around forever...beer, Coca-Cola... the idea of influencing a generation. Films are seen by millions of people. It's a numbers game, if you could hit one per cent who are influenced to buy your product simply because they saw a star wearing it, making a cool move. Then I think product placements are worth the money. Versace...Hilfiger. When you consider that films and videos are aimed at the youth market...you begin to see the power.

IT'S KINDA CRAZY TRYING TO LOOK LIKE SOMEONE IN A VIDEO....HAVE YOUR OWN STYLE.
That's why there are stylists...

SONY

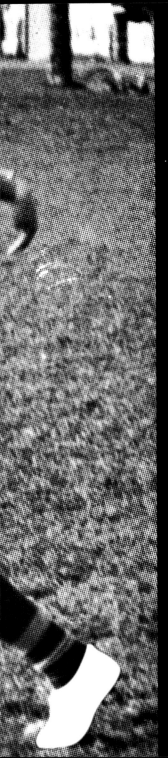

Once upon a time trainers were no big deal. Shocking, isn't it. But true. When I was growing up in America in the late 1950s and early 1960s sneakers [as we call trainers in the USA] were just for sports. And only boring, airhead "jocks" did sports. For you see [and this is the really amazing thing] in my day sports weren't cool.

What was cool was Modern Jazz. Imagine John Coltrane, Thelonius Monk, Chet Baker or the MJQ in their trim, stripped down, minimal, thin labelled suits with their sharp ties and...sneakers. Yes, I know, it's just the sort of look which would go down a treat with today's Acid Jazz musicians but back then sneakers would have sent all the wrong messages - cheap, childish, athletic, hot and sweaty. To be truly laid-back and cool what you needed was a pair of pointy Italian shoes, maybe loafers with little tassels on them. Maybe something in suede.

Speaking of which, Rockabillies were cool. I'm not talking about the rough and ready, bashed-up denim cowboy look, that came later. No, focus on those early photographs of Elvis with his flash suits and hipster posturing. As with the modern jazzers, the original Rockabilly look called for casual yet elegant footwear. And because most of these guys had come from the wrong side of the tracks, like all people from a poor background [including, of course, the black jazz musicians] they wanted classy shoes. Sneakers [at the time the cheapest thing you could put on your feet] simply couldn't fit the bill. A nice pair of blue suede shoes, however, would be just the thing.

Bikes were cool. Think about Brando in "The Wild One" casually getting off his bike and striding into small town America. Nowadays the meanest, toughest, most threatening Rap musician can wear sneakers and look mean, tough and threatening. But in 1954 when "The Wild One" came out in the USA if Brando et al had been wearing sneakers the effect would have been one of comedy rather than menace. No, for symbolic as well as practical reasons Bikers needed a good sturdy pair of motorcycle boots: in 1954 only nice boys wore sneakers.

Beats were cool. In suburban America where I grew up our mental picture was more Beatnik than true Beat - the guy bashing the bongos in shades and sandals. The real Beats like Jack Kerouac and Neal Cassady wore work-wear denim and, in Kerouac's case, a casual collegiate style. The most famous photograph of these two was taken by Neal's wife, Carolyn Cassady. Unfortunately, it cuts them off at knee-level. Could they have been wearing sneakers? I put the question to Carolyn Cassady who lives in London and who put up with untold silly questions from me when I was researching the "Streetstyle" exhibition for the Victoria and Albert Museum. "No, absolutely not", was her reply, "Neal would have been wearing Oxfords and Jack his hiking boots".

On the road. But not in sneakers. It's particularly interesting in Kerouac's case. Once a college athlete, he was far sportier than those of us would-be Beatniks would have been able to get our heads around. We wanted the pale, unhealthy, out-of-it artist in a garret look which would establish our anti-jock credentials. Despite the uncomfortable irony that Jack Kerouac had played college football [and looked it] we wanted to see our Beat heroes as anti-sports as well as anti-establishment. [In fact, we took the two as synonyms]. Hugh Hefner was cool. In the early 60s we would see him surrounded by gorgeous bunny girls in his mansion wearing a dressing gown and slippers, smoking his pipe. Or we would see him at the office in one of those sharp, modern jazz suits with, say, Italian loafers. No sneakers. Clearly the only exercise this *Playboy* was getting was in the sack.

In all of these examples there is a clear equation: if you wanted to be hip/cool/with it and make it with lots of girls you didn't wear sneakers.

So, what changes? Most importantly our attitude to sports. Ironically, it changed back to what it was 100 years ago when everyone was [or wanted to be] out playing tennis, riding bicycles, sailing, horse-back riding and so on. The collapse of stuffy old Victorian values coincided with the rise of outdoor, liberating, go-for-it fun sports. And it had a profound influence on fashion, with garments specifically designed for doing sports gradually shifting into everyday apparel. Within this perspective it would seem that the anti-sports tendencies of the 50s and 60s were an anomaly. Now, obviously, things have gone full steam in the opposite direction with even the most unfit members of our society ambling lazily about in track-suit and trainers. The 80s shifted the equation back to cool=sporty.

Additionally, our attitude towards sports had to become more democratic. The athletic activities which everyone wanted to get into in Edwardian times were based in the upper classes. While, arguably, the sneaker has its roots in the tennis shoe [and therefore the upper class] its more widespread development came with basketball, for example, the Converse basketball shoe which was introduced in 1916 as the first brand name product for this purpose. Played across a much wider social spectrum, basketball gradually lost its white, collegiate associations and became a key route to success for black ghetto kids. That social inversion of the late 60s and early 70s, whereby middle class white kids wanted to emulate poor black kids [consider Tom Wolfe's *Radical Chic* which was first published in 1970 and featured Leonard Bernstein hosting a benefit party for the Black Panthers], swept everything associated with the ghetto into mainstream fashion - including, of course, sneakers.

Within the ghetto, however, one more change was required. Throughout history those from poor backgrounds have always sought to signal success by investing in expensive adornment, clothing and [most of all] shoes. While the well off Radical Chic of the 70s could proudly slum around in cheap sneakers, those from poor backgrounds needed something classier. Happily, sportswear manufacturers began introducing state-of-the-art designer ranges with out-of-this-world price tags and the humble sneaker became a status symbol.

From sending all the wrong signals in the 50s and 60s - uncool, jock, clean-cut, cheap - to sending all the right signals today - go-for-it, sporty [now=cool], street credible yet classy - the sneaker, more than any other item of clothing, demonstrates the key transitions of our recent social history. For the sneaker to become hip the world had to be profoundly transformed - with sports once again becoming fashionable, with new trends bubbling up from the have-nots rather than trickling down from the filthy rich, with authenticity deriving from who you are rather than who your parents were. In a very real sense, therefore, the sneaker is the definitive icon of our fin de siècle 20th/21st century lifestyle.

Who know, one of these days I may even buy myself a pair.

MICHAEL JORDAN SIGNS TO NIKE AND
"RE-DESIGNS" AN EXISTING MODEL.
ORIGINALLY, THE NBA BANNED THEM!
RED, WHITE WITH BLACK SWOOSH

IT BECAME A COLLECTORS ITEM.
YOU COULD FIND THE SAME MODEL IN
DIFFERENT COLOUR COMBINATIONS:
WHITE/BLUE, BLACK/BLUE, BLACK/WHITE.
THERE WAS ALSO THE FAMOUS L.A.
LAKERS COLOURS[!]. AND THE PROTOTYPE
VERSION:BLACK VYNIL WITH GOLD SWOOSH
AND 'AIR JORDAN' WINGS SOLD IN JAPAN
IN 1997 FOR 10,000,000 YEN

VERY SIMPLISTIC. AN ITALIAN VERSION
WAS MADE IN EMBOSSED LEATHER.
FLASH, TO REFLECT MICHAEL JORDAN'S
PLAYING STYLE. SUPPOSEDLY.
[WHITE ONLY]

RADICAL DEPARTURE. MORE OF A
SPOILER- TYPE SOLE. A NEOPRENE
INNER BOOT, THE NEW 'FLYING JORDAN'
LOGO. [BLACK OR WHITE WITH RED OR
WHITE SOLE]. THERE WAS ALSO A WHITE
VERSION WITH BLUE PLASTIC ON THE
SOLE. THIS MODEL WAS RE-ISSUED IN
1996

AS MICHAEL JORDAN BEGINS TO
INDULGE HIS FETISH FOR CLASSIC
CARS, THE NIKE DESIGNERS ADD A
"SEAT-BELT SYSTEM" AND THE LOGO
TURNS INTO A BONNET BADGE.
[BLACK AND BLUE]. VERY SIMILAR TO
THE 1988 MODEL.IF YOU LOVE BOXES,
THEN THE 1989 BOX IS A MUST, THOUGH
YOU'D HAVE TO BUY YOUR AIR JORDANS
IN ITALY: THE LID OF THE BOX WAS THE
'WINGS' LOGO DIE-CUT - CHECK OUT
NAPLES. [BLACK, WHITE AND CREAM]

FLAMES, REMINISCENT OF "TOP GUN",
ARE ADDED TO THE MOULDING,
EVOCATIVE OF MICHAEL JORDAN'S
SWOOPING ANTICS. PLUS REFLECTIVE
MATERIAL ON THE TONGUE REACTS TO
PHOTO FLASH. [WHITE WITH BLACK
SOLE]. SOME PEOPLE SAY IT'S THE
BEST-LOOKING AIR JORDANS EVER. THE
SHOE CAME OUT IN BLACK OR WHITE
EACH WITH DIFFERENT COLOUR SOLES
[BLACK, RED AND PURPLE/ TURQUOISE],
AND A VERSION APPEARED WITH '23'
EMBROIDERED ON THE SIDE

VERY FUTURISTIC. LOTS OF DIFFERE[N]
COLOURS AVAILABLE. NOTABLY A WH[ITE]
VERSION WITH RED, BLUE OR BURGUN[DY]
SOLES. THERE WERE TWO HOLES IN T[HE]
TONGUE TO PUT YOUR FINGERS IN. IF [YOU]
WANT TO TIGHTEN UP YOUR JORDAN[S]
PLUS EXTRA VENTILATION ON THE SIDE[.]
THE MOST FAMOUS VERSION IS BLAC[K]
WITH FLASH RED BITS ON THE SOLE

S THE US DREAM TEAM GEAR UP OR THE OLYMPICS A NEW MODEL ELEBRATES GLOBAL TV VIEWING, WITH TEXT IN SIX LANGUAGES NSCRIBED INTO THE SOLE. [BLACK ND WHITE]. THE MOST FAMOUS ERSION IS THE WHITE SHOE WITH ILVER BITS AND THE GOLD "FLYING ORDAN" LOGO OUT OF BLACK; ALSO HIS SHOE HAD THE NUMBER "9" MICHAEL JORDAN'S POSITION IN HE DREAM TEAM] ON THE HEEL, NSTEAD OF "23"

WHAT HAPPENED HERE? THE JORDANS "AEROSPACE" HAD THAT REALLY KIDDIE LOOK. THEY WERE BLACK OR WHITE WITH MULTI-COLOURED PAINTINGS AROUND THE SOLE, AND THE LACES WERE HIDDEN BY TWO BIG STRAPS! BASICALLY, THEY WEREN'T A NICE SHOE: EVEN TODAY JORDANS COLLECTORS DON'T WANT THEM BECAUSE NOBODY'S ABLE TO RE-SELL THE THINGS

A RADICAL CHANGE FROM THE 1993 VERSION. THE SHOE IS MUCH SIMPLER, EVEN IN ITS COLOUR RANGES [THE MOST FAMOUS BEING THE NORTH CAROLINA MODEL IN WHITE AND LIGHT BLUE]. COMBINES LEATHER AND NUBUCK WITH THE JORDAN LOGO APPEARING ON THE SIDE OF THE SOLE. THIS SHOE ALSO CAME IN ALL-BLACK WITH NUMBER "45" ON THE HEEL [JORDAN'S POSITION IN THE BIRMINGHAM BASEBALL TEAM]

MODEL NUMBER TEN, COMPLETE WITH TEN STRIPES ON THE SOLE, EACH MARKING A PARTICULAR ACHIEVEMENT IN MICHAEL JORDAN'S CAREER, E.G., NUMEROUS MVP AWARDS. [BLACK, WHITE, GREY OR BROWN, WITH EIGHT VERSIONS OF THE STRIPY SOLE AND A HOST OF COMBINATIONS]

THE FASTEST SELLING SNEAKER EVER, WITH PATENT LEATHER UPPERS AND CARBON-FIBRE PLATES IN THE SOLE, A MARRIAGE OF FASHION AND TECHNOLOGY, PERHAPS? [BLACK AND WHITE, BLACK AND RED, WHITE AND WHITE]

THE LOW-CUT VERSIONS WERE ALSO VERY SUCCESSFUL, ESPECIALLY THE WHITE "SNAKESKIN" SHOE. AGAIN THERE WAS A VERSION WITH NUMBER "45", AND THE FAMOUS "SPACE JAM" EDITION WHICH IS ALL-BLACK WITH A BLUE SOLE AND PURPLE "FLYING JORDAN" LOGO

RADICAL CHANGE FROM THE 1996 MODEL. IF YOU'RE USED TO JORDANS, THIS SHOE IS PROBABLY THE MOST UNCOMFORTABLE OF THE LOT. IT TAKES A LONG TIME TO GET USED TO WEARING IT. THE DESIGN OF THIS MODEL IS QUITE SIMPLE. AND SO ARE THE COLOUR COMBINATIONS [RED/WHITE, BLACK/WHITE, BLACK/RED, BLUE/WHITE]. THE FIRST JUMPMAN IS LAUNCHED, BUT BASICALLY IT'S THE SAME MODEL

THE FASTEST SELLING SNEAKER EVER!

>> THE MOST COMFORTABLE JORDAN EVER,
PLUS EXTRA FLASHY BITS!!!! (WHITE, WHITE WITH DENIM,
ALL-BLACK WITH RED BITS AND VARIOUS SOLES).
>>THE JUMPMAN LINE COMES INTO ITS OWN WITH A RANGE OF DIFFERENT MODELS....

>> STOP PRESS...1998...
WITH A HOLOGRAPHIC '23' AND
'FLYING JORDAN' LOGO IN THE SOLE.

17/06/97

10:52   Eileen, Chicago
          eblack@artic.edu

Well the whole team was expected to come to the rally, and the police had completely shut down the streets (Colombus Drive and Jackson), in fact the entire area where the bus was supposed to arrive. Now, the only way into the school is through the doors where the police were, so I show them my ID and they let me through! So here I am standing on the front lawn (with my ever present camera, you never know when something's going to happen) and the whole shebang's getting ready to start. On the radio, you can hear the reporters in the helicopters saying stuff like, "The bus just made a left hand turn off Lake Shore Drive, and they're heading down Michigan Ave towards the park." Mind you, these are my fucking tax dollars paying some 300!!!! police officers to stand around and give these guys an escort in a damn bus. While we're all waiting, the stinking mayor shows up and he doesn't even have a police escort!! Well low and behold, up pulls this white Range Rover, and the window rolls down as a police officer directs it to park. I'm standing about 50 yards away, and can clearly see that it's Scottie Pippen. So I start clicking away, and guess what pulls up? A beautiful black Mercedes-Benz (an S-16 if I'm not mistaken), and a black Hummer. It's Jordan in the Benz and Rodman in the Hummer. I swear to God, I started giggling to myself, all the while snapping away. The weird part was that all this took place behind the stage, so the crowd didn't even know that they were there yet, so it was really quiet. Then the bus pulls up and all the rest of the players get off. It was eerie the way there were so many police officers around. Bike cops, mounted police, motorcycle cops, scooter cops, and freakin' crossing guards!! I got a couple of pictures of them taking the trophies out of a truck, and then I had seen enough. As I'm walking away, from the crowd's reaction, they had finally reached the stage, because the noise was deafening.

RODMAN

PIPPEN

THE MICHAEL JORDAN WHO WAS THE NICEST THAT I'VE DIRECTED BECAUSE HE WAS RETIRING AND NIKE WANTED A SHORT BIOGRAPHY OF HIM, AND IT WAS A SORT OF GOOD-BYE THING."

SUBJECT: AWESOME IDEA ON YOUR BOOK!
DATE: MON, 13 JAN 97 23:32:49 -0800
FROM: BUBBA <BUBBA.JUNKYARDJEANS.COM>
ORGANIZATION: J U N K Y A R D J E A N S
TO: VISION@CYBERIACAFE.NET

I have been collecting for over 5 years now and 1 year of it as a job. Now I buy and sell used sneakers to make a living. But all the time I buy and collect for myself. I have over five thousand dollars invested in my shoe collection. With everything from Bob Kusey originals from the 50s to all years of the Jordan shoe. I even have 1 metallic blue Jordan first edition which I paid one thousand dollars for. Thanks. BUBBA

At the moment I've got a little bit of a Jordans collection the ones, the twos, the threes, the fours, fives, the sixes. I sold them after that. The fives are the ones. The one after that had the see-through sole. I had a blue and then to Charlie from Out of the Blues. And a blue-purple pair but the leather was cracked. They've got these other ones out now called The Jump Man, not a Jordan but they've got the logo which looks like a Jordan. But it's gone off the wall. FRAZER COOKE

MICHAEL JORDAN IS THE GREATEST SPORTS PERSON ON THIS PLANET. HE IS THE COOLEST PERSON ON THE PLANET. MICHAEL JORDAN IS PROBABLY GONNA RETIRE AT THE END OF THE YEAR AND REEBOK HAVE GOT THE NEXT BET WITH ALAN IBERSON. HE IS A BAD MAN. HE PLAYS FOR THE PHIL AND HIS SNEAKERS ARE SOLD OUT. HE WON ROOKIE OF THE YEAR. THIS MAN IS JUST A HIP HOP HOODLUM. HE DRIVES A TRUCK ALL OVER THE PLACE YOU GOT THESE GUYS COMING ONTO THE ARENA WITH THEIR HIP HOP POSSE, CARRYING GUNS, IT'S LIKE A .....VIDEO. THE REASON HE'S SIGNED HIS WHOLE COLLECTION TO REEBOK, IT'S JUST PURE HOME BOY FASHION. SOMETHING'S GONNA HAPPEN BECAUSE HE'S TAKING BASKETBALL SOMEWHERE WHERE I DON'T REALLY THINK THEY GANNA GO IT'S LIKE WU TANG CLAN PLAYING BASKETBALL AND IT'S STREET BASKETBALL. HE MADE JORDAN LOOK LIKE A MORON, SHOWED HIM UP SO BAD. HE TRASHED JORDAN. HE WAS LIKE, STUPID OLD MAN YOUR TIME'S FINISHED, IT'S ME AND IT'S PURE GANGSTER REEBOK HAVE GOT HIM. DERICK PROCOPE VIBE

MICHAEL JORDAN BRUSHED ASIDE QUESTIONS ABOUT THE DIFFERENCE BETWEEN THE MILLIONS HE EARNS FROM NIKE AND THE WAGES OF THE WOMEN WHO MAKE HIS SHOES WITH THE SUGGESTIONS THAT IT WAS NONE OF HIS BUSINESS." FROM "LADS, GET YOUR KIT OFF!"

MCCLELLAN BIG ISSUE OCT 6-12 97.

SCOOP JACKSON: "...I ACTUALLY LOST A GIRLFRIEND OVER SHELL-TOES."

HOW MANY SNEAKERS HAVE YOU GOT?
I've been wearing Adidas since my third year at high school, which is 1979. Hold on let me check the other closet...16. At school I had a pair of Abdul Jabba. Playing basketball and I twisted my ankle to the point that I thought it was going to break, it went from a standing position to touching the floor, but nothing happened it was fine and that was when I thought these shoes are the dope and that's the reason I've always been with Adidas. Shell-toes are status symbols now in the States because there are so many choices it's not mandatory that you can get em and they're really in style. Real ball players kick the shit out of those creamies, some brothers still play in them. But after it's all over and you're walking around in shoes, your style and your profile in those shoes, if you've got a pair of shell-toes on you know you've got dukes.

IN ENGLAND WE KNOW YOU AS THE CO-PRESENTER OF CHANNEL FOUR'S BASKETBALL PROGRAMME, AND IN THE LAST COUPLE OF YEARS THE SPORT'S REALLY TAKEN OFF. THE KIDS OVER HAVE BEEN BUYING THE JORDAN, PIPPIN AND RODMAN SHOES, WE KNEW THEIR NAMES, AND NOW WE CAN ACTUALLY PUT THE FACES TO THE SHOES...
That's the whole marketing scheme behind the big companies, and it's worked in America. Since the late 70s they started giving shoes identities by associating them with particular athletes. And Nike just got really, really, really lucky with Michael. There is no other way to put it. As nice as Michael is nobody expected it to take the way it did. Nike decided to take a chance on being very creative with a basketball shoe. The colour scheme on Michael Jordan's shoes is what sold them, the first time they had done a shoe with no white on it...

I HEARD THE NBA TRIED TO STOP JORDAN FROM WEARING THE SHOE BECAUSE IT DIDN'T MATCH THE CHICAGO BULLS' UNIFORMS.
No. Let me sort that out for you. The original uniformity rule that goes along with the NBA came from the Boston Celtics. They would wear green shoes but there were so many different variations in the team with the green that it didn't match. That was when the uniformity rule came in.

DO YOU THINK SNEAKERS COST TOO MUCH?
The Penny Hardaway, you know those are $180. I saw those shoes last year and I was like, oohhh weeeee it's going to be tight when they put these on the market, but people are buying them man. What happened with Penny Hardaway was that he was really smart. Nike got an agreement with Arizona University. He was on the stage during the final quarter, having those shoes on and when he won the whole thing he was the only one on the squad that had them on, so he got free publicity right then. You got 30 million people watching and you win theNational Championship that's alright free publicity for the Penny shoe. All Star games is where it really picks up. Different shoes mean different things to different players. Sometimes it's money driven and sometimes it's just love of the shoes. Some players are shoe fanatics also. Kenny Holloway told me he left Adidas to go with Nike strictly because they had more shoes. With Rodman, it wasn't about big money, it was Converse were going to treat him better than what they did at Nike. It had nothing to do with the shoes, he didn't even care about the shoes.

ARTHUR JAFFA TOLD ME THERE WAS A PLAYER WITH THE WASHINGTON BULLETS WHO TURNED DOWN A SHOE DEAL WITH NIKE. HE TOLD THEM, YOU'RE CHARGING TOO MUCH FOR THE PEOPLE IN MY COMMUNITY.
That was Chris Webber. I think Converse was supposed to pick him up, but I don't know whether they did. Michael Jordan's not that community concerned. Chris has always been a community concerned athlete, and he's going to remain that way, he's still in touch. Gym shoes especially at this level have became a kind of a status symbol for the walking poor. When you're walking around trying to play your new Jordans somebody's going to want something from you, there's always somebody who can't afford what you've got and it's not smart to flaunt in front of them. But it's supply and demand, I mean, this is a business, it's not Nike or Adidas or Converse's responsibility, or the athletes, to put other people's priorities in shape. If this family's going hungry but you're buying your baby a pair of $100 gym shoes, then he's not eating because your priorities are messed up. Take responsibility and make your child understand that gym shoes really don't mean shit. That's the best way to make a change.

YOU WERE SAYING THAT MICHAEL JORDAN HAS GOT A JUMP MAN SHOE WHICH ARE MANUFACTURING.
Michael bought the logo and called the company Jump Man. It's not seen as competition by Nike, but Michael's going to have to do something when he leaves basketball.

HOW MANY YEARS DO YOU RECKON HE HAS LEFT?
Next year. He should have retired last time because he was tired and fed up with all the media stuff. In sport, you can't take a leave of absence, you have to retire and the comeback. Michael still feels he has something to prove. What Michael's done for gym shoe culture is amazing, but it's not like he did it alone. There was the whole Converse concept before, they had Doctor J, Bird, Magic, Doctor Shake, that led to Michael. Basketball athletes are more popular than any other sport because it's easier to sell a basketball shoe. They're universal, high-top, low-top, you can wear them in winter or summer. It's about casual clothing being accepted in society, but the shoes aren't going to last more than four or five months. They're made out of polyurethane and they're not as durable as they used to be. The companies come out with new styles because every four months someone is going to be wearing out a pair of shoes. I can understand the technology behind the shoe industry, they're trying to make a better shoe, but they're not selling these shoes to people to play basketball in. I want to see what happens when Nike runs into their wall, when the NBA runs into the wall. The popularity of basketball is going to go up, but nothing lasts forever... remember baseball had the whole thing for about 100 years. I want to see a black-owned and manufactured shoe company, and hopefully it will be me or somebody else, they'll break into the market, not that the shoes are going to be better, but it would just be nice to see a black-owned company get a piece of this pie because of the constituency of the market. And it may be Chris Webber....

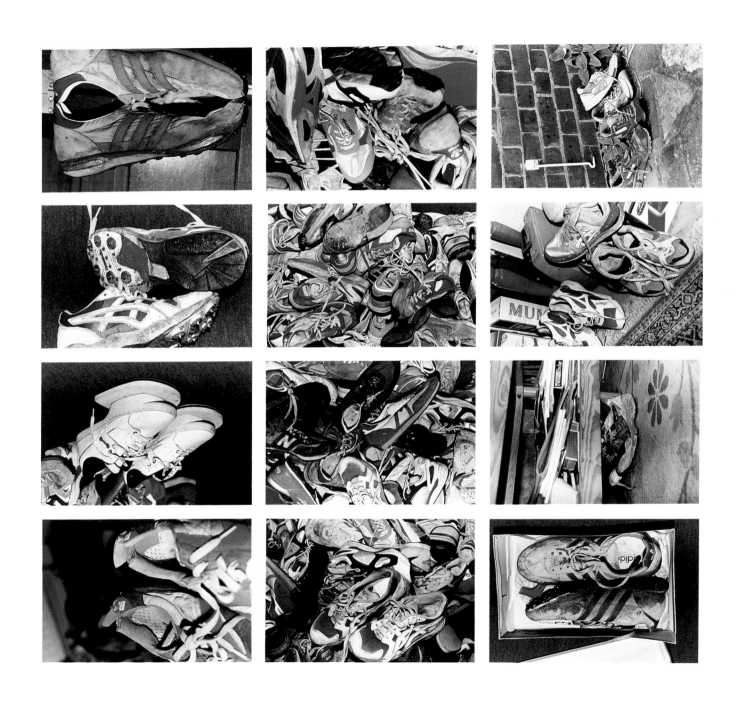

I can never throw any of them away. They bring back too many memories—happy and painful. They are a Testament to the countless nights and days lost pounding parks and tracks in search of the perfect run, the perfect race, in the perfect pair of shoes.

John Bryant, Deputy Editor of **THE TIMES**

I'm John Regis. Great British athlete...200 metre British record holder, but I won't bore you with all that...Been to the Olympics, World Championships, Commonwealth Games, European Championships. Been there, done it, got the t-shirt.

WHAT SHOE COMPANY ARE YOU WITH?
Nike for three seasons. Things go in cycles. Back in the 80s the world was dominated by middle distance runners because they were the personalities. Nowadays the public want to see the more explosive events, accordingly Nike have decided to sponsor more sprinters.

DO YOU HAVE ANY SAY IN THE DESIGN OF A SPIKE?
Absolutely. This new Nike spike, I was in at the early stage of its development back in 94, because they used a couple of models, myself, Michael Johnson, John Drummond and a couple of other athletes...me for my size, because they wanted feedback from a smaller athlete and a couple of in-between sized athletes. And rather than have laces they've got Velcro over the top. We had teething problems, people didn't take to Velcro, but they've sorted that out...and as far as I can see it's a perfect spike. We are the models. Whatever we wear, the public sees and the public wants to be involved in it.

DO YOU THINK SNEAKERS HAVE TOO MANY GADGETS?
I need trainers to run in, all that other stuff weighs them down...all these new fangles, if that's what the public want, fine...

WORDS OF WISDOM JOHN?
Nike is the best, because they actually believe in the product. I think if people make enough noise about it I'm sure their prices will come down.

WELL, Jackie Ajyepong, BEING A HURDLER WERE YOU ALWAYS INTO TRAINERS?
It wasn't something I was really fashion conscious about as a kid, because I wore school uniform most of the time.

OUTSIDE THE SCHOOL GATES?
Puma, Slazenger, Nike, Adidas, Dunlop Green Flash. The more I got into sport the more I got into trainers. It wasn't fashion, it was all part of the job. You couldn't wear trainers to go out because you were always in them so you'd make an effort to wear something else.

WHAT WERE YOUR FIRST PAIR OF SPIKES?
Puma, the luminous ones....I had a bright red pair.

WHAT WAS YOUR FAVOURITE MIZUNO SHOE?
I wore Mondo Control and the Contender range, they're very comfortable. The problem I have is that because I had a lot of Achilles problems I wear trainers that aren't so high. And Mizuno have a thing at the back, like a pad.

BUT THE TRAINERS ARE VERY HARD TO FIND IN THIS COUNTRY, I DON'T KNOW WHY......
It's because of advertising. They don't advertise enough.

BUT ISN'T SALLY GUNNEL WITH MIZUNO?
Yes........

SO YOU WOULD HAVE THOUGHT THAT WITH HER WINNING THE OLYMPIC GOLD THEY WOULD HAVE REALLY PUSHED THE ADVERTISING TO SAY THAT AN OLYMPIC MEDALLIST WEARS MIZUNO.

My name is Tony Jarrett, I'm a British athlete.

HAVE YOU GOT A SHOE DEAL?
Yeah, Brooks. They do more leisure.

HOW MANY SHOE COMPANIES HAVE YOU BEEN WITH THROUGH YOUR CAREER?
Three. Puma, which was my first one, and then Asics and now Brooks. But I can't even count how many trainers I've got. I've got box-loads of them all stacked up at home.

DO YOU FEEL THAT IF SOMEONE SEES YOU WEARING A PARTICULAR SHOE THAT WOULD MAKE THEM GO AND BUY A BROOKS SHOE, BECAUSE AT THE MOMENT BROOKS DON'T REALLY SAY ANYTHING. THE ONLY PERSON I REMEMBER WEARING THEM WAS ZOLA BUDD. I THINK YOU ARE THE FIRST SPRINTER TO BE WEARING BROOKS.
Yeah, Brooks are mostly for long distance, but they've started to branch out into sprint. Now even spike shoes come in different colours. You want them to match your track-suit. As a company they're building up, making some good trainers and I'm helping them build up some spikes...it's going to be good.

I'm Michelle Griffiths, triple jumper, represented Great Britain at the Olympics and at the World Championships. I'm with Nike on a year on year off basis. When I was about 11, for a birthday present my oldest brother gave me Adidas Sambas. I used to play football with him and I always remember thinking, these trainers are absolutely kicking.

HOW DO YOU FEEL ABOUT TRAINERS COSTING TOO MUCH?
There's no way I'd pay £70 for a pair of trainers for my child...a nice pair of Clarks will do. But kids probably say to their Mum or Dad, I want those same trainers... I remember how much I wanted Michael Jordan trainers. I grew up on them. Now I'm jumping in the basic Nike shoes. But they're light, there's been a big improvement in the last six years. So watch out for me jumping 150 metres in Nike shoes.

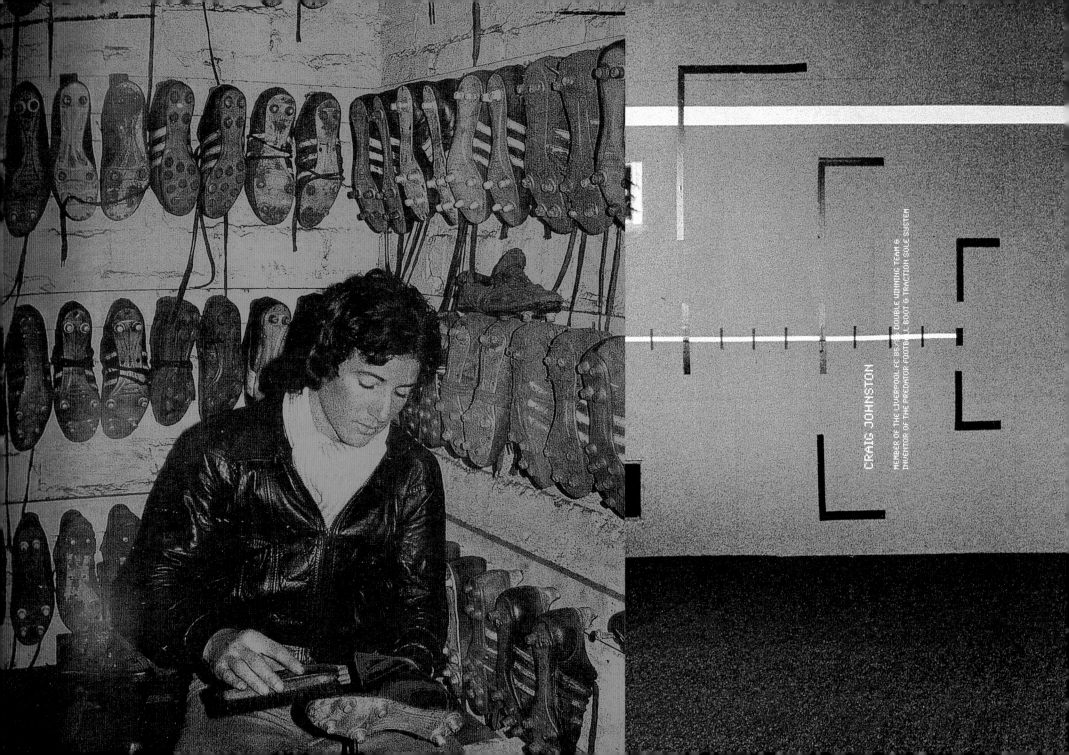

CRAIG JOHNSTON

MEMBER OF THE LIVERPOOL FC 85/86 DOUBLE WINNING TEAM &
INVENTOR OF THE PREDATOR FOOTBALL BOOT & TRACTION SOLE SYSTEM

HELLO CAN I TALK TO CRAIG PLEASE?
WHO IS IT?

...ABOUT THE BOOK ON TRAINERS.
OK, WON'T BE A MINUTE...

HELLO? CRAIG?
HI....MY FIRST MEMORIES ARE OF THE DUNLOP DIPLOMA,
THEY WERE $6.99 AND THEY WERE SORT OF LIKE TENNIS
SHOES. THE ONLY TWO THINGS I EVER WORE WERE MY
FOOTBALL BOOTS OR PUMPS AS FAR BACK AS I CAN
REMEMBER., I USED TO KICK A TENNIS BALL AGAINST A
BRICK WALL AND THAT WORE OUT MY SCHOOL SHOES, SO
MY NICKNAME WAS ACTUALLY "SCRUFF". I'M TALKING
ABOUT TWO WEEKS FOR A HOLE TO DEVELOP IN THE
SCHOOL SHOES AND THE SOCK TO HANG OUT THE FRONT.
SO IT WAS A SORE POINT IN THE FAMILY. BUT I THOUGHT
THAT IF I TOOK THE STUDS OUT OF MY SOCCER BOOTS
THEN I COULD WEAR THEM TO SCHOOL. I HAD THIS
VISION OF BEING ABLE TO WEAR THE SAME SHOES TO
SCHOOL FOR TRAINING AND PLAYING SOCCER IN THE
CAR PARK.
WHEN I WENT TO ENGLAND, MY JOB WAS TO CLEAN BOOTS
FOR THE PROFESSIONALS AND THE TRIALISTS. THEN I
GOT INTO THE FACT THAT GRAHAM SOUNESS WAS THERE
WEARING PUMA. PUMA WERE THE MAIN BRAND BUT
THERE WAS ALSO GOLA. BACK THEN THE OLD LEATHER
STUDS HAD NAILS IN THEM AND HAD TO BE FILED DOWN
EVERY DAY, AND EACH PLAYER HAD THREE OR FOUR
PAIRS OF SHOES. SOUNESS SORT OF TOOK ME UNDER HIS
WING AND HE WOULD GIVE ME HIS SECOND HAND OLD
BOOTS. BACK THEN THE LEATHER WAS MADE OF VERY
THIN KANGAROO SKIN AND THE BOOTS WOULD ONLY
LAST ABOUT THREE WEEKS, SO THEN I'D TAKE THEM
OUT TO THE CAR PARK AND KICK THE SHIT OUT OF THEM.

WHEN WAS YOUR FIRST SHOE DEAL?
THE PROS USED TO LET THE APPRENTICES WEAR THE
NEW BOOTS FOR A COUPLE OF WEEKS. YOU'D JUMP IN
THE BATH IN THE NEW BOOTS AND PUT SOAP ON THEM
TO MOULD TO AND FIT YOUR FEET. AT MIDDLESBROUGH I
WAS HAPPY TO WEAR SECOND HAND BOOTS, SO I NEVER
HAD A BOOT DEAL. WHEN I MOVED TO LIVERPOOL,
PATRICK SPONSORED ME, BUT I FOUND THE LEATHER WAS
VERY THICK AND THE SOLE WAS BULKY. THEY WEREN'T
FOR ME, AS I WAS USED TO ADIDAS AND PUMA. PATRICK
AREN'T SO BAD NOW.
WITH THE PREDATOR BOOT AND TRACTION SOLE SYSTEM,
I REMEMBER ADIDAS DIDN'T BELIEVE THAT THE SHOES
WERE AS GOOD AS I SAID THEY WERE, SO I WENT TO
MUNICH AND GOT BECKENBAUER...I GOT RUMENIGGE...I
GOT A GUY CALLED HANSEY MULLER (BECAUSE I USED
TO WEAR A PAIR OF ADIDAS HANSEY MULLERS) AND I
ASKED THEM TO TRY THE BOOTS AND FILMED THEM SAYING
THERE WAS DEFINITELY A DIFFERENCE. THEN I TOOK THE
FILM BACK TO ADIDAS, AND WHEN THEY HEARD THEIR
OWN PROS SAYING, "THERE'S DEFINITELY SOMETHING IN
IT"....

WHAT YEAR WAS THAT?
I FIRST APPROACHED THEM IN 1990 AT THE WORLD CUP
IN ITALY.

HOW DID YOU DREAM UP BOTH SYSTEMS?
WELL IT'S CLEAR FROM THE HISTORY I JUST TOLD YOU.
BECAUSE OF MY LACK OF ABILITY I HAD TO ACQUIRE
SKILLS. I ALWAYS THOUGHT I WAS VERY SUB-STANDARD,
SO I USED TO TRAIN FOR AN EXTRA TWO HOURS A DAY. I
WONDERED WHY I COULDN'T BEND OR DIRECT THE BALL
LIKE THE GREAT PLAYERS, AND BECAME FASCINATED BY
THE SCIENCE OF SWERVING, STRIKING AND CHIPPING A BALL.
I THINK PEOPLE TAKE FOOTBALL VERY MUCH AT SURFACE
LEVEL, ESPECIALLY THOSE WHO PLAY IT. YOU KNOW
GLEN HODDLE CAN SMACK A BALL FOR 60 YARDS WITH
THE OUTSIDE OF HIS LEFT FOOT AGAINST THE WIND,
INCH PERFECT, AND AFTER SEEING HIM DO THAT STUFF
I'D THINK ABOUT HOW HE DID IT. INSTINCT IS ONE THING.
BUT IF YOU TAKE THE TIME TO THINK ABOUT IT, WHAT
THESE PLAYERS CAN DO TO MOVE THE BALL IN THE AIR

IS QUITE STUNNING, AND WHEN YOU GET DOWN TO FIELD
LEVEL AND SEE THE POWER AND ACCURACY IT'S QUITE
FRIGHTENING, AND I WAS FASCINATED BY THAT.
GOING BACK OVER HISTORY, PUMA HAD A BOOT CALLED
THE FA WHICH HAD A RUBBER SHOE, BUT IT DIDN'T REALLY
WORK AND THEY WERE VERY EXPENSIVE AND WORE OUT
QUICKLY. THAT WAS ALWAYS ON MY MIND. SO WHEN I
WAS TRAINING KIDS, I TRIED TO EXPLAIN HOW TO WHIP
THE BALL AND SPIN IT, AND I'D SAY, "GRIP THE OUTSIDE
OF THE BALL AND FOLLOW THROUGH AND SPIN IT". SO I
THOUGHT ABOUT TABLE TENNIS BATS, RIPPED THE RUBBER
OFF A BAT. INSTANTLY IT GRIPPED THE BALL, AND AT THE
SAME TIME IN AUSTRALIA, AN ELDERLY CHAP APPROACHED
ME WHO HAD A SIMILAR IDEA. I LEFT IT TO LIVE IN
GERMANY. THEN I WENT TO GLEN HODDLE AND JOHN
BARNES, FRIENDS I TRUSTED AND BELIEVED IN AND
SAID, "WHAT DO YOU THINK OF THIS?", AND THEY ALL
THOUGHT I WAS ON TO SOMETHING. SO I USED MY
BROADCASTING SKILLS TO CAPTURE ALL THE INFORMATION
AND ANALYSE IT, SO THERE WAS DOCUMENTARY PROOF.

WICKED...BUT I REMEMBER WHEN THE BOOT CAME OUT I
WONDERED HOW YOU WOULD GET IT PAST FIFA AND
THE FA. SURELY IT IS AN UNFAIR ADVANTAGE?
I WENT TO FIFA HOUSE TO SEE MR BLACKER, THE
GENERAL SECRETARY, AND HIS ORIGINAL INSTINCT WAS
THAT IT WAS AN UNFAIR ADVANTAGE, BUT I TOLD HIM
THAT I THOUGHT THE GAME NEEDED MORE GOALS AND
MORE POWER, AND THAT GOLF AND TENNIS PERFORMERS
HAVE LOOKED TO TECHNOLOGY TO IMPROVE PERFORMANCE.
SO, WE TALKED HIM OUT OF IT.

TECHNOLOGY HAS MADE IT EASIER...?
YEAH. I ALWAYS WANTED TO BE THE BEST IN THE WORLD
AT SOMETHING, AND I TRIED FOOTBALL AND FAILED DISMALLY.
BUT BECAUSE OF MY UNIQUE EXPERIENCE WITH THE
PREDATOR THERE IS NOBODY IN THE WORLD WHO
KNOWS MORE ABOUT PERFORMANCE SOCCER SHOES. SO
I'VE REALLY FOUND MY THING IN LIFE NOW? AND THE
FACT THAT I GOT INTO THE SCIENCE OF IT AND STARTED
TO USE DIGITAL ANALYSES AND CREATE SOFTWARE THAT
DETERMINES THE FLIGHT CHARACTERISTICS OF A BALL
THROUGH THE AIR, AND THEN TO REVERSE ENGINEER THAT...

THAT'S WILD MAN...
NO, THAT'S BEAUTIFUL. IT'S A BEAUTIFUL SIGHT. YOU SEE
SOMEONE REALLY BELT A BALL AND IT'S STUNNING. AND
WHEN AN INCH CAN MAKE THE DIFFERENCE BETWEEN
WORLD CUP GLORY AND DEFEAT, IF SOMEONE HITS THE
BAR, YOU THINK, IF I CAN IMPROVE A PLAYER BY TWO OR
THREE PER CENT, OR MOVE A BALL IN THE AIR BY AN INCH.
THAT'S A STUNNING THING.
AND A FINAL POINT. THE MOST CLASSIC SHOE OF ALL
TIME IS STILL THE COPPA MONDIAL. THEN THE WORLD
CUP. THOSE TWO SHOES. EVERYBODY HAS TRIED TO COPY
THEM AND RIP THEM OFF. UMBRO IS THE ONLY BRAND
THAT HAS GOT CLOSE. IF I WERE TO NAME THE HARLEY
DAVIDSON, THE ROLLS ROYCE, THE FENDER STRATACASTER
OF SHOES....IT IS THE WORLD CUP, AND ITS BABY BROTHER,
THE MONDIAL. AND IF YOU WANT THE TOP FOUR OF ALL
TIME YOU'VE GOT TO ADD THE SAMBA AND THE PUMA KING.

WHAT'S FUNNY IS THAT I HAVEN'T SEEN ADIDAS TRY
TO DO A PREDATOR VERSION OF THE SAMBA.
WELL, I HAVE BEEN HARPING ON AT THEM SINCE DAY
ONE, AND THAT'S WHAT I'M PUSHING FOR, TO MAKE
PREDATOR VERSIONS OF THESE CLASSIC MODELS.
PERFORMANCE WILL GET MORE AND MORE CRITICAL,
AND IF WE'RE ON THREE PER CENT NOW I RECKON WE'RE
GONNA GO UP TO FIVE, SIX AND SEVEN PER CENT.

«STOP PRESS...PREDATOR ACCELERATOR LAUNCHED FOR
FRANCE 98 WORLD CUP, TO BE WORN BY BECKHAM...

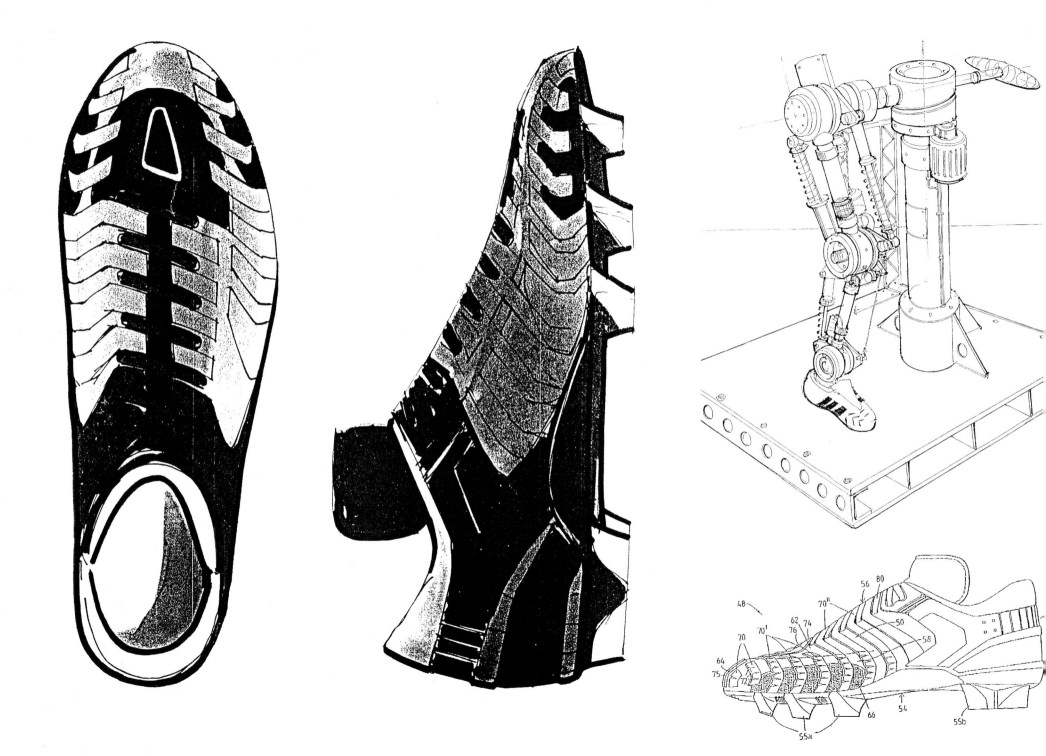

48

56 80

70″

62 74

70′ 76

70

64

75

72

55a

66

54

50

58

55b

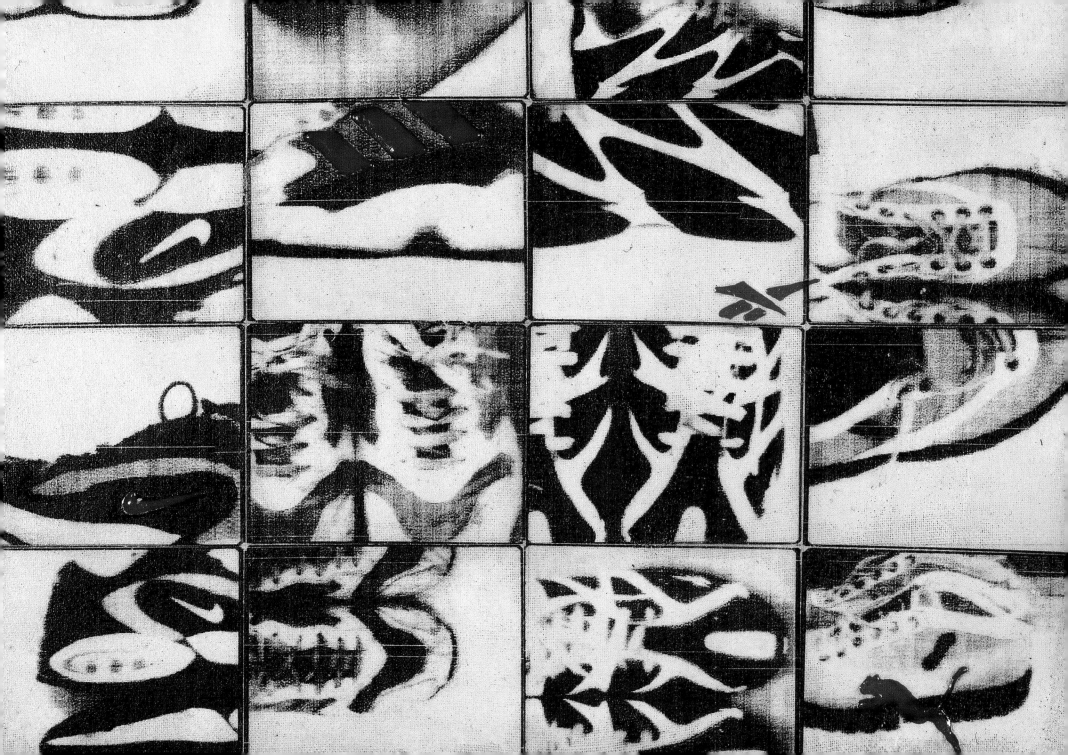

"ALI BOM BI YAH"

CHANTED DURING THE ALI/FRAZIER FIGHT 'THE RUMBLE IN THE JUNGLE' ZAIRE 73

PRINCE NAZIEM
ALL I'VE GOT TO SAY ABOUT SNEAKERS IS...

...COME ON YOU'RE AN ADIDAS MAN.
EXACTLY. THAT WAS WHAT I WAS JUST GONNA SAY. NOT JUST BECAUSE I AM SPONSORED BY ADIDAS, RIGHT.
BUT WHEN I PUT ON A PAIR OF TRAINERS AS COMFORTABLE AS ADIDAS IN EVERY WAY AND IN EVERY DEPARTMENT
AND IN EVERY SPORT THAT YOU THINK ABOUT, ADIDAS IS THE LEAKS, AND IT WAS THE LEAKS IN 94, THAT YOU
KNOW, WE'RE GOING TO HAPPEN IN 97, COME 98 NOW, THE SHIT'S STILL GREAT, 99 ALL MINE, COME THE YEAR
2000 NO ADIDAS, JUST WORK THAT OUT FOR YOURSELF G MY MAN.

YEAH, ARE THEY GOING TO MASH YOU MAN?
WE'LL SOON 'IN SHAHLAH WHICH MEANS GOD WILLING. IT'S ALL DOWN TO IF GOD'S WILLING.

WHAT SIZE ARE YOU?
WHAT SIZE AM I?

...YEAH
I'M SIZE SEVEN IN A TRAINER.

...I OFTEN REMEMBER THE INCREDIBLE IMAGE OF A BOXING MATCH WITH MUHAMMAD ALI. IN HIS FIGHT HE TWIRLED AROUND IN ADIDAS BOOTS DEC-ORATED BY SALVADOR DALI...

TONY HAWK, AIRWALK SKATE TEAM RIDER

HOW DO YOU SAY TRAINERS IN YOUR MOTHER TONGUE?
SKATE SHOES.
WHY DO YOU WEAR TRAINERS?
BECAUSE SKATEBOARDING HAS COME A LONG WAY SINCE 2X4S, CLAY WHEELS AND BARE FEET....AND NO OTHER SPORT IS CONCERNED WITH OLLIE PATCHES.
ARE TRAINERS BETTER THAN SEX?
THEY MUSTN'T BE, BECAUSE I USUALLY TAKE THEM OFF BEFOREHAND.
WHAT'S THE WEIRDEST THING THAT HAPPENED BETWEEN YOU AND YOUR TRAINERS?
ABOUT TWO YEARS AGO I PUT THEM ON, AND MY SIGNATURE WAS STITCHED INTO THE TONGUE. THEY'VE BEEN LIKE THAT EVER SINCE.
HOW DO YOU WEAR YOUR LACES?
CRISS-CROSS. CLASSIC-STYLE, TIGHTENED MORE WHEN I SKATE.
HOW OFTEN DO YOU CLEAN YOUR TRAINERS?
HARDLY EVER, UNLESS I STEPPED IN SOMETHING.
WHAT'S THE MADDEST THING YOU'VE DONE FOR A PAIR OF TRAINERS?
STARTED SKATEBOARDING FOR A LIVING.
WHAT TRAINERS CAN'T YOU STAND?
THE GAUDY GREEN GELATINOUS DOUBLE-TONGUED FRESH-GUY BLINKING ONE MADE FOR THE NO FEAR CONSUMER.
WHEN DID YOU BUY YOUR FIRST PAIR AND WHY?
IN 1978 I BOUGHT A PAIR OF VANS BECAUSE I THOUGHT THAT TO BECOME A TRUE SKATER IT WAS MANDATORY TO WEAR THEM.
HOW DO YOU REACT WHEN PEOPLE STEP ON YOUR TRAINERS?
IF I'M WEARING THEM, I SAY OUCH.
DO YOU HAVE SPECIFIC TRAINERS FOR DIFFERENT SPORTS?
ONLY TWO TYPES: MY SKATE SHOES AND MY WEDDING SHOES.
ARE YOU PROUD OF YOUR TRAINERS?
DEFINITELY.

GEOFF ROWLEY, AIRWALK SKATE TEAM RIDER

WHAT'S THE CRAZIEST THING YOU HAVE EVER DONE FOR A PAIR OF TRAINERS?
I don't get crazy, especially not for shoes.

IF A TOP BRAND COULD MAKE YOU A SHOE WHAT WOULD IT BE LIKE?
I already have a pro shoe coming out on Airwalk. It has a design all its own,
with hi-tech features and styling never before seen in a skate shoe. It's going
to change things.

DO YOU HAVE SPECIFIC TRAINERS FOR DIFFERENT SPORTS?
I have some Airwalk hiking shoes for when I go hiking or stalking animals.

WHAT'S THE OLDEST PAIR OF TRAINER YOU'VE GOT?
A pair of Airwalk Enigmas and Nexts, both legendary skate shoes, that were
given to me by Sin, the head of design at Airwalk.

DO YOU KEEP YOUR TRAINERS WHEN THEY ARE DEAD?
I throw them in the bin outside and the lady in the apartment below fishes
them out for some reason or other. She likes to recycle. Or she's mad.

**APART FROM WEARING YOUR TRAINERS ON YOUR FEET, DO
YOU DO ANYTHING ELSE WITH THEM?**
I eat them! Who wrote these questions?

DO YOU WEAR SOCKS WITH YOUR TRAINERS?
Always. Otherwise your feet quickly become cheese ridden and mouldy.

WHAT TRAINERS WOULD YOU NEVER BE SEEN DEAD IN?
There are too many to list.

FAX

.. to .... SARI RATSULA VANS
. from .... :::
. subject ......
. pages .... STEVE CABALLERO
. date ....
.... 13/5/97

WHY DO YOU LIKE TRAINERS?
I love skate shoes made by Vans because of style and comfort.

HOW MANY DO YOU OWN?
A lot, probably more shoes than my wife!

ARE TRAINERS BETTER THAN SEX?
I can't compare the two. I guess it depends on the fit.

WHAT'S THE WEIRDEST THING THAT'S HAPPENED BETWEEN YOU AND YOUR
TRAINERS?
The weirdest thing is that I see them on people all over the world

RAREST?
My "Natas Kaupus" signature shoes, made by Etnies in France, in 1989. I have them
still in the box with a sticker.

WHAT'S THE CRAZIEST THING YOU'VE DONE FOR A PAIR OF TRAINERS?
What I do now, ride a skateboard!

DO YOU CUSTOMISE?
I like to Superglue the stitches so they last longer.

ARE YOU PROUD OF YOUR TRAINERS?
Very proud to have a signature shoe with my name on it.

DO YOU KEEP DEAD TRAINERS?
If they have some life I give them away to skaters who need them.

DO YOU KEEP SPARES?
Up in the attic.

DO YOU KNOW ANY INTERESTING FACTS ABOUT A BRAND
Yeah, does Nike condone slave labour?

APART FROM WEARING YOUR TRAINERS, DO YOU DO ANYTHING ELSE WITH
THEM?
I store them in my closet.

FAX

.. to .... :::
. from ....
. subject .... SARI RATSULA VANS
. pages .... LANCE MOUNTAIN
. date ....
.... 23/5/97

HOW DO YOU SAY TRAINERS IN YOUR MOTHER TONGUE?
My mother would call them tennies, I call them skate shoes.

DO YOU LIKE TRAINERS?
Yes. Never liked skateboarding barefoot

HOW MANY TRAINERS HAVE YOU GOT?
A lot, but I only use one pair at a time.

ARE TRAINER BETTER THAN SEX?
My relationships with shoes never last but I've had the same wife for 12 years.

DO YOU COLLECT?
For the last four years I've been buying every pair of Jordans that come out, for my
son. And I've got a few pairs of skaters' shoes.

WHAT'S THE WEIRDEST THING THAT'S HAPPENED BETWEEN YOU AND YOUR
TRAINERS?
Have one fall off while skating and run down a 12-foot-high cement bowl in my
sock. Also, there was a time when skateboarding was very small, no one did it,
and if you saw someone on the street with Vans, with an ollie hole, you knew they
skateboarded, and you'd be so stoked and would probably talk to them.

WHEN ARE TRAINERS DEAD?
When the support is wilted.

DO YOU CHANGE YOUR TRAINERS DURING THE DAY?
No, don't use chill shoes.

INTERVIEW WITH CRISTIAN STEVENSON.
MAKER OF THE SNOWBOARD FILMS "ODD MAN OUT" AND
"DAY TRIPPER, (STILL TRIPPIN)".

The first pair of Nike Air Jordans were on sale in Washington DC, and my Daddy, he knew I was a big basketball fanatic, and I would play every day after school for 3 hours on the courts right below my house, so my Dad went down to George Town in DC the only shop that had the Michael Jordans and he waited for two hours because he knew how much those shoes meant to me, and he came back and he threw the shoes down, and dude it's like kind of like meeting god I guess, you know what I mean...so I put on the shoes, hit the courts, and you know I was so proud because I was only 14, 15 years old and you've got these shoes on....and I was little back then, I was only about 5.5 so I was a guard kind of a kid and I had a good outside shot, so this guy picked me pretty early because...I think it was the shoes because you know, hey that guy has got Jordans on....but I was a bit nervous because there was a lot expected of me so I was throwing three pointers from outside and I was sticking them, no back walls, full on net, just net, net, net... and that was one of the best games of my life, with my first Air Jordans.

STATIC STATIC CYCLE

SILENT EXERCISE MACHINE

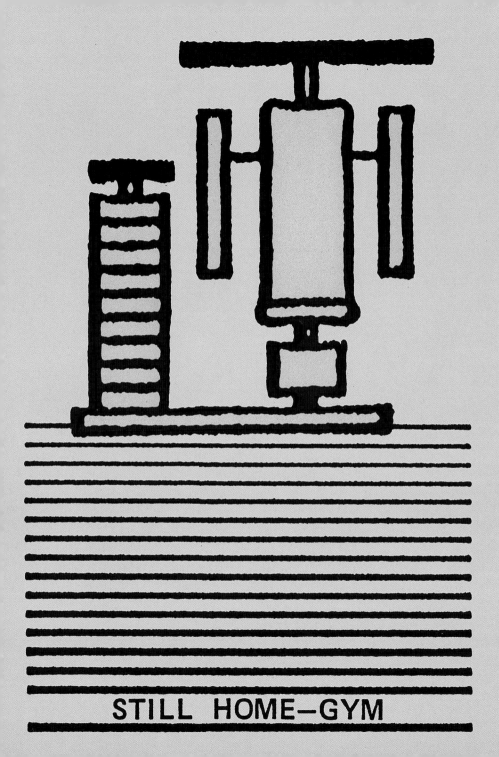

STILL HOME-GYM

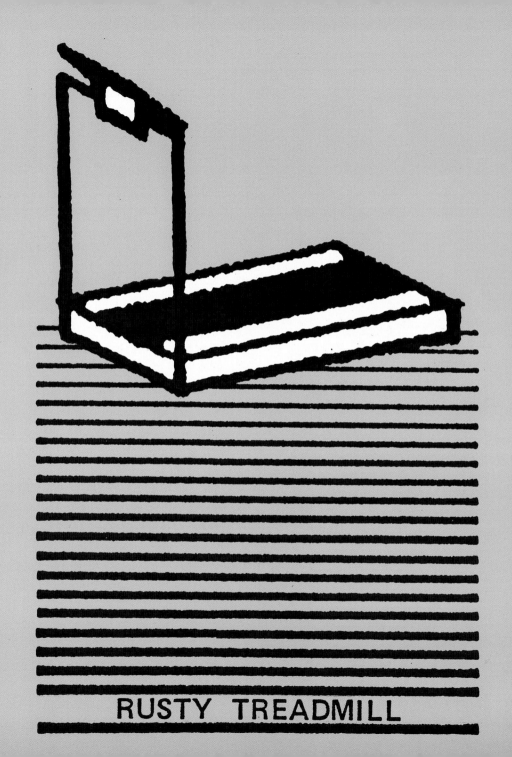

RUSTY TREADMILL

JOGGING (
INNA BAB
WIT A KRISS
ANNA THIK

"JOGGING" BY FREDDIE McGREGOR

N THE SAND
LON LAND
TRACK SHOES
OBBY SOCKS

YES DREAD. GIVE THANKS FOR THE REASONING OF REALITY AND I AN I WILL KEEP TRAINING...

MARCUS: AH STAR YOUR TRAINERS LOOK DEBT, YOU KNOW!!!!!!!

JAMEL: SO ME RUN THINGS, JUST KICKING UP THE COMPETITION.

MARCUS: WHERE YOU GET THEM, AND HOW MUCH THEY COST????

JAMEL: NOW THAT, ME NAR TELL YOU!!!!! STAR!!!!!!

MARCUS: SEEN! YOU THINK COS YOU HAVE A LITTLE HUNDRED POUND TRAINERS ON YOUR FOOT, YOU'AR RUN THINGS, STAR!!!

MARCUS: OK, OK, OK, JUST COOL MY BREATHIN, IT IS NOT AS SIMPLE AS THAT, THERE'S ONLY ONE WAY TO SQUASH THIS....YOU SEE THE RASTAMAN OVER
THERE HANDING OUT LEAFLETS AND SELLING INCENSE. LET HIM SQUASH THIS, COST HE AIN'T DEALING WITH TRAINER! HE IS DEALING WITH JAH....SEEN.

JAMEL: YA, YA, THAT SOUND SAFE STAR....HAIL RASTAFARI.

RASTAMAN: JAH LOVE YOUTH MAN, ENOUGH RESPECT, WA'DE'I'AR'SA' (OR, WHAT ARE YOU SAYING)

JAMEL: DREAD, YOU KNOW THAT OUR CHOICE OF TRAINERS IN TODAY SOCIETY HAVE BECOME A STATEMENT OF INDIVIDUALITY....
SO MUCH TO THE POINT WHERE, THOSE OF US WHO KNOW STREET CULTURE, SSSSHHHH HOLDIT DOWN. HOLD IT DOWN....HR HR HR HR DON'T SETTLE FOR NOTHING LESS, THAN THE BEST.....

RASTAMAN: YES YOUTH MAN, I AN I OVERSTAND DEM REASONING. BUT BEFORE ONE CAN LIBERATE ONE FEET, ONE MUST LIBERATE ONE'S MIND.THE REALITY OF TRAINERS YOUTH MAN,
IS THAT SOME TRAINERS ARE 2 BAD, 2 WICKED AND 2 DAM EXPENSIVE. YOU MENTIONED STREET CULTURE. STREET CULTURE IS THE STRENGTH OF STREET KNOWLEDGE! KNOWLEDGE IS TO KNOW!!!!!!
TO KNOW THAT WITHOUT YOU YOUTH MAN AND YOUTH WOMEN, THERE IS NO TRAINERS.....YOU ARE THE PREREQUISITES OF TRAINERS. AND I AN I SAY THAT WITH NO MITIGATION.
FOR YOUTHS MAKE AND BREAK THE SALES OF....MR.....ADIDAS, AIRWALK, CONVERSE, DIADORA, FILA, KAEPA, K SWISS, LA GEAR, MITRE, MIZUNO, NIKE, PUMA, REEBOK, RYKA. YOU HEAR.........
SO, YOUTH MAN, KEEP TRAINING? TO KEEP FIT MENTALLY AND PHYSICALLY BECAR!.......IT IS NOT DE' PRICE, THAT MAKE IT NICE. IT IS YOUR LOVE OF LIFE, THAT GIVE THE SPICE. JAH. LOVE YOUTH MAN.....

GREG TATE

AND ARTHUR JAFFA ....

Greg: This is the thing about the black community, you don't really know who spends money and who doesn't and where the sneaker budget fits into the overall budget. It's part of your resplendence. It's kinda fascinating because last time I was in London the degree to which people had totally digested hip hop style...goin into a club the atmosphere was just Wutang. I coulda been in Brooklyn. The dynamics...how people related to one another was reminiscent of that kinda edginess. It was so un-Black British demeanour. I call this the Wu Vibe. It's live or die hip hop. It was very different from when I went to my first warehouse party, with the Caribbean background, people with certain style elements mingled....

Arthur: Nobody ever talks about how much black people spend on leisure wear. When integration happened in the schools you had underprivileged black kids coming to mixed athletics parks and they'd get trainers and clothes and stuff. Oftentimes that stuff was better made clothes than what people had. So at the end of a game, as opposed to taking it off they'd wear it around. And that's the beginning of it taking on a certain fashion caché. Athletes were wearing sneakers because they were better than the shoes they had. More durable. So the people who were making this stuff picked up on it. That precedes hip hop. There was a whole generation of people growing up seeing Peter Tosh, Bob Marley and those guys wearing it...Jamaica had the shit down in 74, 75. It's like...constantly trying to erase the source.

Greg: Over here, in the US, is this fountainhead of hip hop. Things become hip because someone in hip hop decides to adopt it. It's like, we're gonna make Tommy, we're gonna make Timberland. But the labels never take on a larger dimension than the culture which creates them. Urban culture is just a euphemism, hip hop has made leisure-wear a billion dollar fashion business in less than twenty years. It has to do with black male style, with masculinity, athleticism. Because hip hop in already in the media. It's the trickle over. It's set in the street, and it's supported by what you're saying in body language. They hang in a comfortable way, which is part of the appeal...projecting an aura of regal-ness.

AND IN THE UK, BECAUSE WE HAD ALL THESE DIFFERENT INFLUENCES WE CREATED A REAL HYBRID FASHION.

Greg: That's the "diasporic" experience. A friend was talking about style in Mali, and it's all about combinations and patterns, just chaotic. From an African sensibility, it's about reconciling things that would be contradictory. James Snead wrote about cutting and breakin as being the great ancient trope of African culture. Hip hop put a certain definition behind the terminology but the actual practice has much deeper roots and has to do with creating a space for contradictions, chaos, clashes and resolving things inside the cultural experience.

GREG TATE, VILLAGE VOICE, NEW YORK
ARTHUR JAFFA, CINE
MATO
GRAPHER, NEW YORK

...YEAH THE THING ABOUT BREAKDANCE IS THAT WHEN IT WAS REALLY HAPPENING IN MANHATTAN, THAT'S WHERE ALL THE CLUBS WERE, BUT YOU KNOW HIP HOP, GRANDMASTER FLASH AND ALL THE REST OF THAT.....BLOCK PARTIES, PEOPLE WORE TRAINERS, KICK ABOUTS, FOR BEATINGS AFTERWARDS, PEOPLE USED TO WEAR SPORTSWEAR BECAUSE YOU COULD GET AWAY QUICKER, THEY WERE RUNNING AWAY FROM A LOT OF POLICE MAN. THE CLOTHES THEY WORE WAS STUFF THAT WAS LIKE KEEP-ING THEM WARM WHEN THEY WERE SPRAYING AT NIGHT DOING ALL THAT STUFF. IT WAS MORE FUNCTIONAL. AND THE THING ABOUT NOW, ITS MORE OF A STYLE THING WHEREAS WITH THE ORIGINAL B.BOYS IT WAS A PRACTI-CAL THING. SHARP, LONDON '96 I LIKE AIR JORDANS BECAUSE I LIKE THE HIP HOP SCENE. I LIKE THAT STYLE. I LIKE WHAT ALL THE BREAKDANCERS USED TO WEAR. I'VE EVEN GOT A PAIR OF VANS FROM THE LATE 70S THAT WERE MADE ESPECIALLY FOR BREAKDANCING CALLED BREAKERS. SIMON GUNNING

HE DEAFANING CHEERS HAD DIED DOWN, THE EXCITEMENT ON THE LONDON ALL STARS
ACE'S WAS VISIBLE TO ALL. FLIPSKI DRESSED IN HIS USUAL BLACK LEATHER ADIDAS
RACK SUIT AND SHELL TOPS RAN BACK INTO CIRCLE AND BEGAN PUSHING EVERYONE
ACK RECREATING THE CIRCLE SO THE BATTLE COULD CONTINUE.
LL EYES WERE NOW ON HALIT'S SWEATING FACE, WHAT MOVE WAS HE GOING TO DO,
WHAT OTHER BIG MOVE HAS HE GOT TO BUST.
LIPSKI'S SKILFUL DISPLAY OF BREAK DANCING HAD SENT THE CROWD WILD SCREAMING
BOY" "BOY" "BOY" AND SHOUTING WITH APPRECIATION. HIS ONE-LEGGED SWIPES,
ANCY FOOTWORK AND HALOS HAD RAISED THE STAKES TO THE LIMIT, HE THEN TOPPED
LL THOSE MOVES WITH AN EFFORTLESS 1990 WHICH SAW HIM REVOLVE AT LEAST FOUR
IMES CAUSING A SYNCRONIZED GASP THROUGHOUT THE SWEAT-DRENCHED VENUE
OLLOWED BY AN ALMIGHTY CHEER. FLIPSKI THEN PROUDLY RAISED HIS HANDS IN THE
IR WHILST ACCEPTING THE APPLAUSE. THE ELECTRIC VIBES IN THE SPATS CLUB ON
HIS PARTICULAR SATURDAY DIDN'T PERMIT HALIT OR HIS INFAMOUS CREW LIVE TO
REAK TO BACK DOWN IN ANY WAY. THIS MUCH ANTICIPATED AND LONG AWAITED BATTLE
AS VERY MUCH ON
RESSED IN THEIR FAMILIAR BLUE PUMA T-SHIRTS, PUMA STATES AND LEE JEANS, THE
IVE TO BREAK CREW'S UNBEATEN RECORD WAS BEING SERIOUSLY CHALLENGED. DJ
INGERS WAS BUSY BEHIND THE TECHNICS CUTTING UP THE CHIC CLASSIC "GOOD TIMES"
O THE HEAD NODDING APPROVAL OF A GROUP OF UP AND COMING DJS.
AKING OFF HIS HEADPHONES HE BEGAN SPEED MIXING FROM DECK TO DECK "GOOD
IMES", "GOOD TIMES", "GOOD TIMES", FASTER AND FASTER UNTIL THE CAPACITY CROWD
RUPTED YET AGAIN INTO CHEERS.
HEN JUST AS QUICK HE MIXED IN ANOTHER CLASSIC "JUST BEGAN", BY THE JIMMY
ASTER BUNCH, THE FAMILIAR INTRO OF THIS B-BOY CLASSIC CAUSED YET ANOTHER
PONTANEOUS UPROAR. AT THAT VERY MOMENT A KNOWING SMILE FLASHED ACROSS
ALIT'S FACE AS HE STEPPED BACK INTO THE CIRCLE.
PATRICK COLDSWEAT

my adidas walk through concert doors
and roamed all over coliseum floors
i stepped on stage at live aid
all the people gave and the poor got paid
and out of those speakers, I did speak
i wore my adidas but i'm not a sneak
the sands of foreign lands
with mike in hand i cold took command
my adidas and me close as can be
we make a mean team, my adidas and me
we get around together, my adidas and me
and we won't be had when caught in bad weather
up and down forever

MY ADIDAS/PETER PIPER

RUN
DMC

GLEN E. FRIEDMAN

Interview with Glen E Friedman during the opening party for his exhibition "FUCK YOU ALL" at the Institute of
Contemporary Art. London. early 1997. Images taken from his books "Fuck you Heroes" and "Fuck you too".

TONY ALVA. 77

The very first sneakers I remember buying? Believe it or not they were shell-toes (Adidas Super Stars), when I was eight or nine years old, cause I used to drag my toes. I wore them the first year they came out. I'm talking about, like 1970 or 69.
I swear to God I wore them back then, cause I used to go like this all the time (dragging toe on floor) it was a habit of mine, so my dad got me shell-toes and ADIDAS WERE THE SHIT cause I was living in New York back then. I had them forever until I moved out to California, and I think I started wearing Vans, when I started skating because Vans though...no one knows. I mean the only reason that anyone ever bought Vans was that they were CHEAP, not cause they were good. They used to be seven dollars a pair in 1975. for the deck shoes. They were the skaters' shoe. I mean you'd look at Tony Alva, and everyone was wearing them and you were able to get the two-tone ones and Wentzle Ruml had the very first two-tone ones which were red and blue. Tony got them later and made them famous, right. I WAS THE VERY FIRST TO ORDER LIGHT BLUE AND DARK BLUE. I KNOW THAT FOR A FACT! (laughs). It's true cause you could go into Vans and get the material yourself and pay a dollar more and they would make them for you. But remember they were only eight dollars, custom made. I was definitely very into sneakers.

I'm vegan now so I won't wear any of my shoes in the Campus collection. I've got nearly every colour and I've got some rare ones, black with silver stripes, burgundy of course with beige stripes, light blue with white, dark blue with beige and grey with beige. Actually I don't have the black with red or the green with white, which I really wanted badly, but you know they re-made them all. I had them when they made them originally. I also have a pair of shell-toes with lizard skin and I did have some shell-toes with reflector stripes, cause from working with Run DMC I used to get a load of this shit. But now I just wear Jack Purcells cause I'm vegan. I have worn Nikes. You know the ones which came out in "Terminator"? I wore those, but I like shoes with laces that are "a part".
I don't like the u-turn at the bottom. I can't wear shoes like that. They bother me, they disturb me. I think they're for girls or something...like your shoes I hate, those are girl's shoes... (pointing to Paul's black and purple Cortez). But you know what I'm saying. I like it when they're separate here...that's why I don't like the Gazelle, I only like the Campus.

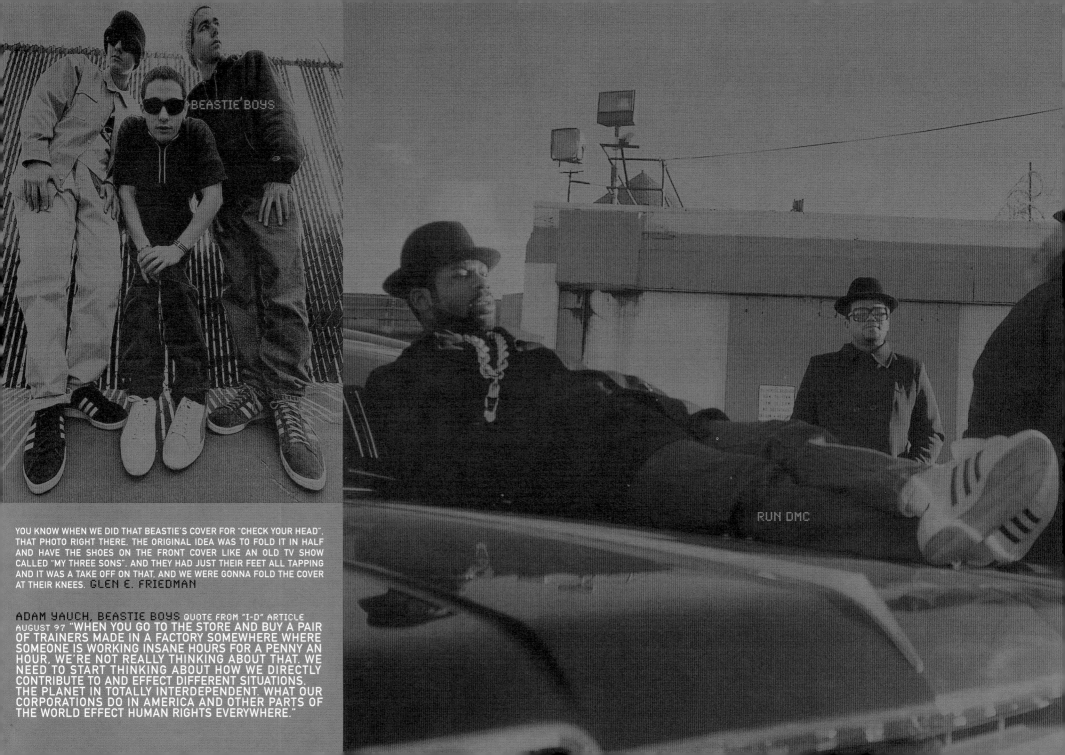

BEASTIE BOYS

RUN DMC

YOU KNOW WHEN WE DID THAT BEASTIE'S COVER FOR "CHECK YOUR HEAD",
THAT PHOTO RIGHT THERE, THE ORIGINAL IDEA WAS TO FOLD IT IN HALF
AND HAVE THE SHOES ON THE FRONT COVER LIKE AN OLD TV SHOW
CALLED "MY THREE SONS". AND THEY HAD JUST THEIR FEET ALL TAPPING
AND IT WAS A TAKE OFF ON THAT, AND WE WERE GONNA FOLD THE COVER
AT THEIR KNEES. GLEN E. FRIEDMAN

ADAM YAUCH, BEASTIE BOYS QUOTE FROM "I-D" ARTICLE
AUGUST 97 "WHEN YOU GO TO THE STORE AND BUY A PAIR
OF TRAINERS MADE IN A FACTORY SOMEWHERE WHERE
SOMEONE IS WORKING INSANE HOURS FOR A PENNY AN
HOUR, WE'RE NOT REALLY THINKING ABOUT THAT. WE
NEED TO START THINKING ABOUT HOW WE DIRECTLY
CONTRIBUTE TO AND EFFECT DIFFERENT SITUATIONS.
THE PLANET IN TOTALLY INTERDEPENDENT. WHAT OUR
CORPORATIONS DO IN AMERICA AND OTHER PARTS OF
THE WORLD EFFECT HUMAN RIGHTS EVERYWHERE."

JAZZY B INTERVIEWED BY PAUL AYRE

You know that I'm a footballer right?...so that's what it stemmed from, having trainers that needed to be comfortable...but I go back to the days of Gola, Mitre, I'm talking Winfield, like four stripes. In actual fact I was in a shop the other day in Carnaby Street getting a pair of new school football boots and the guy was saying that he's got the old original stuff, the Penerol boots, the Franz Beckenbauers. It was a very important part of growing up. Being a victim of fashion, a trainer is as important as a pair of Doc Martens or even Monkey Boots. The old Italian suits and the Stan Smiths, the white ones...green flash used to run with a suit with the old label on the cuff. I'm talking about the days of white football boots, were they Kevin Kegans, no Allen Ball! I'm talking the 70s.
THAT'S TRUE, THEY WERE NAILED INTO THE BLOODY BOOTS.
One time when everyone was wearing track suits and the sneaker to go with the track suits...What was that big sports shop in Wood Green, under the bridge?
YOU'RE TALKING ABOUT DUVALS.
DUVALS!..yeah, that was it.
DUVALS, AND THAT WAS HARRINGEY.
Harringey, I'm sorry, yeah.
IT WAS THE SHIT FOR A TIME, AND THEY WERE WICKED PEOPLE IN THERE.
Roots and culture, Reggae music, that's my thing, and man back in the day, would have been calling you a sticks man or something, that was like running style...And nowadays, everything is narrowed down to just Adidas and Nike for myself personally. And Nike has become synonymous with all of our wear, so much so that they ban it from clubs which is stupidness. I guess they see it as a youth thing, because they think that the youth can't afford to buy shoes, but the sneakers cost more than the shoes. fuck with it.
SO ARE YOU AN OLD SKOOL OR NEW SKOOL MAN?
Well I like to move with the times.
IT'S REALLY FUNNY, A LOT OF THE PEOPLE I INTERVIEW SAY THEY ARE INTO THE OLD SKOOL...BUT THEY WEREN'T EVEN AROUND AT THE TIME...
True say...
SO HOW MANY SNEAKERS DO YOU HAVE?
Maybe at one time I had about 180...but that was a long time ago...in 89 to 90.
AND YOU GAVE THEM AWAY?
I've got a big family you know.
WHEN YOU GO TRAVELLING ABROAD, DO YOU LOOK FOR SNEAKERS?
Me and H went to Korea...and we actually went to the places where they make the sneakers...you go to these underground markets, at the time we was buying for the shop as well, and um yeah man we was out there for days just buying sneakers.You know hip hop culture, or black culture period, has influenced fashion and influenced sneaker companies. Check Nike or Adidas, that's built on the black dollar or black pound, but they'd never admit it. We'd be talking till the end of the cake you know, but at the end of the day it's business in one sense or another and it's all shit.

Fabel: I was about 10 in 1975-76 when I started to see some kids breakdancing. It started in the Bronx, but Spanish Harlem caught on very quick. The attitude for the most part was all about competition. You had to have the dopest moves, the most flavor.

The brothers started to wear sweatshirts with their names or the name of their crew, like gangs used to do. Then we took it to the next level. The graffiti writers started to paint their jackets, not stoned-washed jackets, but extra strong denim so you could do nice pieces on them. Even pants were covered with graffiti.

Ken Swift: One of the main things about B-boying was footwear. I used to wear Converse 69s. They had a very thick rubber sole. We didn't have a lot of money, so we wanted to keep our sneakers as fresh as possible. On some of the models, like the Adidas Superstar, the side of the shoe used to get fucked up too quickly. When I was dancing with them I scratched the white leather all the time.
So we started to dance and move differently to avoid scratching our sneakers too much. We adapted our way of breaking to the sneakers. The thing was to do your footwork so smooth that you almost never touched the concrete. We were saving up on sneakers in almost a scientific way. It was very important, cos $35 for a pair was a lot of money back in the days.

Fabel: Then it went to the level of laces. You were not allowed to do them, it was a real taboo. You had to wear your laces undone otherwise you were a sucker. We started to copy graffiti artists' characters. That's where the word phat came from. Everything was big, exaggerated. So it went from phat laces to even phatter laces. I used to have half-inch elastic laces with two or three pairs of socks on my feet, so my sneaker would look like it'd been drawn by a graffiti artist. We were wearing those 70s jeans and rolled them one side to show the different layers of tube socks. You had to look flashy when you were dancing, almost like Native Americans wearing different colored feathers.

GRANDMASTER FLASH
When I was coming up it was Converse and Super Pro-Keds with the red and blue lines on the top. Those were phat, word up.
WHERE DID YOU GROW UP?
In America, New York City.
WHY DO YOU THINK THAT SNEAKERS HAVE BEEN SYNONYMOUS WITH HIP HOP CULTURE SINCE THE EARLY DAYS?
Basically because it's a very comfortable sort of footwear. When we're dancing and doing our thing, when we're DJing or MCing, you gotta be comfortable when you're ripping the house down.

AFRICA BAMBAATA
WHAT SNEAKERS WERE YOU WEARING WHEN YOU FIRST STARTED OUT?
It's hard to say, could have been PF Flyers, Nike or Pro-Keds. The sneaker market is so big now it's crazy, you got sneaker shoes, sneaker sneakers, it's all sneaker crazy!
WHY DO YOU THINK SNEAKERS ARE SO BIG IN HIP HOP CULTURE?
Cause they have like a lot of funky styles and hip hop's about the funk, so with the funky styles of hip hop and the funk that they put on the sneakers, so many designs and different elements...we're just giving up the funk to the sneakers! And it's time for some hip hop sneakers to come from the hip hop community.
SO WHAT ARE YOU SPORTING RIGHT NOW, THEN?
Right now I have some Nikes on, I'm a Nike man, I like some Nikes....

WHAT CLOTHES AND SNEAKERS DID YOU WEAR WHEN YOU WERE YOUNG?

What I was wearing? My crew was wearing a lot of Fila, but at that time Fila didn't have sneakers so we stayed in fresh K-Swiss. We'd only wear them for say, three or four days, and then you had to discard them, cause they no good once they start sagging and getting all tacky looking. Fresh K-Swiss or Diadoras, this is what Björn Börg wore and we felt that those were the correct match for the Fila sweat suit, that's what all the players wore.

WHEN DID YOU GIVE UP WASHING SNEAKERS?

Never give up washing sneakers. I gotta go wash my Jordan's right now. The best sneakers are the ones that wash real clean. You can't have dirty sneakers, you check people by their feet.

WHAT DO YOU THINK OF SNEAKER COMPANIES SPONSORING HIP HOP ARTISTS?

I mean, personally, you know, as far as getting sponsored, I wouldn't mind getting sponsored, but whenever they want to give me sneakers that's it, they just give me the shoes! I could buy the shoes! I'd like somebody to give me some money to wear their shoes, then I'd wear them everyday. But, you know, when somebody says they're gonna sponsor me they'd be like, OK, Ice we're gonna give you three pairs of sneakers, I could buy three pairs of sneakers! I don't need that kind of sponsorship.

SO, WHAT'S YOUR FAVOURITE SNEAKER RIGHT NOW?

My favourite sneaker right now, I'm wearing these Jordans. They fresh because they wash clean, you don't have to buy a new pair every week. And I still wear K-Swiss, real tuff, and Nike Cortez, the gang bangers' shoe.

WHEN I WAS TALKING WITH DJ MUGGS HE WAS SAYING THAT THE CRIPS AND THE BLOODS WERE WEARING THEIR DISTINCTIVE COLOUR OF NIKE CORTEZ...

Yeah yeah yeah. Muggs tell you about that. Well of course, Cripps will never wear a red pair of shoes and a blood would never wear a blue pair of shoes. There was a while when Cripps were wearing BKs for "Blood Killer" and there was a lot of different shoe things going on. You know, I ain't no gang banger no more so I ain't really involved in the color thing. I got a blue pair and a red pair. THE ESSENTIAL FESTIVAL, BRIGHTON, 97

ICE T

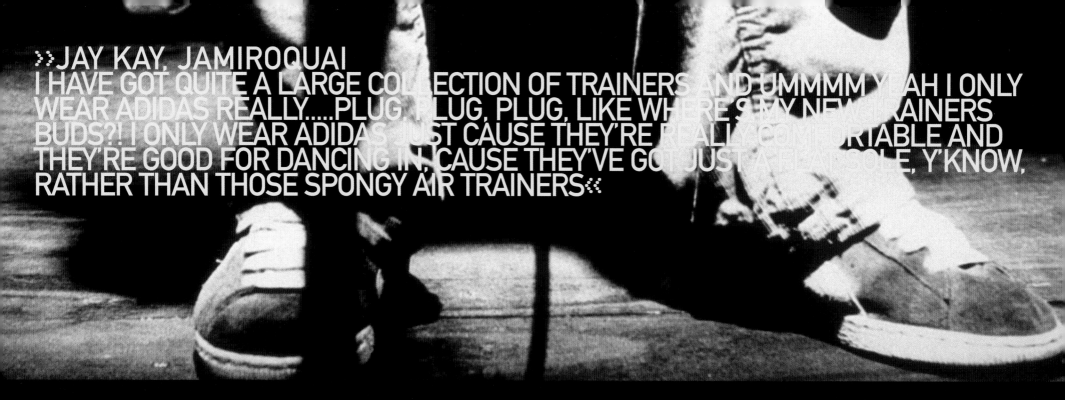

>>JAY KAY, JAMIROQUAI
I HAVE GOT QUITE A LARGE COLLECTION OF TRAINERS AND UMMMM YEAH I ONLY WEAR ADIDAS REALLY.....PLUG, PLUG, PLUG, LIKE WHERE'S MY NEW TRAINERS BUDS?! I ONLY WEAR ADIDAS JUST CAUSE THEY'RE REALLY COMFORTABLE AND THEY'RE GOOD FOR DANCING IN, CAUSE THEY'VE GOT JUST A FLAT SOLE, Y'KNOW, RATHER THAN THOSE SPONGY AIR TRAINERS<<

>>NORMSKI, AN INFORMOUS ALL-ROUND CREATIVE TYPE, LONDON, 97

......the footwear situation...the thing is that it is crap, it is rubbish, it is in fact EXIT, but it's also entrée. It's also in, like it is really important, but when you say a word like "crep", in the world of today, that can be interpreted as in the word of a crêpe, you know them lovely things you put your Nutella sauce on, or it can be like "Crep", like back in the day, 1973..."Put your Crep pan your foot". And that means your plimsolls, your trainers, not your shoes, never your shoes or your slippers or your sandal or your boots. It was never any of those things, it was definitely only your leisure-wear rubber sole. It's kind of funny if you think about it, because Crep, that's how I see footwear, just so that you know, just to get the record straight, I don't see them as sneakers.
Because I'm not really into those kind of Americanisms.......NO. I don't know if that was an Americanism, I mean who knows? Maybe that was a Germanism, that the Americans stole. But all I know is that it is an "ism", and all I know is that I'm definitely not into it because it is too far down the line, it is too far removed. I mean "I got a pair of sneakers" just does not sound British, and being Black British and all that, it does not make as much sense as "Nice Trainers". Like when you came in and I said, "Nice Trainers", automatically and I didn't think about it....But now that we're beginning to talk about it I realise that it is a point of stoppage with me, when I start sounding American about something that is so personal to my feet. And I am definitely absolutely loyal to footwear and understanding a pair of boots, understanding my snowboard boots and understanding my trainers and my roller blades or my skate shoes, which are still trainers but there is a specific type of trainer I wear when I go skateboarding.
....When it comes to the Americans you can't test because you know they've got the baseball boot, the soccer boot, the racquetball glove, the softball glove...and that's one thing I really like about the Americans, their sportswear with regards to footwear. Because they absolutely take utter pride. I don't know if it is due to the fact that they've polished a lot of shoes in their time, but they definitely like the soles, and I know that the best sole that I've ever come into contact with has been on an American person's foot rather than on British feet. But then, if I think about it, it was probably actually on a British person's foot first, because there was many a...Monstrosity!...Yeah, that I can't even dream to think of, that I wouldn't wear. There was many I wanted to wear, like, you know, back in them days. I'm talking 70s. You had Mitre, Adidas..... Adidas was the lick, Adidas Kick....was the ultimate shoe, and I was quite young, under double figures when the Adidas Kick were large. 1974, 75, 76...that was the times of "sideburns are us" in this country and Rastaman was a goin out. And you know everyone who came since that has built the inner-city person that we have now got. Because it has only been 30 or 40 years since this place, London, was trash. That's true...You get me? And you get all these different colours of people come in. And then I suppose the reason why I'm really confusing my awareness of things like trainers with America is because of the amount of times I've taken information from American artists.

But if we think deeply, like we are now, about the beginning of that time, then I was old enough to say, oh I don't want those basketball ones with the little grey things on that you get at British Home Stores, I want the low cut ones that just look a bit cooler. But everyone got them plimsolls because their heels didn't rub, but then when you saw the Converse All Star with the thing on the other side of the heel, oHHHHHH, that looked right...You looked like you were gonna rub your heels together...with the star...so you would aspire to an American manufacturer at that particular time....I remember Dunlop Green Flash was likin. You couldn't touch that shoe, and you had others like Adidas Stan Smith, coming off as the tennis champion...That's really important to me, because I don't care too much about half the trainers that lead the market these days, but I have a deep feeling about back in the day. I'm trying to remember the trainer that made me cry, that I asked for. And I can't, but it was so sly........
Mitre bring it upon another level. Boxing shoes, ballet shoes, dancing shoes, they perfected that area because it was really left up to them to deal with because they couldn't TOUCH the soles of Adidas. They couldn't touch the soles of Converse, and Converse and Adidas technology is what goes into making Nike. So Nike had the dollar bill to follow it up and that's where America beats down the whole world because they have got the ability and the size of an economy to be able to say, "Let's invest this much and just transform the progressive athletic shoe". Transform it progressively to the point where Adidas has had to pull their boots out of their boot cupboard and transform it radically...racing along in the history a little.....Kick, Samba, Mamba, Ringo, with all them kinda shoes...And all of them were Dred. They all had their place in the street. There was always a particular shoe that went under a particular type of denim. You had Lois jeans, Lee jeans, Levi's come late on the British side. We had Farrah, a classic kind of alternative look at apparel, as opposed to just wanting to go on the left-of-field thing with the American look....All them sweet boys who used to bust Farrahs and Mitre Memphis because they look like shoes .....All the Ragga and Rude Boys all went for suede because it looks like money, and I love my suede because it has got that kind of plush finish to it...and you had your Tacchini track-suit...But when I was a young man I never had Jack mate! Still wearing monkey boots. One ting, you get me, in my circle you never used to go and mash up anything to get any of dat. I ended up as a photographer, later on in my teenage years, probably because I was forced to admire other people's stuff. I was not going to be forced to feel that I had to have all of this stuff, but although I had the peer pressure as they grow up. I also had a bit of a balanced training.

WHAT I NORMALLY SAY TO PEOPLE IS THAT IF THEY'VE GOT MORE THAN, SAY TWENTY PAIRS,
THAT'S RESPECTABLE, YOU KNOW WHAT I'M SAYING?
I'VE THROWN HALF OF MINE OUT, CAUSE IT WAS A BIT SILLY. A LOT OF THEM WENT AROUND THE CORNER TO THE OXFAM PLACE.
IS THAT THE FIRST BAG? (LAUGHS)
THERE ARE THESE...NOW THESE WERE MAD THESE WERE. WHEN I FIRST SAW THESE...
THEY'RE PHAT MAN, WHERE DID YOU GET THEM?
CANAL STREET. BUT D FROM OUR CREW. HE HAD A GOOD NAME FOR THEM.....ACIDAS.
BUT I HAD A BIT OF A THING FOR THEM, SO I GOT THEM IN MOST COLOURS. HAVE YOU SEEN THESE YET ON YOUR TREKS?
NO WELL NO, THE ONLY VERSION OF THIS SHOE I'VE SEEN IS THE WHITE ONE...(MUSHROOM REACHES IN THE BAG)...THAT'S IT!
THE ONLY ONES I DIDN'T GET WERE THE ORANGE AND BLUE.
OHH I NEVER SEEN THEM, BUT YEAH MAN THAT'S JUST ROUGH ROUGH ROUGH ROUGH ROUGH ROUGH....
AND THESE I REMEMBER SEEING THESE DOWN IN SOHO. WHAT WAS THAT SHOP CALLED?
RHYTHM RECORDS?
NO NO WELL BACK. WAS IT GROOVE...?
GROOVE RECORDS?
WAS IT? YEAH ON THE CORNER. WELL ANYWAY I REMEMBER A BLOKE STEPPING OUT WITH A PAIR OF THESE ON
AND HE'D OBVIOUSLY JUST COME BACK FROM THE STATES AND WE WERE ALL LIKE...(EXPRESSION)... "WHAT ARE THOSE".
WHAT TIME WAS THAT MUSHROOM?
I CAN'T REMEMBER. BUT...WELL ACTUALLY MILES BROUGHT THESE BACK FROM JAPAN.
WELL PUT IT THIS WAY I HAVE NEVER EVER SEEN BLACK AND RED AND I'VE NEVER SEEN PURPLE
AND YELLOW, THESE ARE JUST PHAT! NOW THESE, THESE ARE SHOCKING. OH WILSON...
THESE WERE FROM JAPAN AND WE CALLED THEM
WILSON ROBOCOPS AND GOLDIE WAS TRYING TO GET THESE OFF ME FOR YEARS. THEY DID THEM IN
ALL-BLACK AS WELL. BE CAREFUL WITH IT PAUL. THE PLASTICS PERISHED ON IT.
THAT SHIT SHOULDN'T REALLY HAPPEN.
WELL IT'S LIKE THE ADIDAS YELLOWING-UP.
THIS STYLE WAS A BIT LATER ON.
YEAH THAT'S THE FIRST AIRFORCE. HAVE YOU SEEN THE ONES WITH THE ICE BLUE SOLE?
THAT'S A CLASSIC SHOE. AND YOU DON'T OFTEN SEE MANY BROWN AIRFORCE.
HOW MANY AIRFORCE HAVE YOU GOT?
I DUNNO I'VE THROWN MOST OF THEM AWAY...HERE'S SOME ALL-BLACK. AND THESE I GOT IN ABOUT 1986. BUT THEY'RE GOING YELLOW.

YEAH WHEN YOU TALK ABOUT SHELL-TOES, THIS IS LIKE THE PROPER STUFF, LOOK AT THE LEATHER. ON THE NEW ONES, THE
LEATHER ISN'T THE SAME, IT'S LIKE PLASTIC, THIS IS THE PROPER STUFF, AND WITH THE SNAKE SKIN STRIPES.
WE WERE WEARING THEM WITH THE GOOSE JACKETS....
THE SHELL-TOES AND GOOSE, IT WAS SO SO FRESH, I WAS TALKING TO FAB 5 FREDDY ABOUT ALL THAT AND HE
WAS SAYING IT WAS JUST CHEAP PRACTICAL CLOTHING THROWN TOGETHER AND IT LOOKED SO SO FLY.
YEAH ANYWAY I'LL BRING THE SECOND BAG IN. NOW THESE CORTEZ. AFTER A COUPLE OF DAYS OF WEARING
THEM YOUR FEET WERE LIKE A PAIR OF SOFT MARROWS. BECAUSE THERE'S NO SUPPORT IN THEM.
THEY'RE A LOUNGING SHOE REALLY, YOU CAN'T DO ANYTHING ELSE IN THEM...
AND THERE'S NO VENTILATION.
THAT'S TRUE, THAT'S TRUE, BUT WHAT I LIKE ABOUT A CORTEZ, IS THEY CAN GET OLD AND A BIT BEATEN UP AND THAT
NOW. THIS IS WHAT I CONSIDER THE ALL TIME QUALITY TRAINER. FILA. YEAH. I GOT THEM IN JUST ABOUT EVERY COLOUR. WE USED
TO GO OUT TO NEW YORK. WHEN FOOT LOCKER USED TO GET ONE-OFF LINES AND WE'D ARRIVE AT NIGHT AND BE DOWN THERE
LOOKING THROUGH THE FOOT LOCKER SHUTTERS AND YOU'D BE LIKE, "RIGHT I'M COMING DOWN HERE TOMORROW TO GET THOSE".
AND TAKE A LOOK...THIS IS THE ADIDAS CAMPUS FROM JAPAN AND THIS IS THE ADIDAS CAMPUS FROM AMERICA. BOTH EARLY-80S.
AND WE WERE INTO THE JAPANESE ONES BECAUSE YOU CAN SEE IT'S A DIFFERENT SHOE. PADDED AND MUCH BETTER MADE. SEE
HOW IT'S WORN. LOOK AT THIS. THE AMERICAN ONE IS ALL SHRIVELLED UP.
DO YOU KNOW WHAT SNEAKERS YOU WERE WEARING WAY BACK?
WELL THE FIRST ONES I EVER WANTED WAS A PAIR OF HI-TEC TECS. I KNOW THEY SOUND A LITTLE WONKY NOW. AND AFTER THAT I
THINK IT WAS PUMA G VILLA'S. PEOPLE WILL LAUGH ABOUT THEM NOW BECAUSE THEY WERE FOOTBALL FIGHTING SHOE. WELL ALL
THOSE KIDDIES WERE WEARING THEM AND ALL THE B-BOYS WERE WEARING THEM. BUT NOW YOU SEE PEOPLE LIKE PUFF DADDY
WEARING THEM ...CAUSE THEY'VE RE-RELEASED THEM.
YEAH, BUT WITH DIFFERENT COLOURED SOLES, LIKE ICE SOLES. BUT THAT WAS A TUFF SHOE WHEN THAT CAME OUT.
YOU CAN'T FUCK WITH THAT. AS YOU SAY THE B-BOYS AND THE FOOTBALL CASUALS LOVED THEM ALONG WITH DIADORA
AND GAZELLES, FIRST TIME AROUND.
YEAH AND EVERYONE USED TO GET THEIR STUFF AT NIK NAKS. IT'S MAD BECAUSE I USED TO BE IN A LITTLE CREW BEFORE THE WILD
BUNCH. AND THEY ALL USED TO BE INTO FOOTBALL FIGHTING. AND ON SATURDAY EVERYONE WOULD COME IN THE ROOM. WE HAD
TURNTABLES AND THAT. ALL ARMANI JACKETS ON. GAZELLES AND STANLEY KNIFES AND THEY'D BE LIKE. WE'RE ALL OFF DOWN THE
FOOTBALL WHAT YOU SAYING? AND I'D BE LIKE. NA NAA. AND A COUPLE OF US WOULD STAY BEHIND ON THE DECKS. THE THING IS I
CAN REMEMBER WHEN PEOPLE IN THIS COUNTRY WEREN'T REALLY CLUED-UP ON TRAINERS. ONLY THE HIP HOP KIDS..AND I CAN
REMEMBER GOING OUT TO NEW YORK. GOING THROUGH CUSTOMS AND YOU'D SEE A BAGGAGE HANDLER WITH A PAIR OF TRAINERS ON
AND YOU'D BE LIKE. WHAT'S GOING ON HERE THEN? SO IT'S ONLY RECENTLY THAT ALL THE TRENDY PEOPLE HAVE PICKED UP ON IT.
NICE ONE.

PUBLIC-SCHOOLIN',
GUN TOTIN',
ADIDAS WEARIN',
GANG SHOOTIN',
WELFARE NEEDIN' KIDS

...PRIVATE-SCHOOLIN',
HEALTH CARE HAVIN',
REEBOK-WEARIN',
COLUMBUS LOVIN',
TWO BIT RACISTS...

>> THE SNOOP DOGGY DOGG INTERVIEW
KENSINGTON METROPOLE, LONDON '96

HOW LONG HAVE YOU BEEN WITH REEBOK? about two weeks.

WHAT WERE YOU WEARING BEFORE? Converse. they used to give me a lot of free shoes. Converse is a gangsta shoe back home you know what I'm sayin...if you ain't got a lot of money you get yourself a pair of Converse for $20. and I was sporting them and I was just down with them. but Reebok they looked out for me in a major way so I can get some shoes for me and my pops. they've been lookin out for my son. I mean it's just major. I love the way Reebok doin me...

IN TERMS OF LA AND THE GANG BANGERS, A LOT OF THE HISPANIC AND PUERTO RICAN KIDS WORE NIKE CORTEZ. the black community was the All Stars. but they wore Cortez too. the blue ones. the Cripps wore the blue ones. but the Cortez were basically for the Hispanics. and now I'm takin it to another level. Reebok is the Doggy Dog and everybody down with it.

NORMALLY REEBOK ISN'T MY BRAND, I'M MORE OF A NIKE MAN. but Reebok showing up you know what I'm sayin?

SO IS IT A NEW THING FOR SHOE COMPANIES TO SPONSOR RAP ACTS? THEY ARE..... they will sponsor rap acts. it's just that it has to be the right.....it's gotta be somebody's policy what they can wear. and the key is I don't feel negative about it. like. what is he wearing Reeboks for? you know. my image right now is in the perfect situation where I can do whatever I wanna do. because I'm not a negative person any more. I'm all about making good music and being positive and the kids love me. and if they see me wearing these Reeboks...I can play basketball in my house. I got the court. and I'm like the Lakers. the Lakers are sponsored as well. They from LA. they just round the corner. it all ties into each other. they using me for the west coast promotion because I'm from the west coast and I'm head of the west coast. and if I'm wearing Reeboks everybody going to start wearing Reeboks cause I'm going to make it cool. especially if they see me. Nick Van Essen and Shaquille O'Neal in the commercial. real tight with the Reeboks. they gonna make me a Snoop Dogg Reebok. they'll put a paw on it right here...damn! it's about time I'm bringin back my Reeboks. and they've got that flag on there too. that London flag on there....

I THOUGHT THEY'D GOT RID OF THAT. no. it's still there. they just put it on the inside of the shoe! are you with Nike? NO, NO, NO.

4

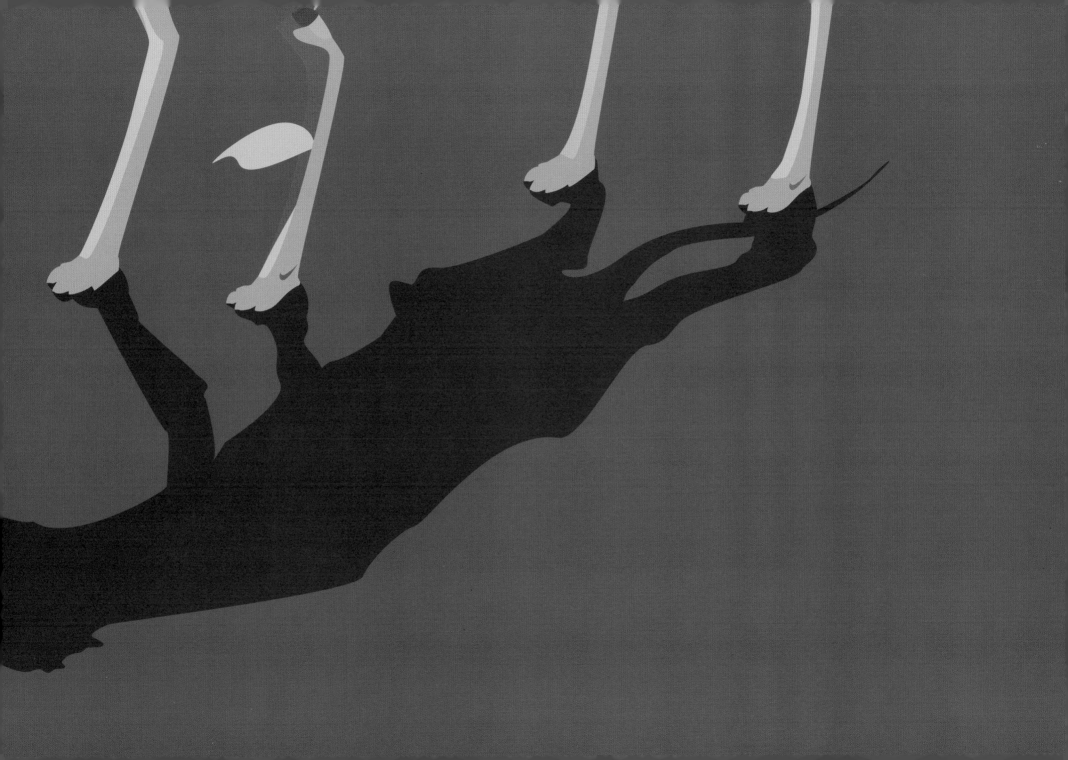

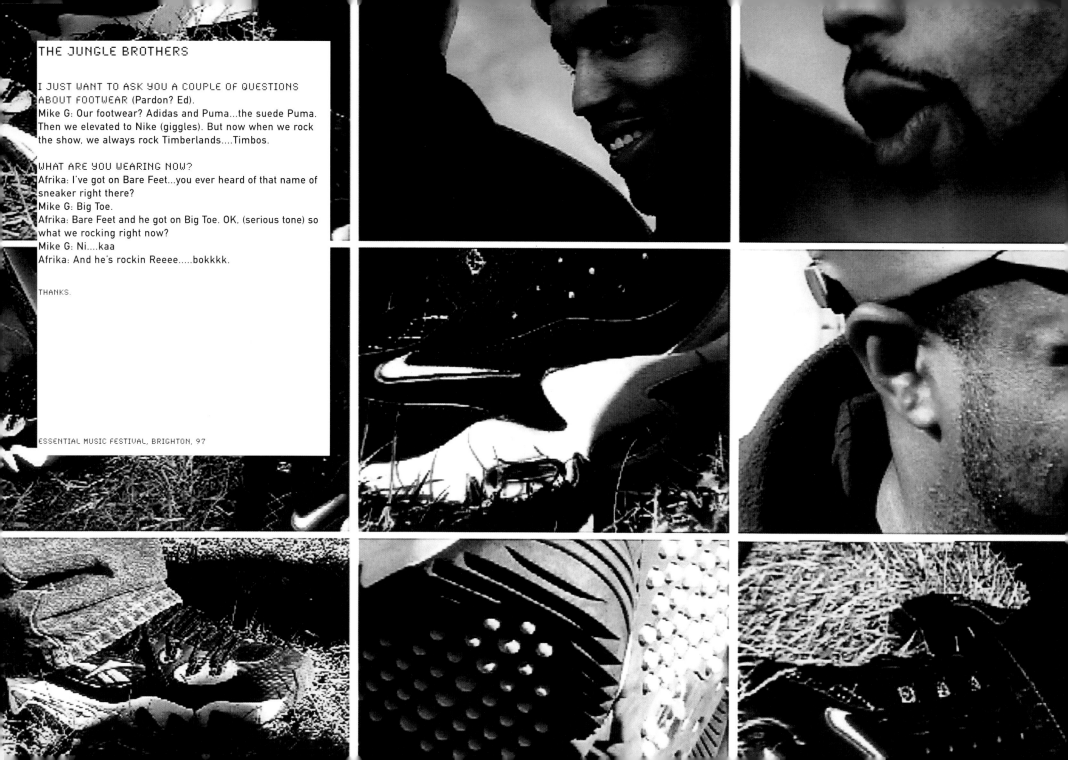

THE JUNGLE BROTHERS

I JUST WANT TO ASK YOU A COUPLE OF QUESTIONS
ABOUT FOOTWEAR (Pardon? Ed).
Mike G: Our footwear? Adidas and Puma...the suede Puma.
Then we elevated to Nike (giggles). But now when we rock
the show, we always rock Timberlands....Timbos.

WHAT ARE YOU WEARING NOW?
Afrika: I've got on Bare Feet...you ever heard of that name of
sneaker right there?
Mike G: Big Toe.
Afrika: Bare Feet and he got on Big Toe. OK. (serious tone) so
what we rocking right now?
Mike G: Ni....kaa
Afrika: And he's rockin Reeee.....bokkkk.

THANKS.

ESSENTIAL MUSIC FESTIVAL, BRIGHTON, 97

JAY-Z AND DAMON DASH

HOW DO YOU KEEP YOUR 85
AIRFORCE ONES LOOKING SO FRESH?
DD: cause I keep buying new pairs!
J-Z: yeah, airforce ones, you've got to
buy at least two pairs every month.
DD: every week!
J-Z: at least two, they've got to look crisp,
they've got to look nice and new.

DO YOU HAVE ANY TREATMENT FOR THEM
WHEN YOU GET THEM NEW?
J-Z: no, that was played out in 88, 89.
DD: when did you stop washing sneakers, 85?
J-Z: yeah, that long ago, they don't do that any
more, that's why you got to buy so many cause
you can't wash em, they don't look the same
like when they're fresh out of the box, there's
nothing better.

WHAT WERE YOU WEARING WHEN YOU WERE
YOUNG?
DD: airforce ones!
J-Z: these are classics, on the street these are
the sneaker to have, it hasn't changed in ten,
fifteen years.

WHEN I WAS IN NEW YORK EVERYONE
WAS WEARING TIMBERLANDS, DO YOU
THINK SNEAKERS ARE DYING OUT?
DD: no, it's the same thing, a classic
boot, a classic sneaker.
J-Z: they're brothers.

SO ARE YOU AN OLD SKOOL
OR NEW SKOOL MAN?

I like both man, I like to put them together. People are trying too hard, they're still trying to pull the tongues out, which I think is a bit naff, do you know what I'm sayin? People have got into more zippers and stuff and B-boyism brought it to the forefront. All the niggaz are wearing them, and I don't mean niggaz in terms of being black, I mean niggaz as in anybody on the street, like Irish fukin thugs, joyriders wearing sneakers, everybody........

SO WHAT SIZE ARE YOU?

I'm a fukin' UK 10 with about 150 pairs. The rarest pair I've got is a Wilson, given to me by Milo who used to be in the Wild Bunch...like Robocop, black leather with a casing around the side. And I've got these Adidas Equipment, they're black, and almost like the shell-toe nose but all black, with a Velcro covering....rare as fuck them buggas man....and obviously like I got Jack Purcells, the originals, and corduroy Adidas, Gazelle style.

GOLDIE

LONDON MUSIC WEEK 97

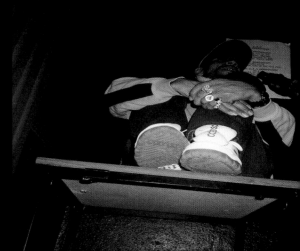

IF I WANT AIR I'LL GET A TRAMPOLINE MATE.

The thing I like about DCs is that you can abuse them. A lot of sneakers, like the Nikes, are like erasers because the companies go, hang on a minute, all the niggaz are buying them so let's give them a material that's gonna wear out a bit quicker so they have to buy another pair. DCs will last you a long time, but a lot of sneakers like Puma States, when you tred on them they're fucked....You know, it's like, Oi mind my fuckin sneakers man! Don't get in the sneaker game man, they're nasty man. And with Stride, they're full of air, you know, let em down and we'll talk.

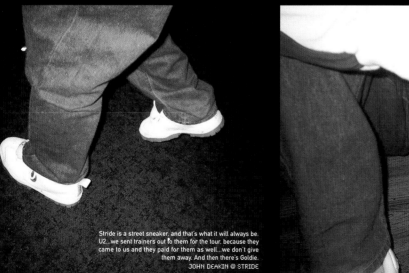

Stride is a street sneaker, and that's what it will always be.
U2...we sent trainers out to them for the tour, because they
came to us and they paid for them as well...we don't give
them away. And then there's Goldie.
JOHN DEAKIN @ STRIDE

WHEN I STARTED DJING I USED TO DO IT ON BASKETBALL PLAYGROUNDS. THAT WAS BACK IN 1988. AT THE TIME I HA
A DEAL WITH NIKE, I USED TO GET FREE PAIRS, WELL, I WAS KIND OF PAID IN SNEAKERS. THEY USED TO ORGANIZ
BASKETBALL TOURNAMENTS IN THE PARISIAN SUBURBS. I REMEMBER ONE YEAR SPIKE LEE DID SOME KIND O
DESIGN FOR THEIR COURT. I REALLY LIKED DJING THOSE EVENTS. I STILL DO, BUT THIS TIME IT'S IN A 17,000 SEATE
INDOOR STADIUM FOR THE MCDONALD'S OPEN, WITH THE WINNER OF THE NBA PLAYING.
I WEAR NIKE SNEAKERS MOST OF THE TIME. THE FIRST PAIR I BOUGHT WITH MY POCKET MONEY, I WAS ABOUT 13, WA
THE NIKE TERMINATOR IN BLACK WITH THE GOLD SWOOSH. I USED TO PLAY BASKETBALL QUITE A LOT, SO I'VE ALWAY
BEEN INTO BASKETBALL SNEAKERS RATHER THAN LOW-CUT SUPERSTAR TYPES. I THOUGHT THE NIKE AIR FORCE O
THE CONVERSE WEAPON WERE VERY GOOD, THEY CAME IN SO MANY DIFFERENT COLOURS. THEY'RE A CLASSI
BASKETBALL SNEAKER, GOOD TO WEAR AND GOOD TO LOOK AT.
I ALWAYS LIKED AIR JORDANS, UNTIL THE MODEL 10, WHEN I THOUGHT...OOOH, MAYBE NOT, IS JORDAN TAKIN
ECSTASY OR SOMETHING. THOSE SNEAKERS WERE A BIT TOO MUCH FOR ME. YOU KNOW, MICHAEL JORDAN WAS TH
ONLY REFERENCE, AND EVERYTIME YOU WATCHED THE ALL-STAR GAME, YOU THOUGHT, I NEED THOSE SNEAKERS NOW
AT THE MOMENT I'M PRETTY SOBER WITH COLOURS, MAINLY BLACK OR WHITE. I'VE BEEN BUYING THEM IN NEW YORI
FOR THE PAST THREE OR FOUR YEARS. THE GOOD THING ABOUT THE STATES IS YOU CAN FIND THE SAME MODEL W
GET IN EUROPE IN WHITE, IN BLACK, OR VICE-VERSA. THERE'S A BIT MORE CHOICE, AND IT'S HALF-PRICE. THAT'
SOMETHING I NEVER QUITE UNDERSTOOD. WHY DO NIKE HAVE PEOPLE IN THEIR EUROPEAN BRANCHES DECIDIN
WHAT COLOURS TO IMPORT FOR EACH COUNTRY? WHY COULDN'T WE GET THE COLOURS THEY GET IN THE STATES O
IN JAPAN? BUT THEN AMERICANS DON'T NECESSARILY GET THE COLOURS WE HAVE.
I OWN ABOUT 55 PAIRS, AND THEY'RE ALL BOXED. I LIKE BOXES. I THINK THE AIR JORDANS AND THE AIR MAX BOXE:
ARE WICKED. THE WORST MEMORY I HAVE WAS WITH A PAIR OF BLACK AIR JORDAN FROM 1989. I PAID 999FF, THE
WERE THE MOST EXPENSIVE JORDANS THAT EVER CAME OUT IN FRANCE. THE SOLE WAS RUINED IN TWO WEEKS
THERE WAS A BIG HOLE GOING THROUGH IT! I WAS SO PISSED OFF. I WENT BACK TO THE SHOP BUT THE GUY REFUSEI
TO CHANGE THEM OR GIVE ME MY MONEY BACK.
I ALWAYS WEAR MY LACES LOOSE, I WANT MY SNEAKERS TO BREATHE.

I HAD THE CHANCE TO GO TO CALIFORNIA IN 1989 TO VISIT MY FAMILY AND SPENT A LOT OF TIME LOOKING FOR COLOURS YOU COULDN'T FIND IN EUROPE. I WENT TO A FLEA MARKET IN SAN JOSE AND FOUND A PAIR OF BLACK AND BLUE AIR JORDAN MODEL 1. THEN I KIND OF STOPPED LOOKING FOR NIKES AND WENT BACK TO MY FIRST LOVE, ADIDAS. I WAS CHASING NASTASE IN LEATHER.

I FOUND A WHITE PAIR WITH WHITE STRIPES, ANOTHER WHITE PAIR WITH GREEN STRIPES, AND ANOTHER ONE WITH GREY SUEDE STRIPES. IN 1992, THOUGH, I WAS SKATING A LOT, AND I WAS WEARING THOSE BAGGY PANTS WITH OLD-SCHOOL PUMAS THAT MY FATHER BROUGHT ME BACK FROM CHINA. AT THE TIME YOU COULDN'T FIND RE-ISSUED PUMA CLYDES, YOU HAD TO LOOK FOR OLD ONES. THE OLD ONES I WAS WEARING HAD VERY THIN SOLES. THE RE-ISSUES IN 93 HAD DIFFERENT SOLES, AND MY FRIENDS USED TO TAKE THE PISS: "OOH, YOU BROUGHT BACK YOUR GRANNY'S SNEAKERS AGAIN..."

GILES

TO:
FROM: ~~Josephine James~~ ~~Simon~~ Joseph Trophilos. Simon Stopford
DATE: ~~21 September 94~~ 16/4/07

Josephine,
Here's the questions... pick your favourites. You can basically just fill in
the answers on this form and fax it back to me, if that's cool and stuff.
Please try and get more than yes/no answers. Thanks again and things.
S x

Most Important Trainer Questions:

1) How many pairs of trainers do you own and which are your faves?

38   ALL ADIDAS.

2) Are trainers better than sex?

NO

3) What's the rarest/ most expensive pair of trainers that you own?

OLD ADIDAS SPIKESKIN SHELL TOES

4) Do you consider your trainers as shoes, footwear, piecs of art or just
trainers?

TRAINERS

5) What trainers would you never be seen dead in?

NIKE

6) Do aliens wear trainers?

OF COURSE

Muchos Grazias to Giles for cooperation !

If you do not receive legible copies of your fax, call the direct line number above

ZOLL 3 4 5 6 7 8 9 10 11 12 INCHES

Made in Indonesia. Fabriqué en Indonesie. Fabricado en Indonesia.

BUSTA FLEX, PARIS, 97

adidas

FARID J, Busta Flex's manager, jumps in the conversation on the Cortez.
Back in 1989, I imported Nike Cortez to France, with two friends, Alex (Lady Soul) and Stef (Home Core). Our shop was near Les Halles and people called us the Kings of Cortez. We travelled to the States and managed to get the rarest models. At one point we had 75 models of Cortez, in different colours and materials.
I remember finding some rare pieces in the suburbs, in a shop owned by a Chinese man who bought black and red Cortez with crocodile and skin swooshes. In Miami, you could find pink or light because the colours varied from east to west coast had a very limited edition pair in beige nubuck c Escape, some black and gold swooshes, grey and blue and silver.
Then you had the different colour combinations of upper and sole. A simple pair of red Cortez came in variations: different materials (suede, leather, nylon different coloured soles (white, all red), different swoo (white, silver...). The most amazing colours were for k you could find a purple pair with an orange swoosh, a flashy turquoise blue with a silver swoosh and turquoise sole.
If you're into Cortez, you have to consider different periods.
The first Nike running shoes was a Cortez shape, though the first model of Cortez was slightly different and came in leather in the classic colours: white shoe, red swoosh and blue line on the sole.
The Cortez came back big time in 1987 when the gang wars were at a height. Bloods and Cripps in LA used to run around and get shot wearing blue or white for the Cripps, and black for the Bloods because the red ones were hard to find. Then there was the third period, starting about three years ago, when you got new models mostly made in Korea. The swoosh is slightly fatter, they're made of suede and nylon, and you can get some really good colour combinations, red/silver, blue/yellow, beige/blue...
And there are the re-editions of the classics, but with little tweaks, like the swoosh embroidered in different colours on the back, a small plastic swoosh on the side, translucent soles.

BUSTA FLEX: I had a pair of beautiful red Nike Terminator with a gold swoosh. I went on holiday in Martinique and wore them all the time. I felt so comfortable in them that I even went on the beach with them, jumped in the sea and played soccer in the sand...still with my sneakers on. They lasted for about one hour. I totally ruined them. There were holes everywhere, it was like a horror film. It was a very depressing holiday.
I also destroyed a pair of Adidas Torsion, my only pair of Adidas ever. I was on my bicycle, and for some reason my foot got jammed in a spoke. That was it. Adidas RIP.
I customise twenty per cent of my sneakers. When I don't want to wear a pair, I create my own model with markers, TippEx and spray cans. I remember bombing some Air Max in golden brown.
I change my sneakers three times a day and have got different pairs for specific activities. I also keep a pair of sneakers in my flat that I put my mobile phone in, so it never falls on the floor. I never wear them. They stay at home. They're my mobile's sneakers.

LADY LAISTEE
PARIS, FEB 97

I USED TO BE IN A BREAK-DANCING TEAM AND CUT KILLER WAS THE DJ. THE COOL THING WAS WE GOT FREE TRAINING SUITS AND SNEAKERS. MOST OF THE PRODUCTS WERE UNAVAILABLE IN THE SHOPS SO I WAS REALLY PROUD. BECAUSE MY FAMILY WASN'T RICH ENOUGH TO BUY ME BRANDED MODELS I USED TO GET FAKE TRAINERS WHEN I WAS A KID. I'M EIGHT MONTHS PREGNANT RIGHT NOW, AND YOU CAN BE SURE THAT MY BABY DAUGHTER'S GONNA HAVE MORE SNEAKERS THAN ME. I GREW UP IN THE PARISIAN SUBURB OF GARGES-SARCELLES, AND THERE WERE FOUR CHILDREN. SO WHEN YOU'RE A 13 YEAR-OLD GIRL AND YOU GET THE CHANCE TO WEAR NIKE SUITS AND SNEAKERS YOU FEEL LIKE THE QUEEN OF THE BLOCK. MY PARENTS BOUGHT ME A PAIR OF ADIDAS FOR MY FOURTEENTH BIRTHDAY AND I REMEMBER SAYING THAT LINE ALL THE TIME: "ADIDAS C'EST LA CLAQUE!". THEY WERE LIKE SAMBAS, IN A VERY DEEP BLUE.

I STARTED TO GET MORE AND MORE TRAINERS, BECAUSE I'D SEE MY FRIENDS WEARING THEM, AND IF YOU DIDN'T YOU FELT REJECTED, YOU WEREN'T COOL ENOUGH. WHEN I GOT MY FIRST PAIR OF ADIDAS, I JUST FELT ALIVE. I REMEMBER MY SECOND PAIR. I WAS WORKING WITH FIVE GIRLFRIENDS AT MCDONALD'S IN THE SUMMER OF 1989, AND SPENT EVERYTHING ON BLUE SUEDE PUMA CLYDES. THEY WERE LIMITED EDITION AT THAT TIME, REALLY HARD TO GET AND WERE ABOUT 800FF. WE USED TO PARADE IN THE BLOCKS, A SIX-GIRL POSSE WITH BRAND NEW PUMAS WITH DIFFERENT COLOURS AND LACES, IT WAS PRETTY COOL. WE WORE THEM WITH TIGHT JEANS. THAT'S HOW YOU HAD TO WEAR JEANS IN THE SUBURBS, BOTTOMS TURNED UP, BIG SOCKS AND THE SNEAKER'S TONGUE OUT. WHAT WE LIKED TO DO THE MOST WAS TO GO BACK TO MCDONALD'S, AS CUSTOMERS, IN OUR NEW OUTFITS.

I ALSO REMEMBER BUYING MY VERY FIRST PAIR OF NIKE AIR MAX. THEY QUICKLY BECAME THE SUBURBAN KIDS' SHOE. WHEREVER YOU GO IN 1997, PARIS, LYON, MARSEILLES...KIDS FROM THE SUBURBS WEAR EITHER AIR MAX OR ADIDAS STAN SMITH. NIKE AND ADIDAS RE-ISSUED MODELS AND IF YOU'RE AN AIR MAX OR STAN SMITH FAN, THEN PARIS IS THE BEST PLACE TO SHOP. I KNOW A PLACE THAT SELLS AIR MAX IN 12 DIFFERENT COLOURS AND STAN SMITH WITH COMBINATIONS IN RED, BURGUNDY, BLACK, BLUE AND ALL BLACK. THEY'RE MORE AFFORDABLE NOW AND I'M A BIT JEALOUS ABOUT THAT. WHEN I WAS 16 I COULDN'T EVEN AFFORD TO BUY RECORDS. I WAS LISTENING TO RAP MUSIC AT FRIENDS' PARTIES, AND WE'D TAPE STUFF BETWEEN US, THE FIRST RECORD I BOUGHT WAS BOBBY BROWN.

I'VE GOT A SPECIAL TACTIC TO WEAR MY CURRENT FILAS. MAYBE I SHOULDN'T TELL YOU, IT'S KIND OF CONFIDENTIAL. I WANT MY SHOE TO LOOK BIG AND COMPACT, SO I USE EITHER FOAM-RUBBER PADS OR EXTRA SOCKS.

MY FAVOURITE PAIR OF SNEAKERS EVER WERE THE ADIDAS CAMPUS LIMITED EDITION: ALL BLUE NUBUCK WITH BLUE STRIPES. I'VE NEVER SEEN THEM ANYWHERE SINCE. THE DAY I DIE, I HOPE I'LL BE ON STAGE, AND YOU CAN BE SURE I'LL HAVE THE DOPEST SNEAKERS AT MY FEET.

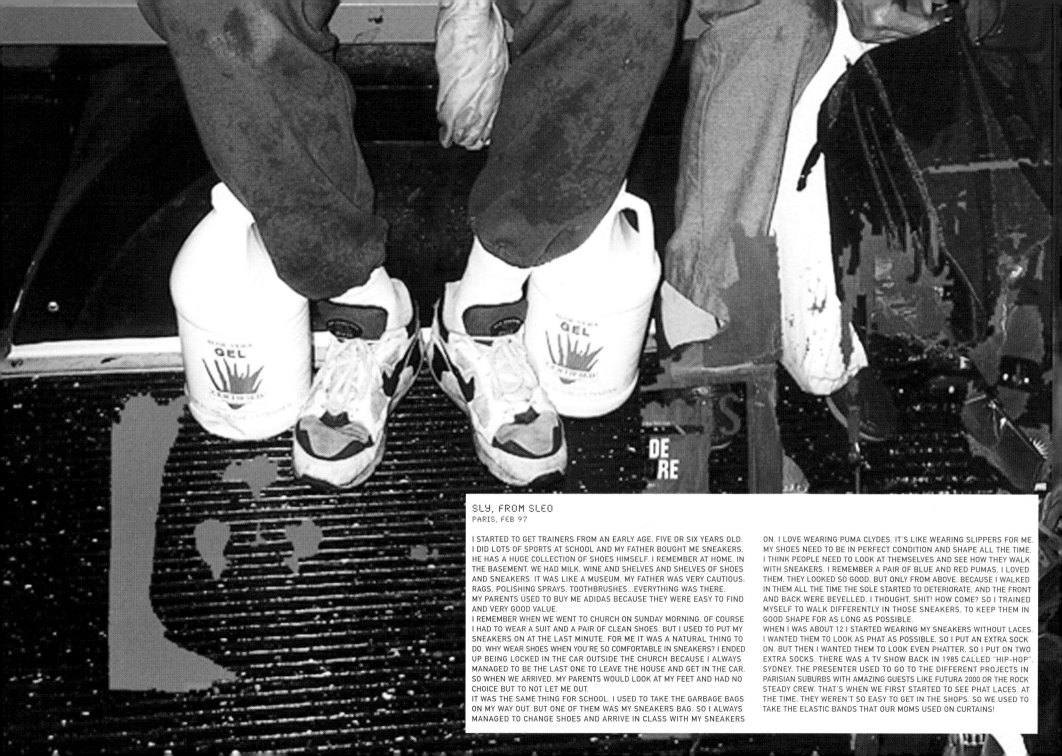

SLY, FROM SLEO
PARIS, FEB 97

I STARTED TO GET TRAINERS FROM AN EARLY AGE, FIVE OR SIX YEARS OLD. I DID LOTS OF SPORTS AT SCHOOL AND MY FATHER BOUGHT ME SNEAKERS. HE HAS A HUGE COLLECTION OF SHOES HIMSELF. I REMEMBER AT HOME, IN THE BASEMENT, WE HAD MILK, WINE AND SHELVES AND SHELVES OF SHOES AND SNEAKERS. IT WAS LIKE A MUSEUM. MY FATHER WAS VERY CAUTIOUS: RAGS, POLISHING SPRAYS, TOOTHBRUSHES...EVERYTHING WAS THERE.
MY PARENTS USED TO BUY ME ADIDAS BECAUSE THEY WERE EASY TO FIND AND VERY GOOD VALUE.
I REMEMBER WHEN WE WENT TO CHURCH ON SUNDAY MORNING. OF COURSE I HAD TO WEAR A SUIT AND A PAIR OF CLEAN SHOES. BUT I USED TO PUT MY SNEAKERS ON AT THE LAST MINUTE. FOR ME IT WAS A NATURAL THING TO DO. WHY WEAR SHOES WHEN YOU'RE SO COMFORTABLE IN SNEAKERS? I ENDED UP BEING LOCKED IN THE CAR OUTSIDE THE CHURCH BECAUSE I ALWAYS MANAGED TO BE THE LAST ONE TO LEAVE THE HOUSE AND GET IN THE CAR. SO WHEN WE ARRIVED, MY PARENTS WOULD LOOK AT MY FEET AND HAD NO CHOICE BUT TO NOT LET ME OUT.
IT WAS THE SAME THING FOR SCHOOL. I USED TO TAKE THE GARBAGE BAGS ON MY WAY OUT. BUT ONE OF THEM WAS MY SNEAKERS BAG. SO I ALWAYS MANAGED TO CHANGE SHOES AND ARRIVE IN CLASS WITH MY SNEAKERS

ON. I LOVE WEARING PUMA CLYDES. IT'S LIKE WEARING SLIPPERS FOR ME. MY SHOES NEED TO BE IN PERFECT CONDITION AND SHAPE ALL THE TIME. I THINK PEOPLE NEED TO LOOK AT THEMSELVES AND SEE HOW THEY WALK WITH SNEAKERS. I REMEMBER A PAIR OF BLUE AND RED PUMAS, I LOVED THEM, THEY LOOKED SO GOOD, BUT ONLY FROM ABOVE. BECAUSE I WALKED IN THEM ALL THE TIME THE SOLE STARTED TO DETERIORATE, AND THE FRONT AND BACK WERE BEVELLED. I THOUGHT, SHIT! HOW COME? SO I TRAINED MYSELF TO WALK DIFFERENTLY IN THOSE SNEAKERS, TO KEEP THEM IN GOOD SHAPE FOR AS LONG AS POSSIBLE.
WHEN I WAS ABOUT 12 I STARTED WEARING MY SNEAKERS WITHOUT LACES. I WANTED THEM TO LOOK AS PHAT AS POSSIBLE, SO I PUT AN EXTRA SOCK ON. BUT THEN I WANTED THEM TO LOOK EVEN PHATTER, SO I PUT ON TWO EXTRA SOCKS. THERE WAS A TV SHOW BACK IN 1985 CALLED "HIP-HOP". SYDNEY, THE PRESENTER USED TO GO TO THE DIFFERENT PROJECTS IN PARISIAN SUBURBS WITH AMAZING GUESTS LIKE FUTURA 2000 OR THE ROCK STEADY CREW. THAT'S WHEN WE FIRST STARTED TO SEE PHAT LACES. AT THE TIME, THEY WEREN'T SO EASY TO GET IN THE SHOPS. SO WE USED TO TAKE THE ELASTIC BANDS THAT OUR MOMS USED ON CURTAINS!

DINO BOTZ, LORDZ OF BROOKLYN
NEW YORK, MARCH 97

I use different names for sneakers. I usually call them kicks or dogs. I wear sneakers to be one step ahead of our competition. I don't wear many pairs right now, probably about 12. I don't know if sneakers are better than sex, but a new pair of sneakers could be equally as satisfying as a virgin: once you break them in you want a new pair. I remember racking a pair of sneakers from a shoestore when I was 10. I walked in with an old pair, and walked out with a new one.
I started collecting sneakers when my foot stopped growing. Sneakers have always been vital in my life, literally speaking: being chased by cops over rooftops, in subway tunnels, backyards, stolen cars. When you grow up in Brooklyn, doing graffiti and other "things", you need the right pair of sneakers. The rarest pair I own are burgundy suede Adidas Campus with gold on it. I was 12 when I had them and I always had a toothbrush on me to keep them clean. I always wear my laces untied, usually fat laces. I choose sneakers with white or dark soles depending on the outfit i'm wearing. I clean my sneakers every day, once a day.
The cheapest pair I bought was Converse All Stars, the most expensive was Nike Air Jordans Model 2. I don't know what's going on with sneakers and designers right now. I can't stand these new space-suit-back-to-the-future-part-2-type sneakers...give me a plain pair of Stan Smiths any day. I used to airbrush the side of my All Stars with a graffiti burner. If a brand would make me a pair of snakers, the style would be cool and laid back, nothing too flashy, sort of like a Cadillac, yeah that's it, the El Dorado of sneakers. I never save up to buy snakers, but when I get paid, the first thing I do is buy a new pair. I could be broke, but I always have a new pair of kicks. When people walk on my kicks, well man, that's a fight in my parrish. I wear flat sneakers for around the crib, heavy sneakers to perform. Sneakers make the outfit, you could have a million dollar outfit on, but if your sneakers are wack, you're fucked! I think sneakers are very good for your feet nowadays, but think about playing basketball in the 50s! I love receiving sneakers as a birthday present, but if you get the wrong size, you're screwed. There are three brands I can't stand: Pony, Olympian and LA Gear.

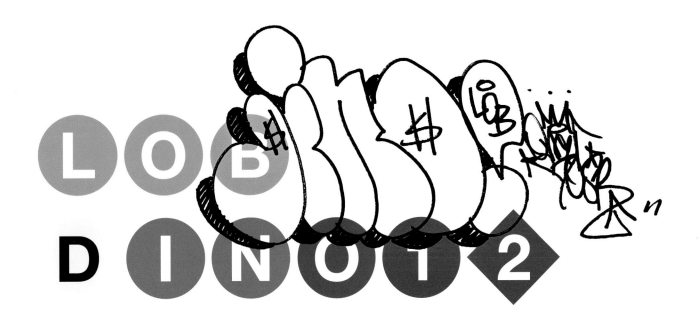

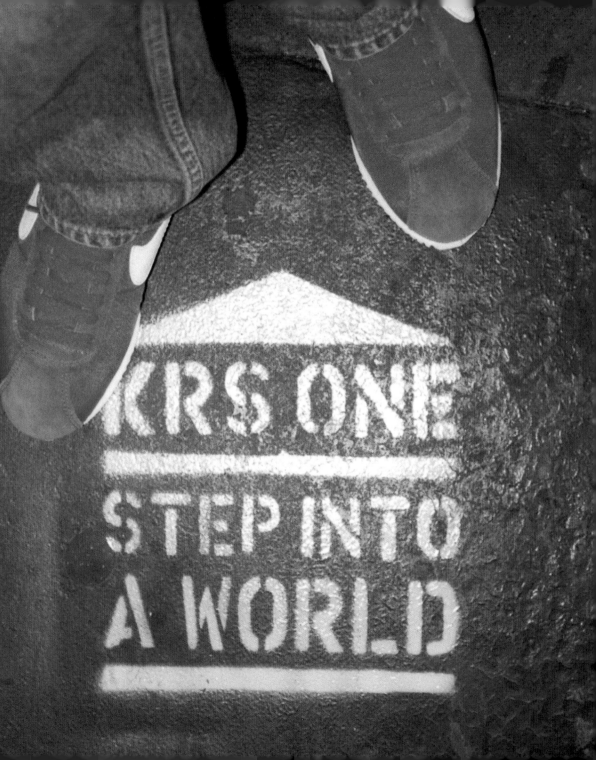

KRS-1

We used to wear shoes that were called Joey. They were clear sandals with plastic. Then we evolved to a sneaker called 69s and Super Bowl Ks, and from there we got leather on our sneakers and Adidas was the first. I think it was Eric Sadler who asked me to be a part of Nike's campaign, to be the voice behind Gil Scott-Heron's music, "The Revolution". So I read the scrip and it had this piece, "the revolution is about basketball and basketball is the truth". I knew it would cause controversy when I said it but the more I thought about it, I thought, what actually is the revolution? Many people think it's wearing a black beret and holding a gun in your hand, talking about the revolution of the white man, but that revolution makes no sense. The revolution basketball gave us, it's not only a cultural revolution but an economic one. To me, if you can shoot a basketball and get up to 3, 4, 5, 6 million dollars, take you, your family and your whole click out of the ghetto, that to me is revolution. So basketball is the revolution, cos it's economic empowerment of black youth who would never have got into that position otherwise had they not shot the root that dug the bird.
Sneakers are a major part of hip hop, basically because the DJ has to stand for long hours, that's the sneaker...the MC has to move across the stage fairly quickly, that's the sneaker...the B-boy breaking into the air doing their thing, again that's the sneaker. If there was ever an official here, the sneaker is it...even if you come to a shoe hip hop party, wear sneakers...
Let me just ask you something now that my mind is round the sneaker. Why do they call them sneakers?*

I DON'T KNOW. WE CALL THEM TRAINERS OVER HERE MAN.

Look at that. In America they call them sneakers because they're used for sneaking around, you make no noise....Trainers obviously, because here you guys like training. We train in them too and I guess you sneak around in them as well. I guess we tend to call things what they actually mean in our active lives, so it is really interesting to look at what cultures call what we are calling the sneaker. Good luck on your book, it really is very interesting.

OK MAN THANKS A LOT FOR YOUR TIME...

PARIS, SUMMER '97
the word "sneakers" was used because they were shoes made with rubber soles, so you could "sneak in" places without making a sound.

NENEH CHERRY

tape malfunction.....
....$£^*^&%FJHkjGLIUY.O*&H(*7^FCRJTYK<ILJOB*&%)O&%U^%WSGVO&

SORRY, WHAT WERE YOU SAYING?
NC: I think I was saying something like "trainers is life!". I've always, always been a trainer person
because I've got all these opposing themes in my personality. You know, somedays I kinda feel like
being a dolly bird, but I can never succumb to it completely, so I'll still have trainers on...laughs...

GOLDIE MENTIONED SOMETHING ABOUT THE FACT THAT YOU AND HIM HAVE THE ONLY TWO
PAIRS OF A PARTICULAR TRAINER!?
I don't know...have we?...laughs...he probably kept mine!

HOW MANY PAIRS OF TRAINERS DO YOU HAVE?
At the moment I'm wearing quite a small selection, about five pairs, but I've got loads in storage.
I've got some really good ones, like this sweet guy made me some customised Nike...I think I got
them from Rifat Ozbek. They were sequinned Nikes.

OH COOL.
Yeah they'd be quite hip now, I might have to get them out.

WHICH BRAND DO YOU PREFER?
I'm a big Puma lady. When I was a kid I used to wear Pro-Keds basketball boots, high-tops, and then
in the early hip hop days I got into Adidas, but I've always been wearing the Pumas with the fat laces.

PHARCYDE

What's up, I'm Slim Kid from the Pharcyde and I'm here today to talk about sneakers...
I've got too many sneakers, 40, 50 pairs basically given to me. These are Nike boots
that I'm wearing, but I've had them for about five years, and they're my favourites.
I like old shoes more so than I like new shoes. I like plain white high-top sneakers.
I think you guys have got some weird arse shoes...really innovative...everybody has their
own character...that says go...I like that.

DO YOU REMEMBER YOUR EARLIEST PAIR OF SNEAKERS?
Yeah, they were baby shoes.

HAS ANY SHOE COMPANY APPROACHED YOU WITH A SPONSORSHIP DEAL?
Yeah, but they have a price tag.

ANY FAMOUS LAST WORDS ON SHOES?
Fuck shoes, we should all be barefoot...no just kidding. Yoh...this is M One from the Pharcyde...

HOW MANY SNEAKERS HAVE YOU GOT MAN?
About 40 pairs...all Nike...cos they're the best...Up Tempo, Penny Hardaway, Air Jordans-
I've got em all going back to 85.

DO YOU REALISE HOW MUCH MONEY THEY'RE WORTH?
I'm not really trying to sell em, just keep em.

DO YOU KEEP EM BOX FRESH OR DO YOU JUST WEAR THEM TO DEATH?
Box fresh...put em in a box and cover em up in a trash bag and seal the bags so that
no dust can get on em.

YOU'RE DEEP.
Sneakers are serious man. Nike gives us promotional stuff too.

FUNNY COS WHEN WE TALKED TO NIKE ABOUT THIS BOOK THEY SORT OF SAID "OH WE'RE
ONLY ABOUT SPORT, WE DON'T DO FASHION OR MUSIC", WHICH IS A LIE BASICALLY.
Well they do, but not in a paid...But the new Pennys man...Hey Marnnie...there's an interviewer
talking about sneakers, would you exchange words with this baby...he's on the Pennys.

THE PENNYS MAN, THEY'RE THE SHIT...OHHH FUCKING HELL, HOLD ON A SECOND I'VE GOT
TO TAKE A PICTURE OF THOSE, EVEN THOUGH IT'S PROBABLY NOT EVEN GONNA COME OUT.
He's taking a picture of the Pennys, 180 bucks in the States, there you go.

Sneakers are fresh they make my feet feel good. There is nothing better than walking into
a mall or down the street in a pair of unseen Nikes. I know it was meant to be.

HOW LONG HAVE YOU HAD YOUR PENNYS?
Got em recently...that's why I'm over here rockin them man...

What's your kind of shoe man? What do you think is number one? If a shoe cost $1,000
and it was made by Nike, Adidas or Reebok, which one would you buy?

OH FUCKING HELL...GREEN AND GREY AIR MAX...
From?

FROM NIKE...ADIDAS HAD A SHOE CALLED SL80 WHICH WAS BLUE WITH GOLD STRIPES...AND FROM REEBOK
THOSE YELLOW INSTA PUMP RUNNING SHOE.
Definitely the shit, I want to see this book.

WELL THERE'S BEEN MOMENTS, IT'S BEEN A TRIP TALKING TO YOU GUYS. EVERY
TIME I TURN THIS THING OFF YOU SAY SOMETHING.
We are Nike collectors. Your mouth is bigger than a pair of trainers, I just felt like saying that to him...

I'VE COLLECTED SNEAKERS OVER THE YEARS, THROUGH THE DIFFERENT PERIODS. NOW I'VE GOT INSTA PUMPS ON. I GOT THE BLACK BEFORE IT CAME OUT. BUT I DON'T HAVE THE BRIGHT YELLOW. I'M GETTING THE NEW EDITION THAT'S COMING...

WELL REEBOK SAID TO ME, WE'RE GOING TO GIVE THEM TO YOU, SO I'M VERY HAPPY WITH THAT. I'VE BEEN REALLY LUCKY BECAUSE I'M NOT TIED TO ONE BRAND. EVERYBODY WAS JUST RIGHT ON ABOUT MY TRAINERS AND REEBOK CONTACTED ME AND ASKED IF I WEAR THEM ALL THE TIME, AND I SAID YEAH. THEY SENT ME A LIST AND THEN A BOX WITH FIVE PAIRS OF BLACK REEBOKS. IT'S QUITE FUNNY. NOW WHEN ANYBODY WANTS TO GIVE ME A PRESENT THEY GIVE ME TRAINERS.
LATELY I GOT A FANTASTIC PAIR OF FILAS. BASICALLY THEY'RE LIKE A SOCK WITH A RED, WHITE AND BLUE STRIPE ROUND A BIT THAT VELCROS ONTO THE ANKLE, WITH A BRIGHT YELLOW INNER SOCK. IT'S LIKE A JELLY SHELL OVER THE WHOLE SHOE AND IT HAS A MASSIVE FEEL ABOUT IT. IT'S STITCHED DOWN THE SIDE OF THE HEEL ON THE SHOE, BUT IT'S HAND STITCHED ON. IT'S AS IF YOUR FEET ARE EMBALMED OR SOMETHING, WHICH IS QUITE WEIRD. THEY ARE THE STORM TROOPER SHOE OF THE 90S...THE REMAKE. VERY FUTURISTIC. AFTER WE'VE DONE THE INTERVIEW I'LL LET YOU COME AND LOOK AT THEM. THE GUY IN OFFSPRING, HE'S BASICALLY A REALLY GOOD CONTACT, HE SAID THEY MIGHT NOT EVEN GO INTO PRODUCTION.

...YOU'VE GOT TO WEAR THEM. I'M NOT SO SAD THAT I'D PUT SOMETHING IN A BOX IN THE LOFT. I JUST LIKE TRAINERS. I ENJOY THEM BEING SO COMFORTABLE AND HAVING SO MANY DIFFERENT COLOURS. I'VE NEVER BEEN A CONVENTIONAL PERSON AS FAR AS MY DRESS SENSE GOES, SO THROWING ON A PAIR OF TRAINERS TO ME IS KIND OF LIKE BEING IN A BAND, IF YOU KNOW WHAT I MEAN? BUT I DO A LOT OF CLIMBING AND THAT'S WHEN YOU CAN GET REALLY PISSED, BECAUSE THINGS THAT NIKE DON'T REALLY WORK, AND I'M HANGING ON BY MY FAITH BECAUSE THE BOOTS ARE SLIPPING LIKE SHIT, BECAUSE THEY WERE DESIGNED WITH FASHION IN MIND. SOME PEOPLE WANTED THAT TYPE OF CLIMBER LOOK ON THE STREET, BUT IT DIDN'T ACTUALLY WORK ON A MOUNTAIN.

STEVEN TYLER FROM AEROSMITH

ARE YOU REALLY INTO TRAINERS? DO YOU ALWAYS WEAR TRAINERS ON STAGE?
ST: WHADDAYA MEAN THESE?
YEAH! WELL NOT PARTICULARLY THESE, ANY?
I HAVE TO.
WHY?
BECAUSE...BECAUSE IN THE 70S I DID SO MUCH...SNIFF...
I WAS SO FUCKED UP ALL THE TIME THAT I USED TO WEAR THESE THINGS CALLED ESPADRILLES, BECAUSE I LOVED THE WAY THEY HAD REAL LONG STRINGS AND I HAD A SPECIAL WAY OF TYING THEM UP AND AROUND HERE, AND THEY LOOKED REALLY COOL. I'D WEAR MY PANTS SHORT YOU KNOW. BUT THERE WAS NO SUPPORT AND I WOULD HURT MY FEET SO BAD, BUT I NEVER FELT IT BECAUSE I WAS ALWAYS...YOU KNOW....AND SO NOW I'M PAYING THE FIDDLER. ON THE LAST TOUR, TOWARDS THE END, I GOT THIS THING CALLED "PLANTIFACIETUS", WHICH MEANS YOU'VE WORN OUT THE BOTTOM OF THE FOOT, SO NOW I FIND THE LIGHTEST PAIR OF SHOES I CAN, THE SOFTEST.

ANY PARTICULAR COMPANY? IS IT ALWAYS NIKE?
NO, THE LAST TIME IT WAS...OH GOD I CAN'T REMEMBER WHAT THE LAST TOUR WAS....WELL AS LONG AS IT'S NOT SOMETHING I TWIST MY ANKLE IN. I HAVEN'T WORN THESE ON STAGE YET I WEAR THOSE OTHER NIKE...
WITH THE SPLIT TOE?
YEAH! I FOUND THEM IN A STORE. I SAID, AHHH THESE ARE COOL...HE GOES, HOW MUCH DO YOU RUN?...I SAID, AHH TWO MILES A DAY...HE GOES, AHH THOSE AREN'T FOR YOU...I SAID, WHADDAYA MEAN?...HE GOES, THOSE ARE FOR PEOPLE WHO RUN MARATHONS THIRTY MILES...
OH RIGHT!
I SAID, WHAT THE FUCK IS THE DIFFERENCE BETWEEN TWO MILES AND THIRTY! AND I'VE HAD THOSE SHOES FOR THREE YEARS AND I WEAR THEM ALL THE TIME, THEY'RE ALL WORN AWAY SO MY TOE STICKS OUT THE END.
AND IT'S ALWAYS SNEAKERS?
YEAH, THEY'RE THE BEST, MY FEET DON'T HURT AT ALL.

MICHAEL FRANTI FROM SPEARHEAD
MICHAEL HAS TO HAVE A SEPARATE SUITCASE FOR HIS...

YOU'VE GOT THAT MANY SNEAKERS MICHAEL?
I'VE GOT MORE SNEAKERS THAN I CAN WEAR, BUT THE THING IS YA BOOK'S CALL SIZE DOESN'T MATTER, SIZE DON'T COUNT. SIZE DOES COUNT COS I WEAR SIZE 14, AND I CAN NEVER GET THE SNEAKERS I WANT, AND IT WASN'T UNTIL NOW THAT THE SHOE COMPANIES SEND ME SHOES ALL THE TIME. NIKE FITS MY FEET. BUT THE THING THAT I LIKE THE BEST AS FAR AS THE LOOK, I LIKE CONVERSE ONE STAR LOW-TOPS BUT I ONLY WEAR THEM ON FORMAL OCCASIONS. HA.

SNOOP WAS SAYING THAT A LOT OF GUYS IN LA USED TO WEAR ONE STAR...
...CHUCK TAYLORS...I'D WEAR PRO-KEDS TOO...THE FIRST LEATHER HIGH TOP, THEY WERE THE HEAVIEST SHOE EVER INVENTED. BUT MOST OF THE TIME FOR PLAYING BALL IN HIGH SCHOOL IT WAS DOCTOR JS HIGH-TOPS. I THINK THAT WAS THE FIRST LEATHER HIGH-TOP THAT CONVERSE PUT OUT, BUT WHEN THE NIKE AIR FORCE CAME OUT, THAT WAS A WHOLE DIFFERENT ORDER...WITH THE FIRST VELCRO STRAP.

IN THE STATES YOU GOT EM IN ORANGE, GREEN, RED...A WHIRL OF COLOURS.
I'VE BEEN WEARING THESE JOINTS A LOT, THESE NIKE HIKING BOOT THINGS...THEY'RE JUST A LITTLE MORE RUGGED FOR ME. ESPECIALLY WHEN WE'RE TRAVELLING A LOT, CARRYING SUITCASES THROUGH AIRPORTS, SETTING UP FOR A GIG OR IF YOUR GONNA BE OUT IN THE SNOW, THE RAIN.

WHAT DO YOU THINK ABOUT THE PRICE OF SHOES?
THE SAD THING ABOUT THE ESCALATION IN PRICE IS THERE IS NO ESCALATION FOR THE WAGES OF THE LABOURERS WHO MAKE THE SHOES...IF YOU CAN AFFORD IT AND YOU WANT IT, THEN I THINK THERE'S A LOT WORSE THINGS TO SPEND YOUR MONEY ON. AS FAR AS STATUS SYMBOLS GO, THAN SHOES. I REMEMBER BEFORE SNEAKERS IT WAS HOW MUCH COKE COULD YOU SNORT? NOW IT'S WHO'S GOT FLYER BOOTS! BUT THE THING THAT REALLY SUCKS, ALL THE SHOE COMPANIES ACROSS THE BOARD USE CHEAP LABOUR IN SOUTH EAST ASIA. AND BECAUSE THEY'VE SPENT SO MUCH MONEY ON PAYING OFF THEIR SPOKES-PEOPLE THE ADVERTISING PRICE IS PROBABLY THE BIGGEST PIECE OF THE ENTIRE COST OF THE SHOE. AND IT'S MESSED UP. THE SHOE COMPANIES HAVE TO REALLY SUSS-UP TO THE FACT THAT BLACK PEOPLE ARE THE ONES WHO GIVE THE STAMP OF APPROVAL TO WHICH SHOES ARE COOL... THAT MAKES THE WHITE KIDS WANT TO BUY THEM. SO IN PAYING US RESPECT THEY HAVE TO PAY RESPECT TO THE BROTHERS IN SOUTH EAST ASIA WHO ARE MAKING THE SHOES TOO, BY PAYING THEM.

CYPRESS HILL & LC
DJ MUGGS, SOUL ASSASSINS

ORIGINALLY YOU'RE FROM NEW YORK?
YEAH I'M FROM QUEENS NEW YORK.
OK SO WHAT WERE YOU WEARING?
WHEN I WAS A YOUNGSTER?
YEAH!
PRO KEDS. YEAH PRO KEDS WERE THE BOOM.
WE CAN'T GET THEM IN THIS COUNTRY
IS THAT RIGHT? AND I USED TO WEAR NEW BALANCE...GREEN
ONES AND BLACK ONES WITH THE SILVER "N" ON THEM
YOU NEVER GET INTO ADIDAS OR NIKE?
YEAH YEAH I GOT INTO ADIDAS ROUND ABOUT RUN DMC TIME. I STILL WEAR
ADIDAS. AND NIKE I WEAR ALL THE TIME. NIKE IS MY MAIN SHOE RIGHT NOW
WHAT WERE PEOPLE WEARING WHEN YOU WENT TO LA?
NIGGAZ WAS JUST WEARING CONVERSE ALL STARS
YEAH THAT'S WHAT SNOOP WAS SAYING
AND THE NIKE CORTEZ, THAT'S BASICALLY THAT OUT THERE. NEW YORK,
ALOT OF THE STICK KIDS WAS WEARING NEW BALANCE, YOU KNOW WHAT
I MEAN, CAUSE THEY COULD RUN FAST....LAUGHTER....
I REMEMBER WHEN I WAS A LITTLE KID I GOT SOME NEW TENNIS SHOES, I
COULD RUN FASTER THAN A MOTHERFUCKER YO! I GOT FASTER ALL OF A
SUDDEN....MY MOTHER USED TO BUY MY SNEAKERS FROM THE SUPERMARKET
...THEY WERE LIKE TWO PAIRS FOR FIVE DOLLARS.
SHIT. I'D GO THROUGH THOSE THINGS IN A WEEK. THEY DIDN'T HAVE HUN-
DRED DOLLAR WHEN I WAS LITTLE, THIRTY DOLLARS WAS LIKE "WHAT! THIR-
TY DOLLARS FOR SNEAKERS!!" I USED TO BUY SNEAKERS ALL THE TIME.
NOW NIKE AND ADIDAS GIVE ME FREE SHOES.
YEAH. BUT I STILL CATCH MYSELF BUYING STUFF WHEN I'LL GO TO THE STORE
AND I'LL SEE SOME NIKES...OH MAN THEY AIN'T GIVE ME THESE. I'M GONNA
GET THESE ONES, I'VE NEVER SEEN THESE BEFORE.

HENRY ROLLINS, FHM MAGAZINE, JUNE 97

Never had a cigar. When I was 17, I got drunk a few times. I didn't like it, never have. Don't like the taste, don't like the feeling, don't like throwing up on my sneakers.

MC SOLAAR

At the beginning of French hip hop there were the big Troops, cause we'd seen them on American records and videos. I remember that shop in Paris· Tikaret...They were the only people to import Troops back in 1986-87, and they provided an escort service from the shop to the train station. At a certain time it was Adidas who were very hip hop with RUN DMC. Right now like....Jordan is the hip hop shoe. For me trainers have always been part of hip hop culture because you can do anything with them....it match- es the relaxed aspect that hip hop has.

KORN

ANYONE WHO'S SEEN ANY PICTURE OF KORN WILL REALISE THAT
YOU SPORT A WHOLE LOAD OF ADIDAS! HOW DID THAT COME ABOUT?

JONATHAN:
Basically we're ripping off RUN DMC and Bob Marley and shit....those were the first.

DAVID:
I gots to say one thing. We copied RUN DMC and Bob Marley. So all these other heavy bands out there wearing Adidas, and I don't want to say no names cause you know who you are, you ripped us off bitch...You wearing this shit, you ripped off Korn, eat a dick.

JONATHAN:
But yeah that's why we did it, Bob Marley....

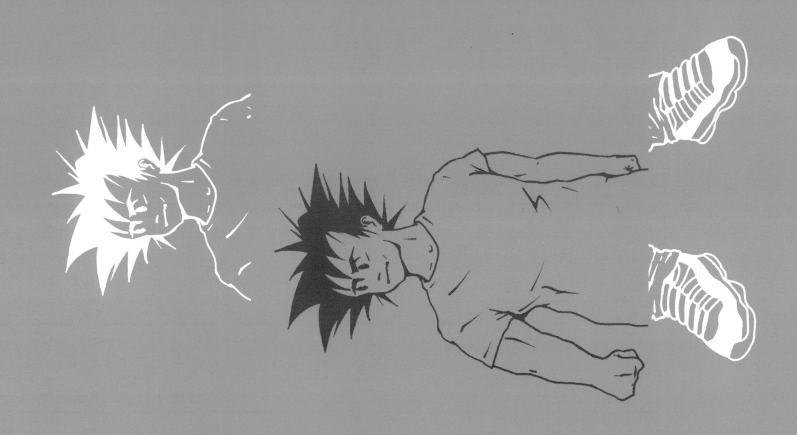

HAVE YOU ALWAYS WORN TRAINERS?
K: Oh yeah pretty much yep.

CAUSE YOU GREW UP IN ESSEX? WHICH PART OF ESSEX ARE YOU FROM?
Well. I was born in Ilford. And I was in Bromdrick. Bit of a change in scene. I suppose I have always worn trainers, apart from when I was a Mod.

YOU WERE A MOD WERE YOU? IF YOU DON'T MIND ME ASKING, HOW OLD ARE YOU MATE?
27. I was a very young Mod...

SO BEFORE YOU WERE A MOD YOU WEREN'T A CASUAL, OR...
I tell you I was a Mod probably before anything else and then Mods went into Casual from there...

SO YOU USED TO WEAR DIADORA OR IT WAS ADIDAS GAZELLES?
I think it was Wimbledon. We were into the Casual thing. I bought this pair of Puma and I weren't really happy. So I took em back and went to get the Nike running shoes with the rainbow colours...It was like, gotta have them. But all the boys in town were taxing people...your track-suits and your jumpers and everything off ya. I was still quite young. 14, 15, and I thought, oh my word no it's the boys I kinda knew a few of them and they were like, alright, how you doing. And someone knew me cause I'd lived on both sides of the town luckily enough. They were cool and they were like, hey you've gotta get these, these are the shoes. It was just a funny little incident. If you could imagine, you've got your 30 notes, the most money in the world. Anyway, they pointed me in the right direction and I got these trainers and felt like I was the bollocks for a few weeks...Then I had a change of scene, really got into...

ROCK?
No I don't really wanna say rock cause that long hair era gets the fist. I just got well into motor bikes. We weren't rockers, and you had to make the statement of being a kinda cool biker. We had Lonsdale boxing boots, leather padded jackets and stuff that would make you look a little more with it, but still protected for the bike...

SO WHEN DID YOU GET INTO THE RAVE SCENE?
End of 1989 beginning of 1990. I'd come back from abroad been there a few years...My mum was well and truly happy about the whole thing. But it's more vague because I can't really remember what I was into then ...

IT WAS ALL A BLUR!
Yeah. I started smoking draw and stuff and trying to kill myself on my bike...and look cool at the same time. After that I got into the party stuff. I wasn't really that fussed what I was wearing on my feet. You used to get a sensible pair of trainers....

THAT WERE COMFORTABLE FOR THE WHOLE NIGHT...
I used to have a run on the Jordans. wearing the Jordans on the bike...I got some used to have a run on the Jordans. and I was in Ireland and the kids were like running out and were in the States. and I was in Ireland and the kids were like running out and were like. oh. 26s man. in grey. And I was like blown out by it all but it didn't really impress me cause that sort of vibe was more with the break dancing and the Casual thing. I was never the Essex boy with the newspaper in the back pocket...

AND THE REEBOK CLASSIC.
Reebok and 501s never. never ever.

WHAT'S SO FUNNY IS THAT YOU WORE THESE JORDANS.
HAVE YOU STILL GOT THEM OR HAVE YOU CHUCKED THEM?
Oh I gave most of them away.

COR THEY WOULD BE WORTH SOMETHING NOW MAN.
Really.

SERIOUSLY. SERIOUSLY. BUT HEY YOU KNOW...
Who cares...

WHO CARES EXACTLY. WHAT'S THE MAKE YOU'RE RUNNING NOW THEN?
I'm really into my Vans and Airwalk. I bounce between the two quite alot.

HAVE YOU TRIED OUT DCS AT ALL?
They are the pride of the bunch in the respect that they get more respect. whereas the other ones I do anything in them...

DO THEY GIVE YOU STUFF? WE'VE FOUND THAT A LOT OF THE AMERICAN ACTS WE'VE BEEN TALKING TO, EVEN THOUGH THESE SHOE COMPANIES WOULD NEVER ADMIT IT, THEY DO GIVE THEM STUFF TO WEAR.
Well the thing is that you get the odd distributor who does you a favour and pops a few your way. but we're not sponsored by them...Get a couple of pairs and ask for more and you're taking the piss sorta thing...I was really into Northwave when they first came out. the big fat ones...cause of the snowboard thing...They are wicked. wicked and then you got a few bumper car copies...They've got some new styles sent through to me that are really. really crisp. But I like my Vans. I like trainers that you can just hang in when you're wearing shorts. that's really more important to me at the moment. I can't wear running shoes and sports shoes with shorts. I dunno. I feel like a holiday maker. I jump on my mountain bike and go and blast off. get some air and jump around. Vans have the grip. They stick on your pedals and they do work and they're really cool to wear. so they are both practical and fashionable to me.

YOU'VE SIGNED A DEAL WITH MADONNA'S LABEL. LET'S FACE IT, YOU GUYS ARE GONNA TAKE OFF IN THE STATES...
I hope so.

IT WOULDN'T SURPRISE ME IF A SHOE COMPANY APPROACHED YOU AND SAID, WEAR OUR STUFF ON STAGE.
It wouldn't happen.

YOU DON'T THINK IT WOULD HAPPEN?
No. we wouldn't do it.

YOU WOULDN'T DO IT?
NO.

EVEN IF THEY DID IT UNDERCOVER. EVEN IF THEY WERE GOING TO DO A KEITH SHOE?
No. no way.

YOU WOULD BE IMMORTALISED.
No.

WHY'S THAT?
Imagine if you were sponsored by British Knights or Troop and suddenly they bring out a load of old cack and you've gotta wear it.

SUPPOSING IT WAS A BIGGER SHOE COMPANY?
Vans and Airwalk and Northwave are the only people that give us shoes. Fuck me. you're only in a band once. you're only gonna be good once and let's take the fucking piss and see if they'll give us a few free pairs of shoes. That is the sketch really. But we'd never get into a sponsorship deal with them or any company. I would never accept anything off anyone. you know. could you wear this in your next video? Because when I arrive for the video I wanna be wearing what I wanna wear. And you've gotta feel comfortable. If they send a pair of shoes you don't feel comfortable in. the video's not gonna work. When I first started dancing on stage...it's the hardest thing to find a pair of shoes you can wear. cause you want something bouncy because otherwise your legs fall off after 10 gigs. So you wanna wear something fat. I'd love someone to come up with something that worked. but um. there you go. I like to get my trainers a bit crisp. Luckily enough I've never suffered from smelly feet. they very rarely die a smelly death. I keep a few pairs a bit cleaner for when I'm going out and stuff. I've got some mates that work out and about and sometimes when I have a change around. so I don't feel like I'm that greedy I give em away...but I do find myself buying a pair of trainers nearly every week....

THAT'S COOL MAN. THAT'S COOL. DEFINITELY. I THINK WE'VE KIND OF COVERED EVERYTHING.
Yeah. def.

WHICH I THINK IS GREAT. BECAUSE I'VE BEEN TRYING TO HUNT YOU DOWN FOR MONTHS MATE!
I'm so useless. I'm useless. But I don't want to let people down.

Wolverhampton. Some wanker stole my shoe when the crowd pulled me into the crush.
The bastard wouldn't give it back so I had to do the rest of the gig barefoot - painful.

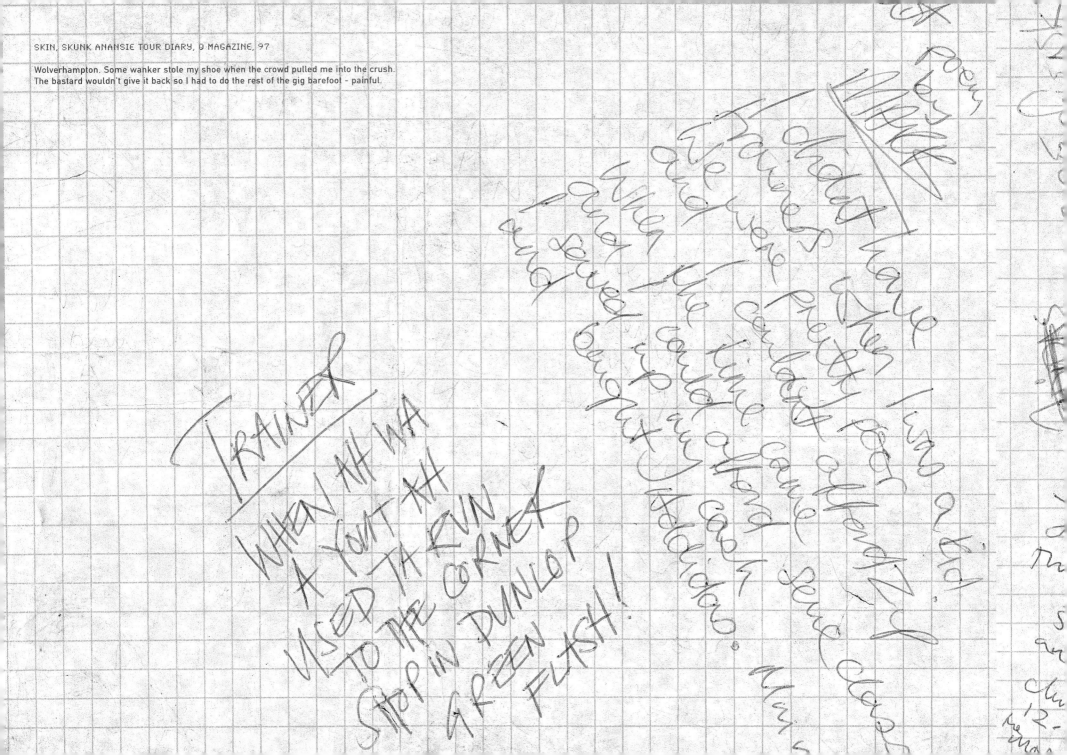

TRAINER

WHEN AH WA
A YOUT AH
USED TA RUN
TO THE CORNER
SHOP IN DUNLOP
GREEN FLASH!

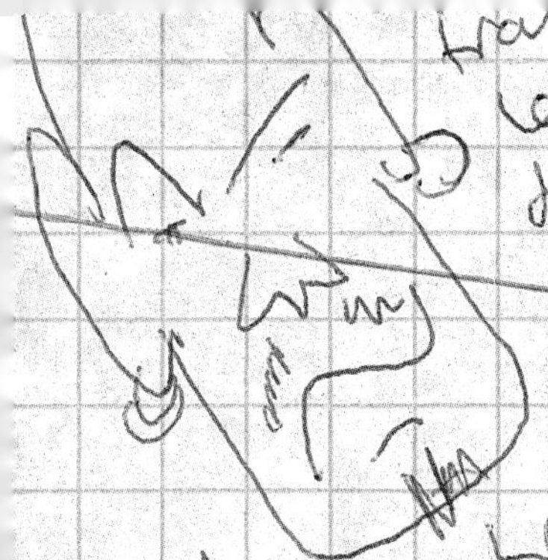

trainers
– no-name
– acupuncture
– Vans
– Airwalk!

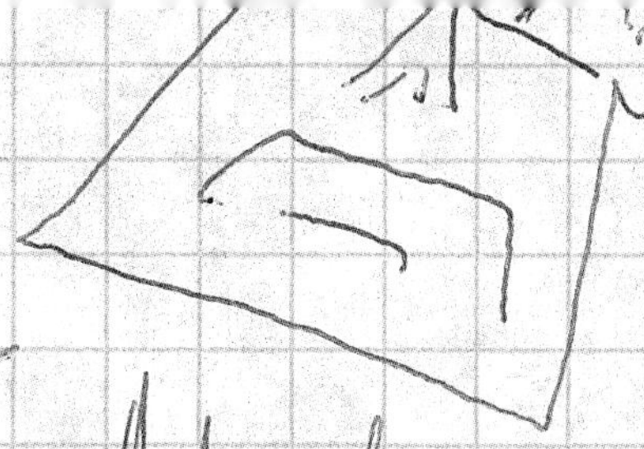

levisbo...
do you wear
them??

ROMA

Mark
trainers – DC shoes
Adidas
Acupuncture
his personal fave
DC shoes
from the USA.

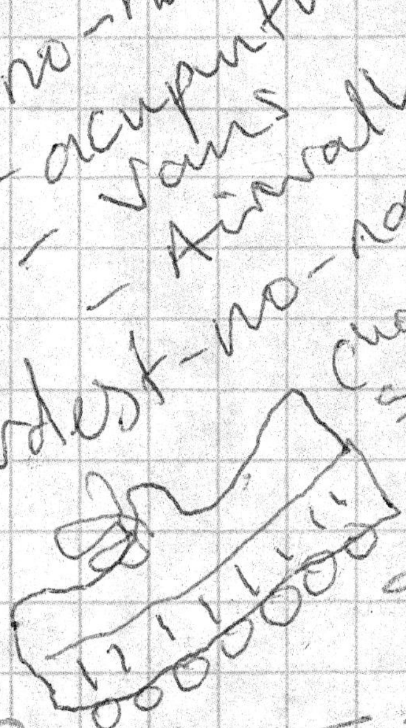

SKON
chocolate
suede
Weirdest-no-name

Skin trainers
Nike
Fila
Acupuncture
no-name
Art
Adidas
+ anything
wierd
and
wonderful.

NA MAN!

TRAINERS
A Pi BOM
BREDA!

for the Record
I drawn in
minutes in
ali nite

FiLA
FUCKINg
ROOL trainers
no-name
Fila
favourite
Fila
Italien
grub

NIKE
OK!

FUCK!

TRAINER MANIA, THE BIRTH BY CARYN FRANKLIN

In the early 80s the allure of the trainer and the buzz to be derived from guiding a sluggish instep between layers of high performance shoe was about much more than proclamations of sporting prowess.

As fashion editor of i-D magazine back then, I was in the perfect place to observe the beginning of a revolution. From this one shoe a whole range of footwear requirements could be satisfied as science fused with ergonomic design to provide the ultimate padded comfort for street survival. Women especially, having already forsaken notions of fragile femininity by refusing to perch on high-rise heels, were keen to swop the ubiquitous brutish boots of the DM variety for plushness underfoot.

Here was a footwear experience that offered much more than go-faster stripes and a hi-tech cushion against harsh urban terrains. In those heady help-yourself-and-have-it-all-80s, a generation yearning for clannish association with any anti-establishment tendency looked for membership elsewhere.

Street credibility, with its sometimes indefinable requirements for living on the edge was worn like a badge of honour. Those who sought it focused on Black America and hip hop culture for substance. Within this movement there existed a potent energy and creativity fuelled by the desire for change, and outsiders searching for a language to express collective and individual confusion could engage with a myriad of rhythmic manifestos pertaining to city-dwelling pressures, identity struggles and political oppression.

The hip hop wardrobe with its ready for action hooded track-suits and padded leather outer-wear utilised the trainer, and this ensemble soon became the dress code for the urban freedom fighter. The trainer, with its ability to adapt to the stylistic requirements of its wearer, offered individuality as well as a reassuring uniform appeal.

As the messengers of this life with their raw and poetic commentary crossed over tomainstream consumption, they gathered followers from all walks. The clothes they wore would influence popular modes of dress from high fashion to high street. Menswear especially would become alive with hip hop styles, colours and motifs and training shoes would provide the biggest area for expansion in the footwear market with prices comparable to those in designer boutiques.

On the Parisian catwalk, Vivienne Westwood accessorised her Witches collection with trainers in March 83 and in subsequent seasons, women now comfortably attired below the ankles with a designer seal of approval employed the shoe to inject contrast into traditional feminine styles.

I wore my cream and blue Converse high-tops with Ms Westwood's billowing knee-length skirt - hemline buttoned and secured to the waistband. The finished effect exposed a generous amount of leg, yet with signals somewhat rearranged to proclaim active engagement with the physical, not passive display of the physique, the trainer allowed for muscular exhibitionism and accompanied the development of certain clubland looks. Sue Clowes offered dramatic textile designs: precariously tied or lose and flapping, while Bodymap promoted slinky body-consciousness. Reassured that we weren't giving off fleshy come-ons with our peek-a-boo fashions we embraced a wholesome philosophy of "there for the dancefloor", and with some conviction carried it off.

Dayglo laces, no laces, padded uppers, customised or box-fresh - in the minds of all youths the trainer was now synonymous with cool. Test driven by a plethora of sporting heroes and sheroes and glorified by music industry luminaries across the board, the trainer would soon adorn the feet of the western world. Household names from Hollywood teamed them with Armani for Oscar award ceremonies while armies of middle aged American women mixed them with pinstripe for the daily march to the office. The trainer could handle every conceivable location as girls and boys from Wisconsin to Wigan adopted them for play in leafy park, craggy gorge and muddy waste.

In the 80s, the trainer - branded or otherwise - would become an essential accessory for modern living. It would go on to become the most technologically advanced foot covering utilising materials able to withstand unimaginable pressures; even a 9mm bullet at point-blank range. Prototypes would be tested to extremes under laboratory conditions and manufacturing giants would pour millions of dollars into attracting new custom. After all that progress, would anyone back at the dawn have envisaged that nearly two decades later, many dance clubs would still operate exclusive door policies prohibiting wearers from entering?

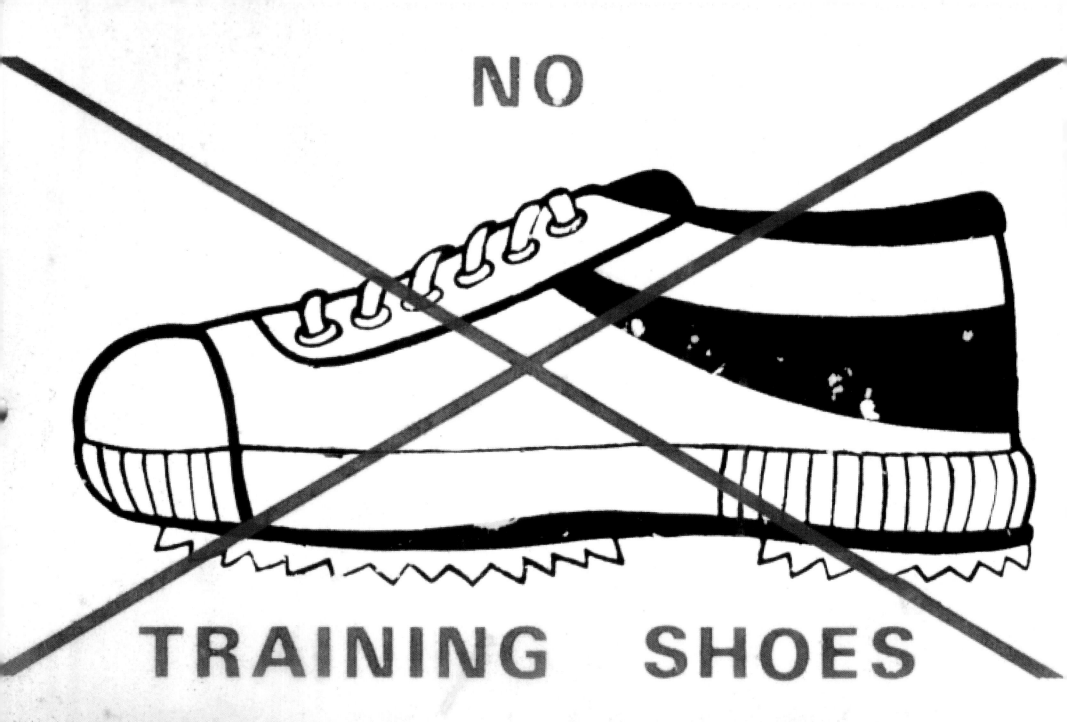

When I was growing up the average trainer we encountered at our local Roman Catholic comprehensive, other than the football boot, was black or white canvas, had a rubber sole and was known to us as a dap, or by the PE instructors as plimsolls. Then, as the 70s drew on, your more affluent schoolboy or serious sporting type adopted the training shoe, the three makes that ring bells being Puma, Adidas and Gola. For yours truly they were a big waste of hard-earned. Shoes to kick a football with were low, low down on my agenda. They were hopeless to dance in, especially in the Northern Soul mode where talc on the dance floor and leather soles provided maximum slipperiness. They did not attract women and, most important of all, were not a status symbol. They were merely an item that nerds who always brought their kit to PE always remembered.

For me there was an infinite variety of common or garden footwear to be enjoyed, shoes that were good to dance in, could be polished and resoled, and were equally at home with jeans, suit or strides. So by the time youths adopted the form I was well out of the woods and denied that the shoes even existed. Even though they were popular with your Rap fellow, and I was into the music I still wasn't interested in trainers. But then again I wasn't into big gold chains and rings or velour track-suits and baseball caps either.

By the mid 80s trainers had really caught on with the plebeian host, along with shell suits and all manner of abused and bastardised sportswear. This phenomenon strengthened my resolve and as the trainer crept further up the leg and got disgustingly diverse in colour and patterning, this resolve grew to ridiculous proportions. In the late-80s, casual garb reached new heights via the existence of hot sweaty house music clubs. Clothes to wear out became clothes to sweat in and the trainer phenomenon boomed. Your Yank loved them, Nike Air and Jordan being names that come to mind. In New York you'd see immaculate Chanel-clad ladies with great big clumping white lumps on their feet. While back in the UK, Freeman Hardy and Willis made their own. Then my Dad started wearing them!

All around me die-hards succumbed, citing comfort as the main reason for adoption. Bastions of the proper shoe fell like nine pins and then a friend of mine wore some I actually liked. These were original, early 70s stock reminiscent of the bumper boot and were government issue for US mental patients and prison inmates.

Until the late 70s, history had conspired against me. Then one day, as I was hurtling down Oxford Street on my bicycle, my brogued foot slipped off the pedal and I came down on the crossbar, balls first, like a ton of breeze block. I collapsed onto the pavement heaving, dizzy in big pain, and an old lady asked if I'd like an ambulance. I said no, dismissively, then after a few more dry heaves came a pitiful, maybe. I resumed my journey still in pain and on reaching my destination was chastised for wearing such silly shoes on a bike, shoes with no grip!

Ha! said I, feeling foolish but brave. Then I went away and found a pair of those trainers in an old shop, Adidas shell-toes, just like my mate's, original stock, brand new for £15. I thought naively that they'd be good for the gym I'd started visiting. I was spotted wearing them by another sartorial mercenary on the way home from the gym, and he said zilch. Then I wore them to work, where they were safely hidden behind my desk, and could only be seen for about five minutes as I walked the hundred yards 'twixt home and office. I wear them now and again, and as the initial shock amongst my friends has worn off, and I've realised that in a world of fluorescent, air-filled trainers my shell-toes are antiquated enough for me to get away with, and I admit they look OK with jeans and chinos. They're not all-white and I care little enough about them not to worry when I drop a tub of acrylic paint on them, or scuff them on the bike.

There was a time when I owned no jeans, trainers or sweatshirts, but now I do. Maybe there's a deep-seated psychological reason why, in that when I was young it took a whole year's saving to buy my capital E Levi's, which cost £180 today. Maybe I did want those expensive training shoes, but negated the urge due to the price. And as for a sweatshirt, the thick, raglan-sleeved model, as worn by Steve McQueen in "The Great Escape", just wasn't available. Maybe I've forgone style in favour of comfort, who knows. I did swear that I would never wear trainers, but I confess that I do now and may God forgive me, especially as I know exactly what I do.

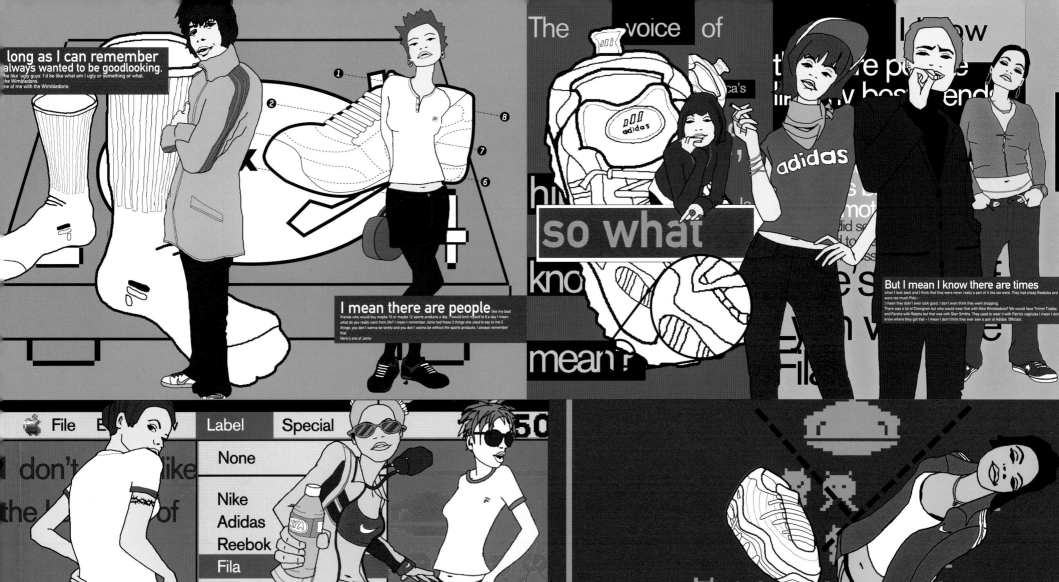

CROSS TOWN CROSS TRAINING BY BRIDGET VIRDEN

Trainer fetishist heaven is, in socially acceptable circumstances, the club. Leisure wear for leisure times. But just how practical are trainers for after dark manoeuvres? According to a recent survey carried out by Puma, 42% of national clubs will allow trainers past the door but 30% operated a selective trainer policy insisting that they must be fashionable and clean.

Starting south of the Thames on the Old Kent Road, on a hectic Saturday night, four of us footwear fanatics put our brand new trainers to the trans-London doorman test. All shoes involved were "box fresh" and points were to be awarded to each brand that gained entry. The players were Puma Cells, Northwave Club, Acupuncture and the favourite skate shoe, the DC.

Spirits are high as we approach the World Turned Upside Down on Old Kent Road. Tony, the doorman, bars our entry. "I can't afford shoes like that, so you're not coming in wearing them, no not even the Reebok pub shoe is allowed. There's no trainers in here."

The shoes came in handy on the long walk up to the Ministry of Sound at the Elephant and Castle (this is south London and there are no cabs!). It's Pushca night and that bastion of glamour is about to kick off. Troops of glitteratti loiter outside. Security tell us, "Anyone can get in if they look truly fabulous in trainers and a g-string." Boy George gets in wearing trainers (not always, Ed), but we don't. As the glittering crowds snigger and point we slump towards a cab and head to...Stringfellows.

Stepping onto the red velvet plush of Stringfellows' pavement carpet, and into the lavish reception area, we become invisible, while the entrance rope is drawn back for a group of double-breasted blazer-wearing chaps. After some time I manage to chat up one of the charming doormen. It seems that not only are my shoes wrong but too much of my body is covered by fabric, and what started as a laugh some hours ago has now induced total paranoia. We huddle together feeling more like out-of-towners, while party people on a club bus pull moonies and try to spit on our heads.

Bar Rumba has to be a safe bet, but Frank, the very personable security guard thinks not. "You get some very nice people wearing trainers, but it can attract the wrong crowd, so we have a no-trainer-policy. I wear trainers myself but not on a night out, I always dress up."

At this point we break into bickering, mobile phones and pagers are consulted, previous engagements are remembered, the humiliation is too extreme. After four venues and four attempts none of us have even been allowed near the cashier, let alone the guest list. The final straw proves to be the Iceni, Mayfair, W1. The trainer-clad doorman waves us through, we stride up the stairs to the desk united in our need for a drink and a tune. I reach for my wallet but a full-on row breaks out, as this is the first night of the Iceni's no-trainer-policy, and no, we can't come in.

The only solution seems to be to head east to Farringdon, the midnight strip that is London's golden-mile of clubbing. Forgoing the delights of the Heavenly Juke Box at Turnmills, which is too easy an old school target, we opt for Happiness Stan's, Smithfields' eclectic superclub. As we approach, the promoters who are being photographed outside, mysteriously scatter at speed, as several are wearing Puma Cells, heartlessly blagged from a staffer at Lynne Franks PR who is one of our crew, and never returned. But, at the door we are finally welcomed with open arms. Case proven? Long live the like-minded.

SUBJECT: I'M LOOKING FOR...........
DATE: THU, 17 APR 97 17:21:33 0900
FROM: ?ISO-2022-JP?B?GYRCPJ5CPBSOSG?
<VJ6J-
Hello. I'm Japanese. I have wanted "adidas master" or "stan smith (red)" for a long time.
But I have never seen them. I will be happy if you give me good news.
MASAHIRO MATSUMURA

I saw that japanese girl on saturday walking down the eastbound platform at covent garden.
Shit man, she had the most amazing Converse I've ever seen: bright red, yellow star and
chevron, all leather man. And fat rubber soles. I don't hesitate to stop girls on the street
when I see unusual stuff on their feet, and you know it's always a good starting point, especially
if you're a shy guy like me. But you know with japanese girls it's kind of different. Even
though this one was really cute, you'd get something like....."They're limited edition, I bought
them in Tokyo, that's where I'm from. You know there are some good shops over there".
Thanks darling, got a return ticket for me?

FROM@JANKWIG.PANIX.COM
RECEIVED 17.5.97 09:42:21
Big problem for me, just shopping in Athletes Foot or Foot Locker, or something, can be
pretty dangerous, since gaping at row after row of Nikes, Converse, Pumas and Avias.and
salivating over white high-tops, and the Chuck Taylor black Cons, and those stripes on the
Adidas. i can get sooooo distracted I forget what I came for. I also gape over that Nike swoosh
mark and often decide what teams I'm gonna root for based on what shoes they all wear.

DATE: THU, 22 MAY 1997 23:18:35 0100 (BST)
FROM: AJ HILL <AH6342 BRISTOL.AC.UK>HILL
BROS ·TO: VISION@CYBERIACAFE.NET

I bought my grandmother a pair of Nike Air Humaras. She wears them when she goes to walk the dog to the postbox
I bought my niece some Adidas shell-toes, she's only two but she still points to them whenever I go round and see her
I bought my mother some black Vans Chukka boots, they're perfect, she says, for being not too smart
I bought my brother some Nike Air Zoom Alphas, he told me he wanted the old ones, fool
I bought my girlfriend some Air Max Totals and she wears them in the gym
I bought myself some Shakendestrukts and haven't worn them yet because they look so good on the mantel piece
I bought my dog two pairs of kiddy Jordans and he ran about the room shaking his four legs like a badly handled puppet

TRACI MCGREGOR
LIFESTYLE EDITOR AT
SOURCE MAGAZINE, NEW YORK, 97

I've been wearing tennis shoes pretty much all my life. I was always a real tomboy, and had to have a pair of the latest kicks on my feet. We didn't have a lot of money back then, so instead of Adidas, we'd get the four stripes! When I got into High School I actually worked at Foot Locker, so I got into all the latest styles. I remember the first pair I bought working at Foot Locker, Adidas high-top Scam Controllers, which I think were Michael Jordan's shoes, in red and white. Now I 'm a shoe-aholic, I have more shoes than I have clothes, I often have nothing to wear them with! The most recent pair I bought were these Fila.

But I was like, a shell-toe fanatic, I have them in black, green, white, just to have them. Still can't nobody beat Adidas, in terms of comfort and style and they use really interesting colors - I had a pair that was white, with tangerine on the tip, and the stripes were purple. They were so cute I had to get a tangerine dress just to dress them up!

Out of everything, clothing or whatever, tennis shoes have always maintained this kinda futuristic feel, they've always been ahead of the times with design and functionality, always ahead of the game. Everything is moving so fast, fast, fast, that sneakers are needed. Everybody is so active, moving around much more than 15 years ago.

I would never call myself a sneaker fanatic but it's a lifestyle that permeates every aspect. I'm a real functional person, very active, and for me to be running around in heels, it just doesn't work.

It's always the thing to have the latest kicks and I don't know if that's just a hip hop thing, or if it's an urban thing, or a black thing or whatever.

It's funny about tennis shoes, they only work when they're new. I would be loving those shoes and then all of a sudden they're a little bit worn, and I'm not in love with them anymore.... That's when it's time to get a new pair. They get old real fast and the styles come in and out so I'll go to Dr J's and buy what's on sale. You have to go to Brooklyn or Queens to get the styles. The thing is, over in Queens we're into colours and most of mainstream America just wants white.

But I think the prices are bullshit. That's why I never buy them when they come out, I always wait until the sale, unless I get hooked. These major companies make so much money off our communities, they don't give anything back. We don't see ourselves in their adverts unless it's some big basketball of football player, and a very small portion of our community is ever going to achieve that. They are not giving back and I think it's a grave injustice because they make millions off of us. It's a shame and I think that we need to realise that.

AKERS SALE
9.99
NO
EXCHANGES
RETURNS
EXCUSES
TALL DEPT
STAIRS

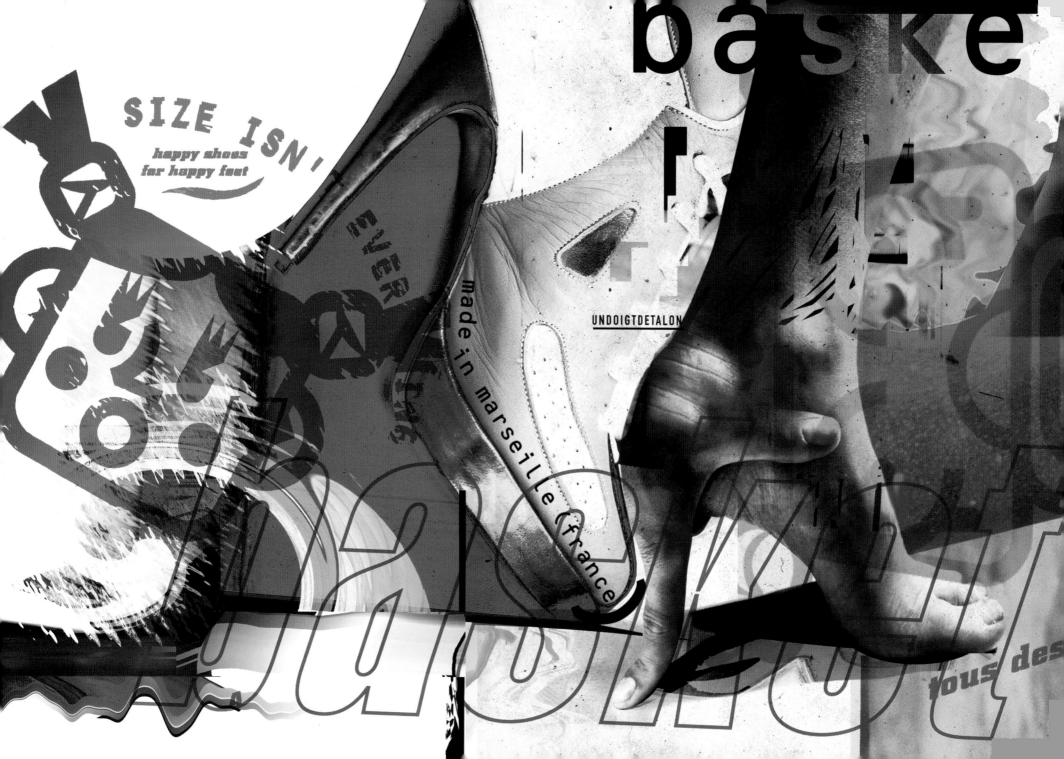

life

BASKET
TALON
AIGUILLE

basket by : Cyd Jouny
graphic desiḡn & photografy
by : tous des K
MADE IN MARSEILLE

lacez vos pieds

basket *life*
is beautifultiful

DP: How you doin?

WELL, WE'RE DOING THIS BOOK, AND AS YOU WERE STYLING WHEN THE SNEAKER BECAME FASHION, I WANTED YOU TO TALK ABOUT WHAT HAPPENED, HOW YOU GOT INTO STYLING FOR "THE FACE" AND "VIBE".

It happened in the 80s when everything was power dressing. People were wandering around in Gaultier suits and beautiful Patrick Cox shoes from Browns, and it was a kind of anti-fashion statement. The first time I even became aware of it was...I used to go to that club Rap Attack...(laughs).

OH GOD!

And Crazy Larry's. And I remember this girl in a pair of Adidas. I think that they were Adidas because Run DMC were huge and Adidas was a big label to have. And that was the first time I ever noticed somebody wearing sneakers in a club. You had a Gaultier jacket, and to wear a pair of sneakers with it was being a bit rebellious, no matter how ridiculous it might seem today. I was drawn to that sort of look. There is still only one sneaker, which is the Air Jordan, the first one, not the red one with the tit, not the red and black one. I've still got a pair of those Jordans, which I'm not wearing now because people keep bugging me in the street, and I'm kinda scared in New York that someone is gonna take them off me. I only wear them out to good functions where people aren't gonna do me for my sneakers.

NO, BUT JORDAN FIVES I THINK...
Because Jordan Fives...

...HAD THE REFLECTIVE THING ON THE TONGUE.

That's the Mother of all sneakers. The first ever Nike sneaker without a swoosh on it. I'd pay any amount of money for a better sneaker. No joke. No joke, I tell you, a friend of mine, his Dad's a really famous photographer. He bought his Dad a pair of Jordan Fives, fresh in the box, five years ago. His Dad, he never opened the box. Two years ago, I'm walking down Greenwich Village. I met my friend. Well man, he's got Nike Fives on. I'm freaking out going "Oh, my God". He had no idea. He just took them back cause his dad never wore them. I went, "You are crazy, I'll give you 500 bucks for them right now". He said, "You can have them" I said "No, not after being on your feet, I don't want them".

That stuff happened, then Nike exploited it. When prices got outrageous and idiots were wearing sneakers, we just went to true stylish fashion. Why pay X amount to buy a pair of sneakers when you can buy a cool pair of old sneakers. Those old Nike Wimbledon were cool. I've been all over the world and have seen some cool things in places like Thailand, stashed away in some old Thai sports shop.

We went up to Kentish Town. There was this really ropey old sports shop on the corner by the tube with an abundance of sneakers, all for £5. Just out the back...the first Shelltoes. So we bought up loads of them. Then we told Duffer where it was and they bought it all. Everything. And, because their stall was kind of trendy then, that sort of started the craze.

Originally, shell-toes, you would be able to get on any street in Manhattan. For two dollars. When I first came to America, in 87, all the tramps wore Adidas shell-toes, homeless people walking around in them. Someone told me a story, that they'd buy a job lot of them and gave them to people. Because there is such an abundance of products in the States that they just forget what they've got.

HOW LONG HAVE YOU BEEN AT "VIBE"?
Two and a half years.

THERE WAS A FASHION SHOOT WHERE YOU HAD MODELS WEARING NIKE TRAINERS WHICH WERE VERY MONOCHROME, AND I REMEMBER THINKING, THIS DOESN'T LOOKS LIKE AN AMERICAN FASHION SHOOT, IT LOOKED EUROPEAN.

That's the advantage of being in America, because I have a different sense of style and I'm aware of the trends and what people want to wear. I like to go into Brooklyn. I need to see what the kids are wearing, to know if they've stopped wearing Tommy Hilfiger and they're wearing Nike. That's where the whole pulse of fashion is right now, it all comes from those kids. When it comes down to a generation gap, those are the kids cos everybody wants to be cool.

There's a big fashion trade show in Atlanta called Super Show, which is an international sportswear show. Put it this way, it's in a super dome and everybody has a stand - Reebok, Adidas, Ellese, Diadora, Umbro - they all have stands on this massive floor.

Nike has a floor to itself. When I went in there they were like aliens, they were just so different to everybody else it was kinda like surreal. It was like, you guys aren't real because your stuff's so bad. You look at other people's stuff and think, it's all right but I'd never wear that. You can't say that with Nike. It's really rapid and really young. They design shoes for guys that are 16

YIFFTA/RONO/MORCELI/AOUITA/NGHGHI/
KIPKETER/DENSIMO/GEBRSELASSIE/ KOMEN/KONCHELLAH/EL GUERROUJ
...GREAT AFRICAN RUNNERS

NHLANHLA MSOMI
SOUTH AFRICAN EDUCATOR, ACTIVIST AND PLAYWRIGHT

During Apartheid you could only get good sneakers from people who'd been abroad, or shops which stocked quality imported gear and no shops in the townships stocked that stuff. The trade embargo meant that imported goods, like Nike, were much more expensive than locally produced goods. They were luxury items, and people who were into trainers wore them as status symbols. Black people were not really exposed to outside culture or anything, for a reason...exposure through the media was heavily regulated.

But music culture was always allowed through. People listened to a lot of soul, like Lionel Ritchie and Whitney Houston. Prophets of the City were sort of on the fringes back then, their hip hop following were from places in Cape Town, mostly from the "coloured" mixed race communities. In the late 80s, there was an hip hop explosion. I think it was due to the media regulations relaxing, and at that time people were looking for alternatives, y'know, that were more militant and hip hop fitted the bill.

And then dress codes started changing and people started getting into sneakers. LA Gear had a lot of black and white sneakers and they were very big. I think they must have had a manufacturer in the country and their shoes and clothing were good quality, quite affordable and attractive. People are definitely not into colours at all. No way, they have to be basic, basic white sneakers. By the early 90s there were shops that sold those things exclusively...and you get the magazines, and see hip hop on TV. Only then did people want those things in a big way, and it took off.

As far as I can see, the hip-hop movement is something that people can identify with, it is black culture, it fits the bill as in feeling proud to be black. Also, it's something that can be used by kids against their parents who don't understand it, it's new, something to annoy them with. Now people are beginning their own local versions of the different dance styles, of hip-hop dress codes and music - which is basically township hip-hop. And with fashion, people are wearing things that they never would before, like hooded tops and necklaces with animal skin and teeth, so it is growing and sort of feeding from the international thing.

Shoes have always been expensive. But this has been counter acted by a huge influx of fake shoes from the Far East, from Singapore, Malaysia, Taiwan etc. They look like the real thing but you only discover down the line that they're fake. The fake shoe industry is threatening to take over from the real shoe manufacturers. You see people on the street wearing Nikes, and Adidas, everything, and it's hard to tell if they're fakes or not. If you went into a shop and wanted to buy a pair of sneakers you could pay up to a couple hundred bucks, which is a hell of a lot of money in terms of percentage of earnings.

But when you look at it, and also at the neighbouring African countries, we've always had middle-class black communities, and kids studying in Europe or the States have always worn the latest trainers and gear. Now South Africa is opening up even more, so it is only a matter of time before the same things start effecting those in the townships. Initially and maybe still, it's a class thing with hip hop culture, not just a black thing. Kids with money can buy trainers and the rest are left behind, like anywhere in the world. Seriously, hip hop presupposes a high level of literacy, something we are still struggling with in black South Africa. Simply to pick up a magazine to see what's going on, to be able to watch CNN to know what's going on, you need to be able to read and understand the international language. So there is that level of literacy which is very significant to all this. You or your parents have to have money to take advantage of that culture. For a significant number of people in Africa, the most powerful economic and political group, the world is becoming a global village via exposure to the media.

MATHIEU KASSOVITZ
DIRECTOR OF "LA HAÏNE"
PARIS, JUNE 97

WHEN I LOOK AT ALL MY SNEAKERS LAYING ON THE FLOOR RIGHT NOW, SO MANY DIFFERENT STORIES COME TO MIND...YOU HAVE INSTANT FLASHBACKS WHEN YOU LOOK AT A PAIR OF SNEAKERS.

I'VE ALWAYS BEEN INTO CLASSIC SNEAKERS: NIKE AIR FORCE, ADIDAS RUN DMC, ADIDAS CONCORD, NEW BALANCE, AIR JORDAN...EVEN THOUGH I'M CRAP AT BASKETBALL AND SPORT IN GENERAL. HOW CAN YOU EVEN THINK OF PLAYING BASKETBALL IN A PAIR OF ADIDAS FORUM MID FOR EXAMPLE: YOUR FEET WOULD BE FUCKED...BUT THE SHOE LOOKED SO BAD MAN, YOU HAD TO HAVE THEM. IT'S A SHOW-OFF-SNEAKER, A SHOE FOR EYE-WASH. THAT PHENOMENA HAPPENED BECAUSE OF HIP HOP. IT LITERALLY CHANGED THE FACE OF SNEAKERS AND THE WAY OF WEARING THEM, AND THEREFORE THEIR FUNCTION. SO WHEN NIKE, REEBOK OR ANY OTHER BRAND TALK ABOUT TECHNOLOGY I THINK, YEAH, COME ON, THEY'RE ALSO B-BOYS SHOES! IT WAS PRETTY DIFFICULT TO FIND GOOD SNEAKERS IN FRANCE IN THE MID-80S. WHEN I SAY GOOD, I MEAN RARE AND FLASHY ONES THAT YOUR FRIENDS WOULDN'T HAVE. OF COURSE THERE WAS TIKARET IN PARIS, BUT THEY SOLD B-BOY'S SHOES LIKE TROOP. THE GAME WAS TO HUNT FOR THE FRESHEST PAIR AROUND, SO YOU WOULD HAVE EXCLUSIVITY FOR A MONTH OR SO, EVEN IF THEY WERE UGLY, LIKE SOME REEBOKS I

HAD - WITH PLASTIC AND POLYURETHANE PARTS ON THE SIDES AND ANKLES, A BIG PHAT LOGO - THAT LOOKED LIKE THEY CAME FROM OUTER SPACE! BUT I WAS THE ONLY GUY ON THE BLOCK TO HAVE THEM, SO IT DIDN'T MATTER IF THEY WERE STUPID. I COULDN'T WEAR THEM TODAY, HELL NO. FOR ME, THERE ARE CLASSICS SHOES LIKE ADIDAS NASTASE, STAN SMITH OR NIKE LDVS, AND THERE ARE SNEAKERS. I CONCEIVE THE SNEAKER MORE LIKE THE BASKETBALL SHOE. IN FACT THE WORD FOR SNEAKER IN FRENCH IS "BASKET". LOOK AT THE ADIDAS METRO ATTITUDE. THAT'S A PAIR OF SNEAKERS YOU BUY FOR THE LOOK...BLACK AND WHITE LEATHER WITH LIZARD SKIN PATTERN, A PURE HIP HOP SNEAKER.

I LOVE AIR MAX CLASSICS. I HAD MOST OF THEM SINCE 1986. THEY HAVE A NICE SHAPE, LIKE A SHARK. MY FAVOURITE PAIR IS IN BLACK AND DARK BLUE. THE ONLY PROBLEM IS THAT IT'S NOT A PAIR ANYMORE...I'VE ONLY GOT ONE SHOE LEFT. I'D BEEN LOOKING FOR THE OTHER ONE FOR AGES UNTIL I DISCOVERED THAT AFTER A QUARREL WITH MY GIRLFRIEND SHE THREW IT INTO THE GARBAGE AS AN ACT OF VENGEANCE...AND KEPT IT SECRET FOR AGES.

SNEAKERS ARE STRANGE OBJECTS. I DON'T KNOW WHY I BOUGHT THOSE YELLOW AND RED ZOOM AIR. I DON'T KNOW HOW OR WHEN I'LL WEAR THEM...I'LL PROBABLY END UP FRAMING THEM.

I FEEL VERY BAD. I GAVE MY BLACK AND BLUE AIR JORDANS MODEL 1, THAT I'D HAD SINCE 1985, TO MY NEIGHBOUR JUST SIX MONTHS AGO. YOU KNOW WHY? BECAUSE THEY WERE A SIZE TOO BIG FOR ME. THEY WERE BRAND NEW, NOT EVEN CREASED! THEN I HEARD THAT THOSE JORDANS SELL FOR UP TO 5,000FF, AND 20,000FF IF THEY'RE BOXED AND SEALED. SHIT! I DON'T KNOW WHY I DID THAT. BUT I'VE GOT SO MANY SNEAKERS, BECAUSE I'VE BEEN BUYING THEM SINCE I WAS A TEENAGER. IT'S LIKE A COLLECTION BUT I'M DEFINITELY NOT COLLECTING. I JUST LOVE SNEAKERS AND DON'T KNOW THE VALUE OF A VINTAGE SNEAKER. I WISH I DID!!! I CAN'T BELIEVE I DID THAT...

"Hello, this is a message for Paul...hope I have the right number...
I'm calling regarding your fax...ah, to do an interview.
He won't be available, but he wishes you MUCH LOVE with it. Okay." Bleep...

SPIKE LEE CORRESPONDENCE, VOICE ON ANSWER MACHINE

stacey,
here's some questions for the sneaker book. are you into being in it? if so can you fill them in and send them back to me or give them to Yvette (I'm not sure when I'm doing the links next). thanks alot for the other day it was a dream! see you soon...remind yvette about coming in and I'll see you then.
thanks stacey, any questions call me.
0171 284 7633
0181 960 1499.

also it would be perfect if you could take some photographs of your sneakers and get us a photograph of yourself which we can put in the book. by the way if you need more space just write on the reverse also.

- what sneakers were you wearing when you were growing up and where was it?

Tracks Sneakers (Baby Blue ones)
It was in Kingston, Jamaica

- what are your favourite sneakers and why?

Adidas! Because they'd be having some wild ones that nobody would think of buying! Original of not there's only a couple of pairs made.

you have unusual taste in sneakers, if so why and what do you

I have a very unusual taste in sneakers (extremely strange taste). - How like to be very different. - I've liked looking at sneakers - I like forked up looking sneakers. The ones people see & say... the first thing they say is damn that's sick!

- can you describe what would be your ultimate sneaker, i.e what would it look like?

you know those japanese sneakers. That's like gloves for your feet. (feet socks) - the nikie comes up black and gold and to each toe. man still become sell those fat little. Ha Ha Ha!

- would you say that you are a sneaker freak?

Hey! Yea! Come take a look in my closets (i.e. Paris, N.Y., London & Canada) Ha Ha!

HA BOTTOM QUITE TRICK!

SPLIT

Dirk Bikkembergs
"When I started designing ten years ago I did a shoe collection inspired by football boots - and it was in the usual colours but was all about cutting, and strange...in the meanwhile I think Nike and Adidas, they're so good at it....why me?....."

Paul Smith
"I like trainers with the wrong things, in the wrong colours...with a suit they look fantastic."

Jil Sander
"Nike...they do it in a very, let's say constructive way."

Nigel Curtis
"I had this idea to combine sportswear with classics, so we have the feeling of trainers and say, Chelsea boots. I want the comfort of trainers but I want something with the sophisticated look of a normal shoe."

Jose levy
"I think you can work on different images with trainers. I can imagine furs with trainers." (yuk. Ed).

Jean Paul Gaultier
"After you try trainers you can't wear anything else...because they're so comfortable. So I make shoes like trainers. but I try to make them not look too sporty. more sophisticated. more city-like."

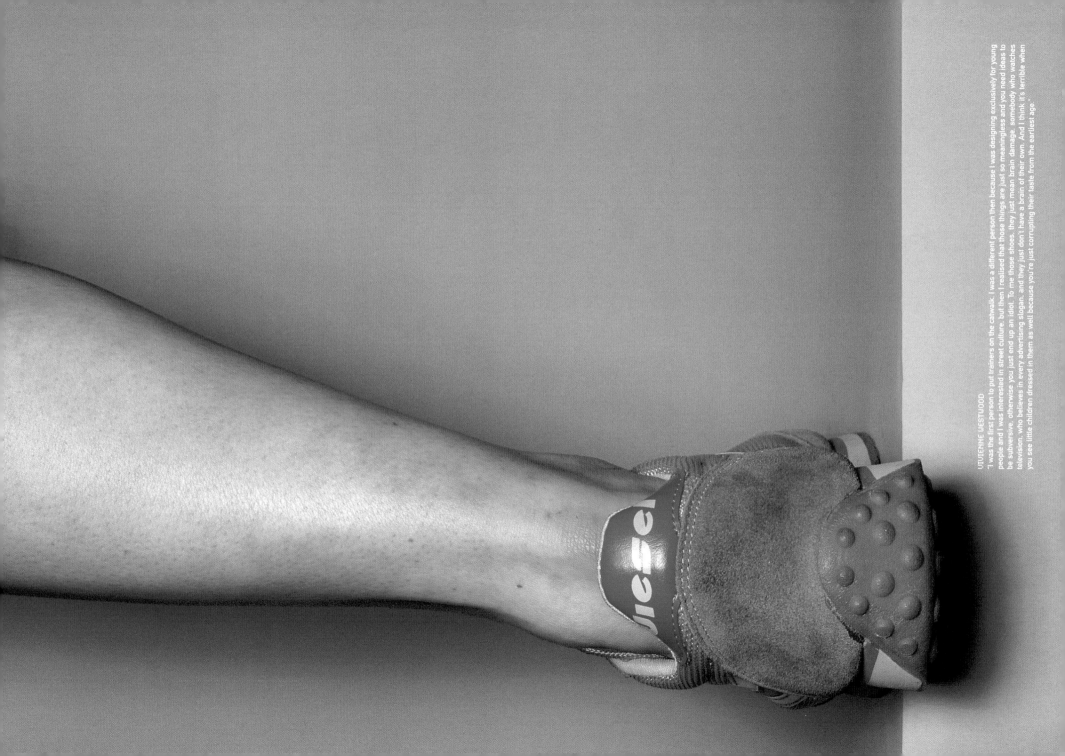

VIVIENNE WESTWOOD

"I was the first person to put trainers on the catwalk. I was a different person then because I was designing exclusively for young people and I was interested in street culture, but then I realised that those things are just so meaningless and you need ideas to be subversive, otherwise you just end up an idiot. To me those shoes, they just mean brain damage, somebody who watches television, who believes in every advertising slogan, and they just don't have a brain of their own. And I think it's terrible when you see little children dressed in them as well because you're just corrupting their taste from the earliest age."

THE CHAPMAN BROTHERS

HOW DID YOU BEGIN WORKING TOGETHER AS BROTHERS?

Jake: We first started playing with each other as brothers and then Dinos said it, that our individual work wasn't good enough, so we decided to work together. Also it raises certain questions about what it is to be an artist, to be an originator of creative products. When you have more than one person making the work it reduces the possibilities for creativity and it means that you're a lot less spontaneous about how you produce art - which means to say that you're turning the production of art into productivity rather than creativity.

DOES IT ENABLE A KIND OF HEALTHY DETACHMENT?

Yeah! One of the prevailing conditions of making art is the idea that to be an artist you have to be egocentric and know how to produce an object which represents or expresses some inner self. With two people you automatically have an adversarial condition where two people tend to fight about whose ideas are prioritised. Then the whole business of making art becomes not about trying to produce coherent things, it becomes about trying to produce schizophrenic things. You're already involved in a discourse, you're involved in a multiplication....

I'VE SEEN YOUR SCULPTURES - THE MANNEQUINS - AND ALSO SOME DRAWINGS. ARE THEY THE FIRST PIECES YOU DID TOGETHER?

In as much as there is any representative theme throughout the work it's a certain relationship with the viewer which is quite sadistic. We are interested in victimising a certain kind of audience, by whatever means necessary, and we've started making films now. We know how to play games very well. Not that people are unwittingly victimised. There is certainly a kind of sado-masochistic economy going on between a bourgeois public and a bourgeois productivity...pub noise...producing nasty objects that people can go and whinge at. It's reciprocal.

There's such a great deal made of controversy in contemporary art, and it seems there are, particularly over the last five years, a lot of funny or quirky ideas, the sort of ideas a lot of people have, but the difference is the artist feels in a position to make it and then call it art....Once you start producing culture you have to work out how much you want to be involved in culture, and producing culture which isn't necessarily edifying. I think that instead of just producing critical culture people have become interested in the ideas of waste rather than....pub noise...it may be necessary to produce a good idea in the worst means possible. We produce things which are so finely made that they exorcise any artistic element, so machine made it looks like no one has touched the thing.

I heard this really funny thing the other day, there was some warning on TV about washing-up liquid. When you wash-up plates you should really rinse them because washing-up liquid gets into your system, so when you eat it lubricates your system, so it just shits out your food. And I think that's a beautiful metaphor for making art, the idea of producing culture which just slips through your arse.

I GUESS THAT THIS IS THE BIG QUESTION JAKE. HOW AND WHY DID THE USE OF TRAINERS COME ABOUT IN YOUR WORK?

We're interested in the idea of genetic perfection, and that includes the monstrosity, everything that's anti-metaphysical, anti-idealist...I mean perfection in the terms of science unhinged from any ethical order. And in some ways, when we made those pieces, they looked like anatomical studies, as though they could have some kind of medical possibility. They looked like aberrations, things gone wrong rather than things gone very right. We wanted to give them some kind of grounding principle, rather than looking like they were a genetic abuse, that they were actually genetic perfection. If you give them trainers it makes them look like they can run really fucking fast, especially if you give them 15 to 20 legs.

Therefore the work becomes about producing something which is not only eroto-genetically strange, but also has athletic skill, velocity and speed. Not something debilitated but something which is absolute perfection. It has the best sneakers possible.

YOU HAVE A PHYSICAL FORM WHICH IS, TO A CERTAIN EXTENT TIMELESS, IS THERE ANYTHING IN THAT, BY USING SOMETHING WHICH IS CONTEMPORARY, YOU ARE...?

Yeah yeah, and also the sell-by-date on trainers is almost instantaneous. As soon as they're in the shops they're almost over and I quite like that idea. One of the presumptions about producing works of art is that you're trying to produce something that is timeless. There's an expectation of art that it should last forever and there's something quite nice about giving it this kind of symbolic full-stop. You're producing an object which looks as though it should be ill, but you're giving the mannequins these trainers which make them run really fast, but also they are frozen at the moment when those trainers were fashionable.

One of the main reasons we use real trainers is that it fixes the object in the same space as the viewer. If we made a sculpture and modelled the trainers it would allow the viewer not to consider their own relationship to the object. But when you put trainers on something, and a wig and eyelashes, it suddenly becomes a little bit like the person viewing, so you get this funny symbiotic relationship.

It's also quite nice because the idea of trainers is about exclusivity and alienation, suggesting that there is some claim to authenticity with trainers, which is fucking hilarious. The idea that the first kid in the school to get the right trainers has some claim to authenticity despite the fact that there's fifty billion of the things being made. So it's one of the funniest representations of mass culture possible. On the one hand it juggles the idea that you can be exclusive, but on the other hand, they have to make enough of the things to make the enterprise worth while. It's a double lie.

Also, you're producing works of art for people who live in a rarefied vacuum. They aren't really familiar with aspects of culture which perhaps they should be. So as soon as you put trainers on a work of art you can be assured that you have alienated those people. In a way they are the most unlikely people to be wearing trainers. It's the same with the titles of the pieces. One of the reasons we called a piece "Two faced cunt", or "Fuck face", is just simply the pleasure of hearing people say it. If a gallery wants to sell the piece they're going to have to say the word.

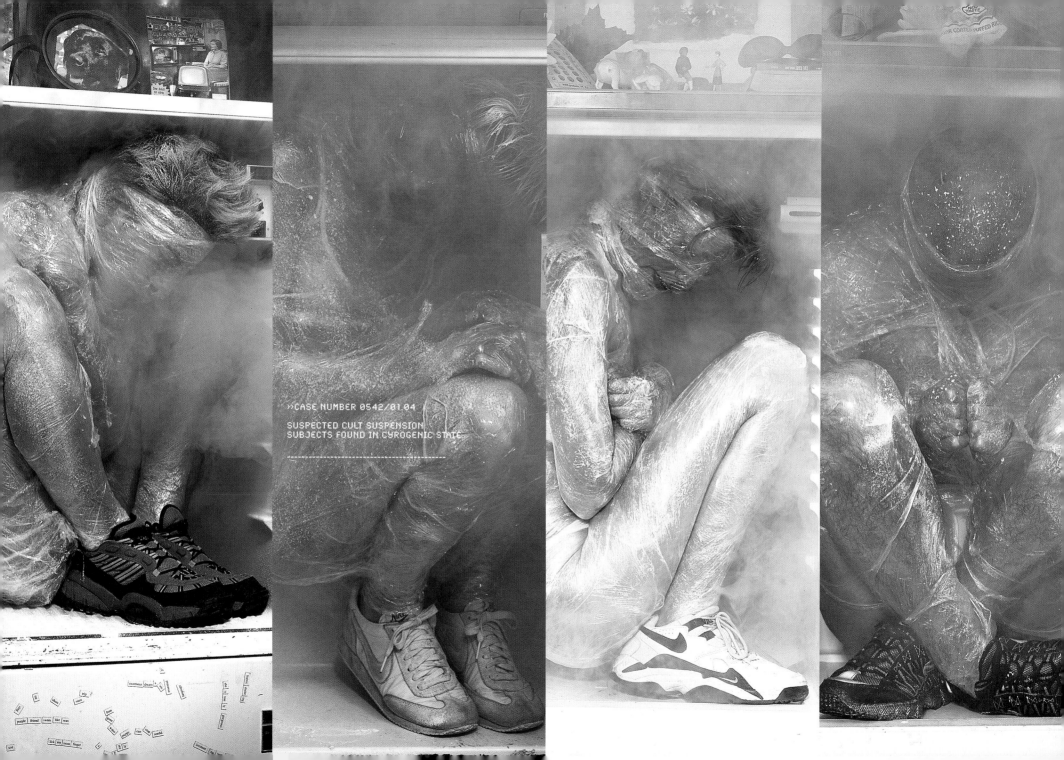

>>CASE NUMBER 0542/01.04

SUSPECTED CULT SUSPENSION
SUBJECTS FOUND IN CYROGENIC STATE

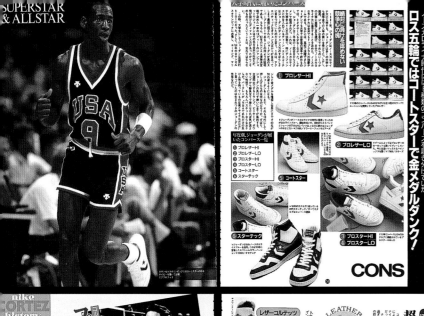

ロス五輪ではコートスターを履き分けて金メダルダンク！

ノースカロライナ時代には6種類のコンバースを履き分けていた

CONS

八七年間、着用していたコンバース

年代別ジョーダンが履いていたコンバース一覧
1. プロレザーHI
2. プロレザーLO
3. プロスターHI
4. プロスターLO
5. コートスター
6. スターテック

WHY JORDAN CAN WALK ON AIR?

HANG TIME 2.03SEC

'NOBODY CAN'T STOP'

SLAM STYLE

Renewal & Maintenance

THEME4 ガンコに汚れたレザースニーカーをみるみる美しくする

ムース／水洗

THEME3 AJI復刻をオリソックリのユー仕上げよう

THEME5 気がついたらプーンと臭ってしまった！

噴霧前 → 噴霧後

---

nike CORTEZ history

超軽量が自慢のスーパーコルテッツに発掘調査の発令

72年のカタログでコルテッツを検証

プリフォンテーン

OREGON

cortez

LEATHER 1st

初公開。これが1stカタログだ

スーパーコルテッツ

NYLON 1st '72

ロングセラーの原点がヴェールを脱ぐ

あまりに意外なルックス。1stをマラソンに思う人続出

意外なスマートフォルムにアスリートの原点を見た

nike

1stにはシューレースのギザギザがなかった！

もしやマラソンでは？

マラソン / コルテッツ

AIR MAX 9 DESIGNER *intervie*

黒ベロ装着のマッ プロトタイプを世界

COMIC

[赤×黒]はAIR MAXが主人公！？

エア・ジョーダン / エア・ミッション / エア・マックス95 / コルテッツ

>>JONATHAN EASYNET.CO.UK
08.11.96

>>

>>YOU CAN GET A COPY OF "COOL TRANS" FROM THE JAPANESE
BOOKSHOP ON PICCADILLY

>>BETWEEN PICCADILLY CIRCUS STATION AND "SIMPSONS" THEY
ALSO HAVE "BOON"

>>THANKS MAN

ショップリストは82ページに！

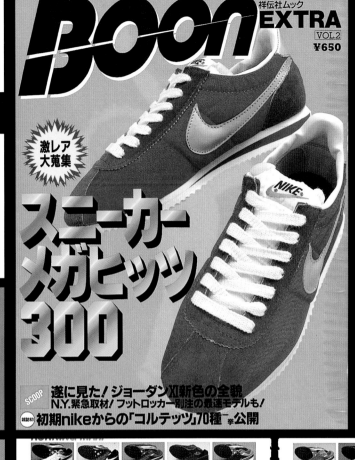

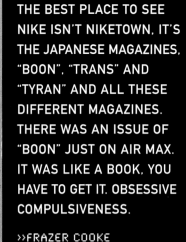

THE BEST PLACE TO SEE NIKE ISN'T NIKETOWN. IT'S THE JAPANESE MAGAZINES, "BOON", "TRANS" AND "TYRAN" AND ALL THESE DIFFERENT MAGAZINES. THERE WAS AN ISSUE OF "BOON" JUST ON AIR MAX. IT WAS LIKE A BOOK, YOU HAVE TO GET IT. OBSESSIVE COMPULSIVENESS.

>>FRAZER COOKE

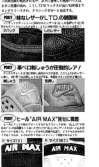

Cortez are always number one but Humpty's got space shoes now

Sneaker Freak

Humpty (right) from East Los Angeles signing Hazard with his friend Art.

Your top sneaker of all time?
Nike Cortez. They're comfortable. And cheap too. All the gangsters wear Cortez so if you have them and a bald head and baggy trousers all the cops are gonna think you are a gang member, no matter what. I still wear them though cause they are firme shoes. They've been around for a long time.

A lot of gang members are wearing running shoes and hi-tops these days?
They do. Like Nike Air Max. All the running shoes are real popular. I just bought a pair of Nike Zoom Flights. They look like space shoes. They have more strong sole, I like sporty shoes. Something I can look good in. So I can look clean cut. Some wear Adidas and Guess but I prefer Nike and Fila.

Humpty staples his trousers for neatness

What do you wear with your sneakers?
Usually a white t-shirt and baggy Ben Davies. I wear them long so you can only see the tip of my shoe. But you know how some guys get their pants all messed up, dragging them in the dirt? I don't want my pants all dirty and torn up. That's why I staple the hem to the sole of my shoe.

My top sneaker of all time

The Nike Cortez is probably the most brilliant shoe ever made. I have had many, many pairs in different colors since I bought my first pair in 1985. You can get the remake in any color imaginable but I prefer the black on white although white on black nylon and leather and black on black leather is nice too. I also have white on red, white on blue, white on black (but I hate that one) and I just like them a lot. They are very simple and clean cut without being boring and they go with everything.

The Nike Cortez was originally designed in 1966 by Bill Bowerman, head track coach at the university of Oregon, for another brand of sneakers. If you buy a pair, you won't be sorry. They are naturally very popular all over the planet but, as I discovered a few years ago, I think most popular with gang members in East Los Angeles.

Gang Sneakers

Victor and **Cindy**, 15, with their new born baby **Veronica** and grandpa**Johnny** from El Serreno. Victor wears black nylon Nike Cortez in this picture but he won't let Cindy wear them. "They're gang affiliated so it could be dangerous for her."

Puppet from AMK in East LA wears black and white nylon Cortez because they are part of the cholo style and look good with his size 60 Ben Davis.

Danny, 22, an ex-gang member from East Los Angeles told me: "I used to be really particular about my clothes. I used to iron my clothes for hours to look good, to impress and intimidate. I'd wear my gang affiliated wear. White t-shirt and my Ben Davies and my Nike Cortez and somebody would know "hey, that guy is trouble right there, walking down the street."They'd know I was from somewhere and that if you messed with me there was gonna be another ten, fifty, hundred other guys to mess with and not only that. You'd know you'd have to duck from guns and everything. And they feel intimidated, they're the one's who feel intimidated. It's weird but it makes me feel allright. I don't care as much now, I just iron them to get the wrinkles out but that's it. I still like wearing the baggy clothes though. I like it. I don't like wearing tight-ass-pants, I tell the guys at work, "hey, your ass is eating your pants. Maybe you like that but I like to be comfortable. I like to be relaxed."

SIMON GUNNING

COLLECTOR & EX-WORLD CHAMPION

DOWNHILL SKATER FORMERLY SPONSORED BY VANS

"THE FUTURE IS RED"

101462.366@compuserve.com

I remember a skatewear company called Vision, and you could go all the way to Brazil and buy Vision clothing, skateboards, decks, the whole thing – all fake – and you could buy any skateboard trucks – I used to skate for Tracker – all fake in Brazil. They're really undercover over there, more than China and Vietnam. And the Italians, big faking centre, you wouldn't have thought... And this country, we make a lot of fakes. Last year in The Times there was an article that hardly anyone read. America approached China about fakes, and China acted. They beheaded 60,000 people publicly, and imprisoned an undisclosed number for faking products. Did you hear human rights organisations talking about that? I'm sure America went "Wooo, we didn't ask you to do that!"

The Air Max 95 is my most requested shoe, in grey and green. And when my girlfriend said to me, do you want a pair?, I said no because all the old men were wearing them in New York. And then about two months later that was it, because all the old men and runners had bought them there were very few left, then the Japanese sussed it out, BOSH. But the problem is that now Nike are saying, we've fucked ourselves up, because they expected to make LOADS OF MONEY MAN...they ain't gonna make shit, cause the Japanese are into rarities, they're not into stuff that you can get every day...Most expensive were a pair of Air Jordans I recently sold for $3,500, the orange metallic ones. It depends on who you're selling to and how much they're willing to pay. It's like going to an auction house to sell a Stradavarius violin.

COLIN HOPE, SIZE 8 (UK)

I work in a trainer shop in Camden which stocks vintage trainers, used and dead stock and some modern trainers. The most collectable? I would say the Jordans are pretty good. Modern shoes...the most desirable are the Air Max and Footscape, and in this country, Rift and the Pump Fury, but the best long term sellers are the Jordans. The unusual colours go for more but I don't really like them. They're ugly. I wear Air Max, but the most comfortable are the Pump Fury. My mum used to buy me Hi-Tech and Gola, cause they were really cheap, but I used to really like Samba, so I saved up and bought them myself. I had a few pairs of running shoes, the Mega Flames and the Waffle Racer. I wish I still had them, they'd be worth £400, £450 now. The most popular shoe in the store is the old canvas high-top Converse. It's not collectable but it's cheap and it seems to be really fashionable in Japan at the moment. They're going away from hi-tech trainers to simple low-tech.

The most expensive second-hand used shoe that I've sold was £800, the Nike Chicago, which is the forerunner to the Jordan, made by Armani in Italy. We also have some very rare shoes, black and red Nike runners with a yellow swoosh and on the back of one shoe it says Elton and on the other one it says John. They were the only pair made and they're not for sale. We're always looking out for rare shoes. I've got the collectable Hong Kong edition of the Fury. There's only 1,997 pairs made and they're in bright colours, black, red and yellow with Chinese writing commemorating the change over from Britain to China. They come with a certificate, bag and pump. We're getting two pairs, and we're having to buy them in at £250 a pair.

I had those shoes for ages, but I wanted that kind of money and nobody would touch it. I sold them over the internet, and I'd say it's probably a world record. I don't really deal with running shoes but I know that some of the early Cortez sell for $1,500, but I've never seen any shoe sell for $3,500 before. It's like Levi's, getting rarer and rarer. We started the collecting off in the early 80s, then the Japanese were doing it and the next minute the Americans are doing it. Now the Japanese are controlling the sneakers market, but it doesn't mean that Nike should set up in Japan and say, guys what do you want? It doesn't work like that. The Japanese are desperate to be Western...they want to be us, they want the rarity value, they want to look around the world and don't want it handed to them on a plate, they want to be rolling the dice and say, yeah, quick, we've got to find this pair! They want the chase.

Nike is still the big thing in Japan, but sneakers are over in Japan because of what Nike has done, unless they can hold back and not give everything. It's like sitting around a table playing cards, Nike is chucking all the cards down and saying, here look what I've got, and the other guys are holding back. But, what they're not realising is that we've seen their cards.

It's a great shame because I think Nike are a brilliant company, but you can't be greedy. They open a couple of Niketown's in Tokyo and wonder why they don't sell much. And that's why all the orders for Nike next year will be down (correct, Ed). In a way that's good because if they don't sell those sneakers they will become rare and the market builds up again. They're frightened to have people like you or me on their team because they view us as rebels, but they don't realise that this is their future. They have to build markets up, not swamp them, watch what is going on, have people on the edge sussing it out, always thinking what's next. Research. Get people on board who know what they're doing instead of sitting behind desks designing sneakers on computers. One person off the street can do the job of a whole marketing team, which they pay millions for...like a cultural sponge just taking in different experiences...I'm not saying the companies need to be trendy...just bring out some special editions...drop certain colours in certain parts of the world. But there is a future...it will be more intelligent, and that goes out to all the big boys, because they're not going to be around if they don't open their brains and let all the information that's out there in. But they've got to produce quality. Look at that film "War of the Worlds". I can see companies having corporate wars within a hundred years. Nike will be fighting Sony and we are the pawns, but we can stop it now.

SNEAKERS ARE JUST A PART OF LIFE AND FASHIONLEADS LIFE. FASHION IS A PART OF US ALL AND WE ALL NEED TO BE ABLE TO EXPRESS OUR INNER FEELINGS WITH THE CLOTHING THAT WE WEAR WHETHER FOR SPORT OR FOR FASHION

THE MAJORS SAY IT IS FOR SPORT AND WE SAY IT IS FASHION. WHEN WILL THE RIGHT HAND KNOW WHAT THE LEFT HAND IS DOING AND UNDERSTAND THAT SNEAKERS ARE FASHION WHETHER FOR SPORT OR FOR THE STREET

MY ADIDAS ROM >>BY SHAWN SMITH
TRAINERS ON THE TERRACES

What exactly do you class as a life-affirming moment? Your first kiss with a girl? How about your first football match? Or the first time you offer your dad out and get a right hiding for your trouble? And - of course - the first pair of trainers you ever bought yourself.

In this writer's case, it was a pair of white leather Adidas Rom - Fifteen quid from a sports shop in Bradford in 1981. What influenced that choice? Two reasons. One was the pure style of the things - those infamous three blue stripes with a thin white rubber strip on the toes, just cool as fuck. The other was the fact that I'd seen Everton lads wearing them outside Elland Road the week before complete with Slazenger v-neck jumpers and wedge haircuts. This new look had started on Merseyside and was starting to spread to other areas and I wanted in. Little did I know at the time just how big a part this image was going to play in my future life. That purchase proved to be the first of many over the next 16 years and was the start of a love affair with trainers that at times was to verge on addiction. Those Roms stood me in good stead for a couple of years - the only other footwear that could compete at that time was a pair of original Kicker boots.

Back in 1981, Adidas Rom were one of the trainers to be seen in - that is, if you were a fashion conscious urban northern male who went to football. Other favourites of the era were Adidas Country (white leather/green stripes), Adidas Stan Smith (all-white leather tennis shoes) and Adidas Sambas (black leather/white stripes and white rubber toe piece). More exotic brands started to appear mainly thanks to lads "acquiring" them while travelling to European away games The first Nikes to appear in Liverpool were allegedly robbed from Paris. 1982 saw another new name on the scene - Diadora and their classic Bjorg Elite. These are possibly the most comfortable pair of trainers I've ever worn. Made of white kangaroo skin leather with a gold flash, these were the dog's bollocks (or possibly Skippy's...). They were also the first trainers I saw to use plastic lace eyelets as opposed to laceholes. These made an appearance in football fashion strongholds like Manchester, Leeds, Liverpool and Middlesbrough but at thirty-five quid a pair they were more popular with our affluent cockney friends. They tended to go hand-in-hand with a garment also sported by the Swedish tennis

ace - the Fila BJ track-suit top, which became a terrace classic. It was around this time that a new lookstarted to emerge from Merseyside as trainers and designer sportswear were abandoned in favour of a more down-market "scruff" look. This included green Peter Storm kagools, tweed jackets, plain crew neck jumpers, suede desert boots and market stall corduroy shoes. Two brands of trainer still managed to hold sway however - Adidas Trim Traab and the ubiquitous Adidas Samba. The Samba became something of a staple in Liverpool and Manchester and - over the next couple of years - the entire north of England. You could spot us a mile off when down in London on matchdays - indeed my mate's non-scallying brother was amazed when they were sussed out on the tube by Chelsea lads while on their way to a midweek Milk Cup tie at Stamford Bridge. "How did they know we were Everton?" - "Adidas Samba" was the simple two word answer, 1984 saw us discover Underground Shoes in Manchester - a shop that imported trainers directly from Adidas' main factory in Germany. All manner of different coloured suede brands were available with the roll call sounding more like a UEFA Cup draw - Napoli, Monaco, Hamburg, Koln, Munchen and more exotic locations such as Madeira, Hawaii and Rhodes - all for a tenner a pair. A personal favourite from this era were Adidas Handball, blue suede/white stripes with a flat brown rubber sole. These have since been re-issued twice by Adidas in 1992 and 1997, and both times I've succumbed and bought a pair.

The mid-80s saw the emergence of all manner of experimentation - even to the extent of purchasing a pair of Nike Flame running shoes and wearing them with the spikes removed - they lasted about three months! During the 1984-85 season, Reebok started to take off and their white leather joggers and tennis shoes have become timeless classics.Joggers were well popular as the decade entered its second half. Indeed they seemed to have country-wide appeal as north/south divides were broken down - well, on the terrace footwear front anyway. Nike mania had finally taken full grip and lads everywhere were just doin' it.

It was around 1986-87 that it all started to go Pete Tong. Adidas followed Nike's lead and moved their manufacturing base from Germany to Eastern Europe and the Far East - consequently

no more factory imports. Underground Shoes closed, rarer trainers became harder to find and new designs were dire. Mainstream sports shops were stocking shite like Troop, British Knight, and Travel Fox instead of old school classics. Disillusioned, I bought a pair of blue suede Adidas Gazelle and decided to retire. My main matchday footwear became Timberlands - the Gazelles and a pair of Nike squash shoes made the trips to Ibiza, and that was it. I'd been forced to go cold turkey and stop buying trainers due to the low quality of "fix" on offer....

Until 1991-92. J-D Sports opened Athleisure in Manchester - a shop specialising in old school sportswear. 1990 had seen the re-emergence of brands such as Lacoste and Fila and some clued-up person with foresight saw a chance to cash in. Athleisure became an oasis in a styleless desert for us late 20s-early 30s well-dressed ex-hooligans. Some old friends were sighted again...the aforementioned Adidas Handball ...Adidas Country ..Nike Cortez....Over the next five years they gave us gems like Adidas Kegler, the ultra-rare Adidas Montreal and Adidas Trim Traab even put in an appearance. My favourite re-issue however has to be Adidas TRX - blue jogggers with fluorescent yellow stripes. They actually appear in the opening scenes of the film "McVicker" as Roger Daltrey fights with the screws for his right to wear trainers. And in 1995 it finally went full circle as Adidas Rom were re-issued. Which is where I came in...What does the future hold? If the marketing men at Adidas and Nike have enough common sense, then they'll keep digging around in their back catalogues. I read somewhere about an Adidas store in Tokyo that stocks just about every trainer ever made by Adidas thanks to a licensing deal which allows their back catalogue to be manufactured and retailed in Japan but not exported. Selfish bastards! However we won't be beaten. The 2002 World Cup is to be staged jointly in Korea and Japan. How many pairs do you reckon could slip into a Head bag un-noticed. Remember the Nikes from Paris?

FRAZER, YOU KNOW YOU'RE THIS LEGEND, YOU'VE GOT THIS LEGENDARY COLLECTION, NO SERIOUSLY.
WHEN YOU TALK ABOUT SNEAKERS A LOT OF PEOPLE GO, OH YEAH FRAZER COOKE RIGHT HE'S GOT A
FUCKING AMAZING COLLECTION...
I KNOW ABOUT IT...

BUT I DON'T THINK YOU'VE GOT MORE THAN ME REALLY...
I DON'T THINK I HAVE REALLY, COMPARED TO ANOTHER PERSON MAYBE...IT'S GOOD MONEY. YOU'VE GOT TO
UNDERSTAND IT'S NOT JUST YOUNG PEOPLE BUYING TRAINERS. WHEN I WAS BUYING STUFF FOR PASSENGER
I BECOME SO INUNDATED WITH STUFF, IT ACTUALLY MAKES YOU HATE IT. THAT'S WHAT HAPPENED TO ME WITH
SHELLTOES. THEY'RE PLAYED OUT A BIT, AREN'T THEY, WELL LET'S FACE IT.
WHEN I WAS AT SCHOOL THERE WAS A COUPLE OF GEEZERS IN THE YEAR ABOVE ME, A CHINESE GUY AND THIS
OTHER GUY AND THEY ALWAYS HAD THE EXPENSIVE TRAINERS. AND I STARTED TO GET INTO THAT. THEY HAD THE
BLUE SUEDE ADIDAS JEANS WITH A SORT OF TRIPLE COLOUR LAYERED SOLE, AND THEN IT CHANGED, IT WAS
HOLLOWED OUT AT THE SIDES. I HAD THE FIRST NIKE WIMBLEDON WITH THE RUBBER TOE BIT. I WENT OUT TO
THE STATES COS MY DAD LIVED IN TORONTO...AND I HAD SOME AIR FORCE ONES IN WHITE WITH A GREY SUEDE
STRIPE, LOW-TOP. I WISH I STILL HAD THEM NOW. AND WITH GOLD, THE SOLES WERE SORT OF A YELLOWY-
ORANGE COLOUR. I WENT TO DEVON OR CORNWALL, AND LEFT THEM UNDER THE BED, PURE ACCIDENT. BUT
THEY WERE COOL ON ME, AND I STILL WEAR AIR FORCE ONES NOW.
WHEN I WAS 13 AND WE DID CALIFORNIA, SAN FRANCISCO, LAS VEGAS, SAN DIEGO, LA, I BROUGHT BACK THE
HANG TEN TUBE SOCKS, COS I WAS REALLY INTO SKATING BIG TIME, AND I WENT TO THE VANS SHOP. SO I GOT
A PAIR OF BROWN, LIGHT BROWN, DARK BROWN AND A T-SHIRT AS WELL, WHICH I STILL HAVE. PEOPLE WOULD
STOP ME IN THE STREET AND SAY, "WHERE THE FUCK DID YOU GET THOSE?" AMERICAN STUFF WAS THE THING.
STREET-WISE STUFF.

IT FEELS LIKE A LOT OF THIS STUFF IS THE MEDIA, AND I COULD BLAME MYSELF BECAUSE I'VE HAD CONNECTIONS
IN ORDER TO COMMUNICATE WHAT I'M INTO. BETWEEN ME AND SOME FRIENDS AND OTHER LIKE-MINDED PEOPLE
WE'RE COMMUNICATING A CERTAIN TASTE TO THE MASS, BUT WE HAVEN'T MOVED ON, SO IT'S HARD TO BE DIFFERENT.
I CAN'T SEE THE SNEAKER THING GOING ANYWHERE, DO YOU KNOW WHAT I MEAN?
I GREW UP IN EAST LONDON, ILFORD AND AROUND THERE. THE WHOLE CASUAL THING WAS REALLY BIG, SO I
HAD SOME STANSFIELDS. I WAS AN UP AND COMING DJ, SO THAT I HAD THE LOIS JEANS WITH A SPLIT AT THE
BOTTOM. I WAS GOING TO CLUBS AND SEEING A BUNCH OF GUYS, PEOPLE LIKE JEREMY HEALEY, AND THINKING,
WOW THIS SNEAKER OF PAUL ANDERSON'S OR WHOEVER, THIS SNEAKER HASN'T GOT A FUCKING SWOOSH ON
IT. THIS IS DIFFERENT AND IT LOOKED REALLY MAD. I WAS HANGING OUT, CLUBBING WITH PEOPLE LIKE NELLIE,
WHO WERE WEARING MY PUMAS. I FOUND THEM IN THE LOCAL SPORTS SHOP IN ILFORD, I FOUND PAIRS THAT
WERE 20 QUID OR SOMETHING, THEN I STARTED WORKING FOR THIS SHOP PASSENGER, AND IN A WAY I ALMOST
CURSE IT.
WHEN WE ACTUALLY THOUGHT ABOUT IMPORTING TRAINERS, IT WAS THE TIME WHEN STUSSY FIRST LIKE CAME
OUT, 88, 89. I WENT OUT TO NEW YORK AND FOUND A STORE THAT HAD MORE THAN 120 PAIRS, $19 A PAIR, ALL
THE COLOURS, ALL THE SIZES. DOCTOR JS OF BROOKLYN HAD EVERY SINGLE PAIR, THEY DIDN'T EVEN GIVE US
LIKE A BREAK IN THE PRICE, AND THEY ALL THOUGHT WE WERE CRAZY TO BUY THEM. SO WE BROUGHT THEM
BACK, WE BROUGHT PUMAS, ANIMAL WITH ATTITUDES, FOUND THE SNAKE SKIN ONES. STARTED SELLING THEM
AND THEY WENT LIKE WILD FIRE. I WAS SELLING THEM FOR 60 QUID A PAIR.
IN SOME WAYS YOU ALMOST GIVE UP YOUR LOVE OF IT, YOU'VE COMMUNICATED THAT TO A WIDER AUDIENCE.
CALL ME A SNOB OR WHATEVER, BUT I BEGAN TO HATE THE FACT THAT I'D ACTUALLY TURNED PEOPLE ON TO IT
BECAUSE I DON'T WANT TO BE WEARING SOMETHING THAT EVERYONE'S GOT, IT'S POINTLESS. TO ME, THE WHOLE
REASON PEOPLE GET INTO SNEAKERS, IT'S TRYING TO ATTAIN THE HOLY GRAIL, ISN'T IT? GET THAT FUCKING
PAIR THAT I LIKE. IF IT'S THE SAME SHOE, ANOTHER COLOUR. IT JUST COMES DOWN TO DETAIL. WHAT IS IT LIKE
NOW...IT'S LIKE STUDENTS.

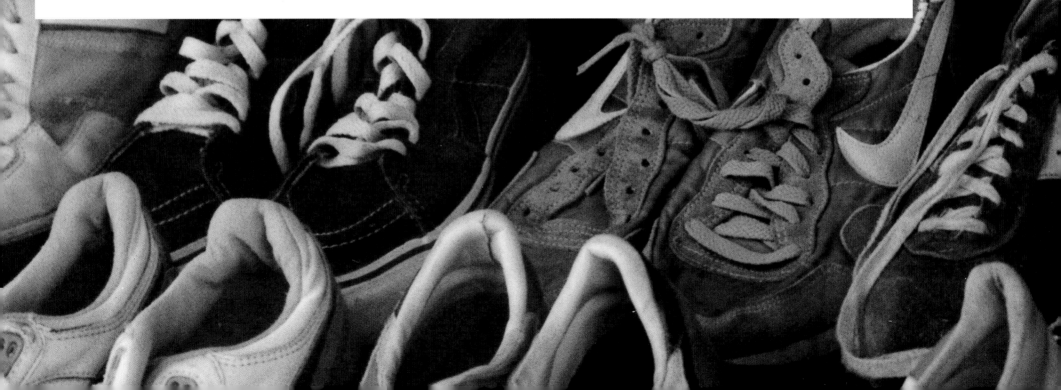

IT'S EVERYONE.
I KNOW J-D SPORT- ARE INTO A CERTAIN SORT OF VIBE...INTO A SORT OF KICKING VIBE, OR AT LEAST THEY KEEP THAT SIDE OF THINGS SATISFIED. WHEN YOU GO INTO J-D IN CARNABY STREET YOU CAN JUST TELL IT'S A MARKETING MAN'S WET DREAM. THEY'VE GOT THE MUSIC GOING FOR KIDS, ALL THE FANCY LITTLE THINGS. IT'S ALMOST LIKE MASS PRODUCED MAR- KETING TO PEOPLE AND...I'D JUST LIKE TO FEEL THAT WE'RE PART OF A GENERATION, WE DON'T WANT THE WOOL PULLED OVER OUR EYES, WE CAN FIND IT OURSELVES. A LOT OF THESE COMPANIES GET IT WRONG.I DON'T FUCKING KNOW WHAT IT IS. IT'S REALLY LAID. WE WERE GOING TO THE SUPER SHOW IN ATLANTA, TRYING TO TALK TO ADIDAS, ASKING FOR OLD STOCK, LEATHER TRACK-SUITS...AND THEY WERE SUCH DINOSAURS, SO SLOW. I HAD KIDS COMING TO ME WITH SERIAL NUMBERS, OBSESSED. AND WE WERE SAYING, "YOU'VE GOT TO BRING BACK ALL THESE COLOURS AND STUFF". BY THE TIME THEY ACTUALLY COTTONED ON, IT WAS TOO LATE. YOU DIDN'T WANT TO KNOW. SO THEN I WAS JUST GOING OUT TO THE STATES TO BUY THE NEWER STUFF. I'M JUST THE BUYER, THEY'D USE MY KNOWLEDGE AND I WENT OUT TO AMERICA AND MADE A LOT OF CONTACTS. ONCE A MONTH I WAS IN NEW YORK WITHOUT FAIL, IT WAS COOL. NEW YORK WAS REALLY HIP THEN. I DON'T THINK NEW YORK'S QUITE SO HAPPENING THESE DAYS. IT'S LIKE A BALL, IT BOUNCES AROUND AND GOES DIFFERENT PLACES. RIGHT NOW IT'S LONDON.
I BROUGHT THOSE AIR RIFT WHEN THEY CAME OUT. I WAS IN NEW YORK AND I WENT TO PARAGON AND A MATE OF MINE SAID, "IT'S THE NEW YORK MARATHON TODAY, YOU'VE GOT TO BUY THOSE THINGS COS THEY'RE THE SICKEST THINGS THAT HAVE EVER BEEN MADE. YOU AIN'T EVER GONNA FIND ANYTHING MORE TWISTED THAN THAT". SO I BROUGHT THEM, AND IT WAS WEIRD, I GOT THEM BACK AND A FEW GIRLS HAD THEM, AND I WAS KIND OF LIKE, I DON'T KNOW ABOUT THESE. AND NOW THEY'RE IN EVERY MAGAZINE.

I SPENT A YEAR LOOKING FOR THOSE SHOES
I JUST FOUND EM. I'M REALLY MORE COMFORTABLE WITH THE MOCKS. THEY ARE SO COMFORTABLE. BUT MINE ARE A BIT FUCKED, I'VE WASHED THEM A FEW TIMES IN THE MACHINE.
NIKE. FOR ME, FOR QUITE A FEW YEARS NOW, HAVE JUST TOTALLY RUN EVERYTHING. THEY'RE REALLY, REALLY GOOD, BUT ADIDAS HAVE LOST IT. THEY WERE RELYING ON THEIR OLD SCHOOL STUFF WHICH IS A BAD SIGN. NIKE SEEMS TO GET IT RIGHT WITH THEIR ADVERTISING. YOU NEVER FEEL LIKE THAT THEY'RE TRYING TO MARKET IT AT YOU, IF THEY DID YOU WOULDN'T WANT IT WOULD YOU? BUT A LOT OF MY MATES IN NEW YORK ARE SNEAKER MANIACS. AND THEY'RE KIND OF SICK OF NIKE BECAUSE OF THEIR OVER-BEARING, CORPORATE IMAGE. PEOPLE ARE WEARING ASICS JUST TO BE DIFFERENT AND THEY HAVE GOT SOME NICE SHOES.

WHAT DO YOU THINK WHEN NIKE SAY THEY'RE NOT ABOUT FASHION?
OF COURSE THEY ARE. LISTEN. WHY WOULD THEY HAVE ALL THOSE COLOURS, WHY DO THEY DELETE THEM? I THINK IT'S SLIGHTLY IRRESPONSIBLE. IN CITIES IN THE STATES PEOPLE ARE FUCKING GETTING KILLED FOR A PAIR OF SHOES. IF YOU'VE GOT A PAIR OF SHOES THAT YOU COULD ONLY GET FOR ONE DAY FOR TWO HOURS, EVERYONE IS GOING TO GET YOU. YOU'RE GOING TO BE PRIME TARGET. BUT WITH A PAIR OF RARE SNEAKERS IT'S A VERY EASY WAY OF LIFE, YOU DON'T HAVE TO BE TOO WILD IN THE WAY YOU DRESS BUT YOU HAVE SOMETHING THAT LOOKS DIFFERENT AND I THINK THAT'S THE APPEAL. YOU DO WALK A BIT TALLER.
BUT IT'S GONE OFF THE BOIL. I DON'T KNOW WHAT IT IS. BUT APPARENTLY THERE'S SUPPOSED TO BE A SILVER AIR MAX COMING OUT. I'VE SEEN ALL GOLD ONES. THING WITH THE NEW AIR MAX IS THEY HAVEN'T GOT THE COLOUR RIGHT. IT LOOKS LIKE AN ORDINARY RUNNING SHOE, AND IF YOU'RE GONNA PAY £110, £120 FOR A PAIR OF SHOES, IT'S GOTTA LOOK FUCKING LIKE A £120 SHOE.
NOW I THINK THAT IT'S VERY HARD TO GET THE SHOE THAT'S A LITTLE BIT SPECIAL. IT TAKES AWAY THE CHASE. BUT I'M STILL OPEN TO IT. LATELY I'VE GOT SICK OF THE WHOLE THING AND WAS BUYING CONVERSE JACK PURCELLS. JUST LIKE BASIC, BASIC, BASIC KIND OF SHOES. YOUR CLASSICS ARE NICE. I QUITE ENJOY IT FINDING THINGS, IT'S LIKE RECORDS. YOU CAN ALWAYS PAY MONEY FOR RECORDS, BUT IT'S A LOT SWEETER WHEN YOU CAN FIND A RECORD FOR LIKE $10 OR A FIVER, BECAUSE YOU'VE LOOKED FOR IT, RATHER THAN RING UP THE DEALER AND ASK CAN I HAVE THAT. SUPPLY AND DEMAND ISN'T IT?

FRAZER COOKE, BUYER, LONDON 97

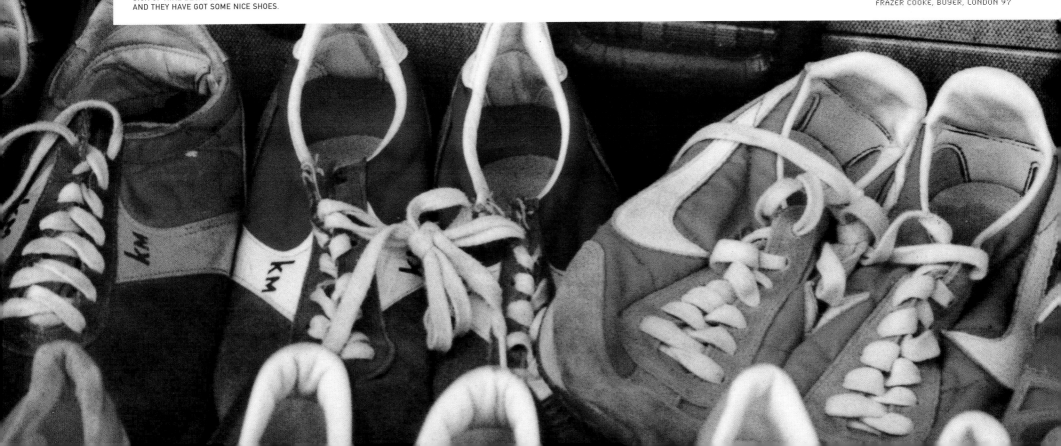

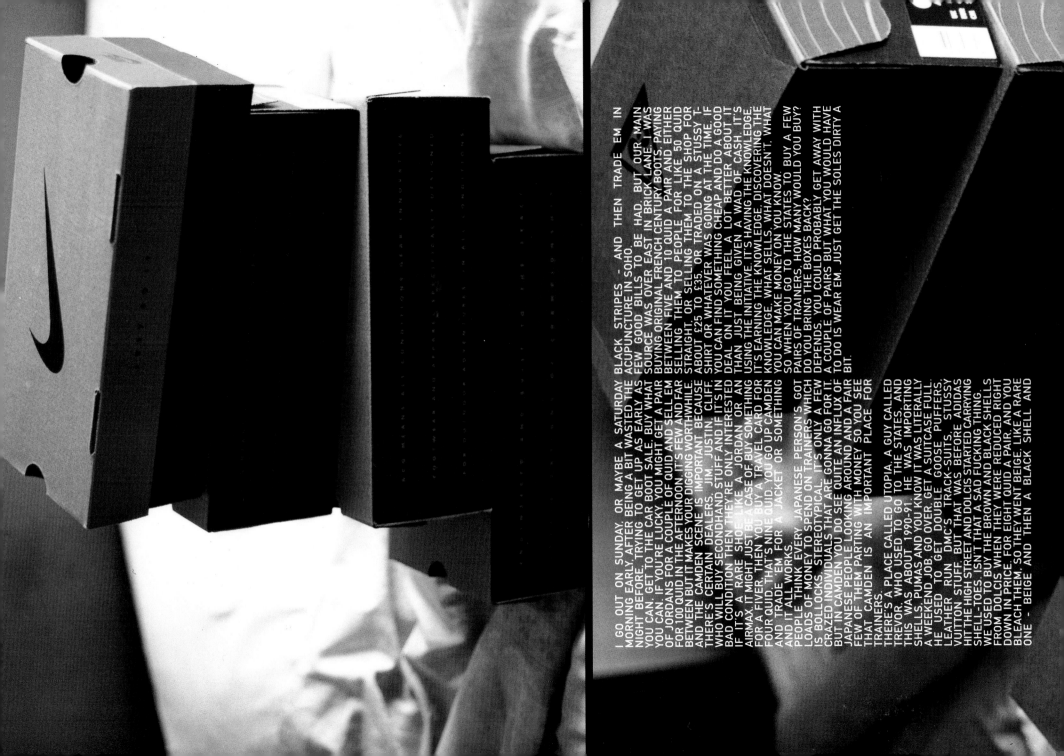

I GO OUT ON SUNDAY. OR MAYBE A SATURDAY MORNING EARLY. AFTER BEING A BIT WASTED THE NIGHT BEFORE. TRYING TO GET UP AS EARLY AS YOU CAN. GET TO THE CAR BOOT SALE. BUY WHAT YOU CAN. IF YOU'RE LUCKY YOU MIGHT GET A PAIR OF JORDANS FOR A COUPLE OF QUID AND SELL EM FOR 100 QUID IN THE AFTERNOON. IT'S FEW AND FAR BETWEEN BUT IT MAKES YOUR DIGGING WORTHWHILE. AND THE CAMDEN SCENE IS IMPORTANT BECAUSE THERE'S CERTAIN DEALERS. JIM. JUSTIN. CLIFF. WHO WILL BUY SECONDHAND STUFF AND IF IT'S IN BAD CONDITION THEN THEY'RE ONLY INTERESTED IF IT'S A RARE SHOE LIKE A JORDAN OR AN AIRMAX. IT MIGHT JUST BE A CASE OF BUY SOMETHING FOR A FIVER THEN YOU BUY A TRAVEL CARD FOR FOUR QUID. THAT'S NINE QUID. YOU GO UP CAMDEN AND TRADE EM FOR A JACKET OR SOMETHING AND IT ALL WORKS.

PEOPLE THINK EVERY JAPANESE PERSON'S GOT LOADS OF MONEY TO SPEND ON TRAINERS WHICH IS BOLLOCKS. STEREOTYPICAL. IT'S ONLY A FEW CRAZED INDIVIDUALS THAT ARE GONNA GO FOR IT. BUT IN CAMDEN YOU DO SEE QUITE AN INFLUX OF JAPANESE PEOPLE LOOKING AROUND AND A FAIR FEW OF THEM PARTING WITH MONEY SO YOU SEE THAT CAMDEN IS AN IMPORTANT PLACE FOR TRAINERS.

THERE'S A PLACE CALLED UTOPIA. A GUY CALLED TREVOR. WHO USED TO GO TO THE STATES. AND THIS WAS ABOUT 1990-91. HE WAS IMPORTING SHELLS. PUMAS AND YOU KNOW IT WAS LITERALLY A WEEKEND JOB. GO OVER GET A SUITCASE FULL. HE USED TO GET DOUBLE GOOSE PUFFERS. LEATHER RUN DMC'S TRACK-SUITS. STUSSY VUITTON STUFF. BUT THAT WAS BEFORE ADIDAS HIT THE HIGH STREET AND DOLCIS STARTED CARRYING SHELL-TOES. ISN'T THAT A SAD FUCKING THING. WE USED TO BUY THE BROWN AND BLACK SHELLS FROM DOLCIS WHEN THEY WERE REDUCED RIGHT DOWN IN PRICE. FOR EIGHT QUID A PAIR. AND YOU BLEACH THEM. SO THEY WENT BEIGE. LIKE A RARE ONE - BEIGE AND THEN A BLACK SHELL AND BLACK STRIPES - AND THEN TRADE EM IN ACUPUNCTURE IN SOHO.

FEW GOOD BILLS TO BE HAD. BUT OUR MAIN SOURCE WAS OVER EAST IN BRICK LANE. I WAS BUYING ORIGINAL FRENCH CENTURY BOOTS. PAYING BETWEEN FIVE AND 10 QUID A PAIR AND EITHER SELLING THEM TO PEOPLE FOR LIKE 50 QUID STRAIGHT. OR SELLING THEM TO THE SHOP FOR ABOUT £25 TO £35. OR TRADED ON A STUSSY T-SHIRT OR WHATEVER WAS GOING AT THE TIME. IF YOU CAN FIND SOMETHING CHEAP AND DO A GOOD DEAL ON IT YOU FEEL A LOT BETTER ABOUT IT THAN JUST BEING GIVEN A WAD OF CASH. IT'S USING THE INITIATIVE. IT'S HAVING THE KNOWLEDGE. IT'S EARNING THE KNOWLEDGE. DISCOVERING THE KNOWLEDGE. WHAT SELLS. WHAT DOESN'T. WHAT YOU CAN MAKE MONEY ON YOU KNOW.

SO WHEN YOU GO TO THE STATES TO BUY A FEW PAIRS OF TRAINERS. HOW MANY WOULD YOU BUY? DO YOU BRING THE BOXES BACK?

DEPENDS. YOU COULD PROBABLY GET AWAY WITH A COUPLE OF PAIRS BUT WHAT YOU WOULD HAVE TO DO IS WEAR EM. JUST GET THE SOLES DIRTY A BIT.

4905 NIKE DUNK LOW BLK/YEL

		EURO	UK	CM
/YEL	USA	42	8	27

Illustration by Oscar Wilson © 1997

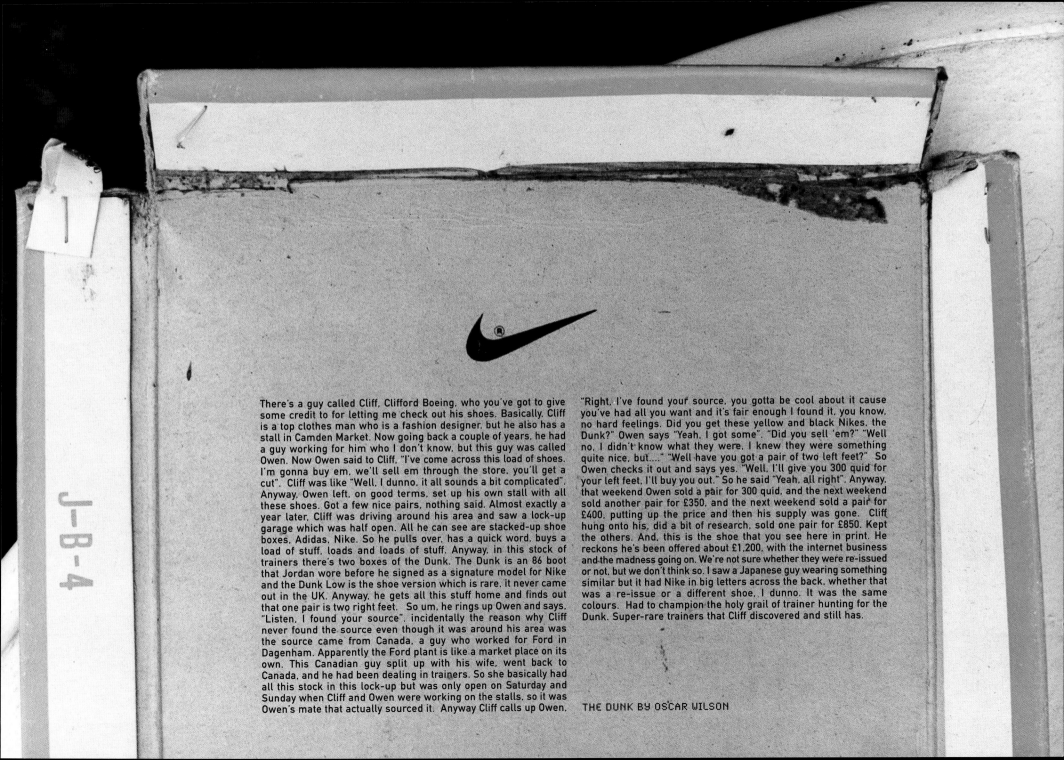

There's a guy called Cliff, Clifford Boeing, who you've got to give some credit to for letting me check out his shoes. Basically, Cliff is a top clothes man who is a fashion designer, but he also has a stall in Camden Market. Now going back a couple of years, he had a guy working for him who I don't know, but this guy was called Owen. Now Owen said to Cliff, "I've come across this load of shoes. I'm gonna buy em, we'll sell em through the store, you'll get a cut". Cliff was like "Well, I dunno, it all sounds a bit complicated". Anyway, Owen left, on good terms, set up his own stall with all these shoes. Got a few nice pairs, nothing said. Almost exactly a year later, Cliff was driving around his area and saw a lock-up garage which was half open. All he can see are stacked-up shoe boxes, Adidas, Nike. So he pulls over, has a quick word, buys a load of stuff, loads and loads of stuff. Anyway, in this stock of trainers there's two boxes of the Dunk. The Dunk is an 86 boot that Jordan wore before he signed as a signature model for Nike and the Dunk Low is the shoe version which is rare, it never came out in the UK. Anyway, he gets all this stuff home and finds out that one pair is two right feet. So um, he rings up Owen and says, "Listen, I found your source". incidentally the reason why Cliff never found the source even though it was around his area was the source came from Canada, a guy who worked for Ford in Dagenham. Apparently the Ford plant is like a market place on its own. This Canadian guy split up with his wife, went back to Canada, and he had been dealing in trainers. So she basically had all this stock in this lock-up but was only open on Saturday and Sunday when Cliff and Owen were working on the stalls, so it was Owen's mate that actually sourced it. Anyway Cliff calls up Owen,

"Right, I've found your source, you gotta be cool about it cause you've had all you want and it's fair enough I found it, you know, no hard feelings. Did you get these yellow and black Nikes, the Dunk?" Owen says "Yeah, I got some". "Did you sell 'em?" "Well no, I didn't know what they were, I knew they were something quite nice, but...." "Well have you got a pair of two left feet?" So Owen checks it out and says yes. "Well, I'll give you 300 quid for your left feet, I'll buy you out." So he said "Yeah, all right". Anyway, that weekend Owen sold a pair for 300 quid, and the next weekend sold another pair for £350, and the next weekend sold a pair for £400, putting up the price and then his supply was gone. Cliff hung onto his, did a bit of research, sold one pair for £850. Kept the others. And, this is the shoe that you see here in print. He reckons he's been offered about £1,200, with the internet business and the madness going on. We're not sure whether they were re-issued or not, but we don't think so. I saw a Japanese guy wearing something similar but it had Nike in big letters across the back, whether that was a re-issue or a different shoe, I dunno. It was the same colours. Had to champion the holy grail of trainer hunting for the Dunk. Super-rare trainers that Cliff discovered and still has.

THE DUNK BY OSCAR WILSON

Adidas Superstar (shell-toe)
Since I saw Run DMC in the "Walk this way" video, that bit where they walk down those stairs on stage and they're all sporting fresh Adidas, no laces, tongues flapping in the breeze, I wanted some of that Old Skool action. They must be the undisputed king of the O-S shoe. I've always kitted shell-toes out with phat laces but never got them as phat as I wanted. I'm always seeing people with some huge lacing thing going on and I'm like, damn how did they get them so wide?
ANDREW DIPROSE

FROM: "THE DUCHESS OF DOMINATION"
FLL3SSC ARTS01.NOVELL.LEEDS.AC.UK
"I think i'll discuss the relative merits of putting padding (folded up socks etc.) inside a shoe to fatten it out (or should that be 'phatten'?)....i ask you, what's worse than a strangled shoe? you could be wearing the rudest nike airs, but if they're tightly laced then you still look like a fool..."

I remember the fat laces...I didn't wear them, except for my Puma Clydes. You have to wear fat laces with Clydes, otherwise you look stupid. Puma Clydes are dance sneakers, almost slippers. I remember those breakers doing the halo until their sneakers flew into the crowd. My friends used to wear fat laces, their sneakers were always very loose, and sometimes they happened to mislay them during concerts...
I've got a pair of Adidas Concord. They're all leather, cream with dark green stripes and sole. But the problem was the laces were too white next to the shoe. So a friend of mine, Vincent Cassel, showed me a trick. I had to dip my laces in a glass of tea for a few seconds and then, miracle, they perfectly matched the colour of the shoe.
MATHIEU KASSOVITZ, PARIS

...back in the days when I was pedalling fat laces that were being sent from New York to Copenhagen to me. I was selling them around for £5 a pop, people I didn't really know would knock on my door to buy these laces.
NIGEL MELVILLE

I ALWAYS THOUGHT, WHAT IS THE POINT IN WEARING LACES, PUMA HAD THAT DISK SYSTEM BUT IT DIDN'T WORK. The thing with spikes is that they've got to have support. What I found with Mizuno spikes is that they're so flimsy, there's no support, and if you're coming off a hurdle you need that. I think laces will always be number one, even though they are a bit annoying, at least they give you the support.
JACKIE AJYEPONG

WHAT ABOUT LACES...?
WHAT ABOUT NO LACES MAN?
FRESH!!! FRESH OUT OF THE BOX YOU KNOW WHAT I'M SAYING....

....but you couldn't run for the bus with no laces! Yeah that's true, but at the end of the day, do you really need laces?
Not really, if you got them a size too small they used to fit like glue. I used to lace them underneath, around the ankle.
And you'd get nuff people in coloured laces that would weave them and all that. What were them fat laces called again?
Block laces or something Yeah And they're tryin to phase that shit out. They're tryin to shut us down with all that Velcro shit.
SHARP, LONDON, 96

"LACES HAVE TO MATCH THE SNEAKER. YOU CAN'T WEAR YELLOW OR BLUE LACES WITH BLACK'N'WHITE SHOES. THEY ALWAYS LACE THEM THE WRONG WAY IN THE SHOP.
THAT REALLY MAKES ME SICK. GOOD LACING CAN REALLY BOOST A SNEAKER, BAD LACING CAN DESTROY THE BEST SNEAKER IN THE WORLD. COLOURED LACES ARE OUT."

FAB 5 FREDDIE   BY PHONE, 97

YOU'RE A BUSY MAN.

Freddie: It's a good topic for a book.

YES, SNEAKERS.

Who's publishing it?

A COMPANY CALLED GOOF GIBBON. OUR BOOK IS A SLIGHT DEPARTURE FROM WHAT THEY NOR-
MALLY DO, BECAUSE IT'S THE CULTURE BOOK. SIZE ISN'T EVERYTHING.

Oh god, that's cool, funny.

WE'RE LOOKING AT SNEAKER CULTURE, AROUND THE WORLD. YOU CAN TELL WHERE SOMEONE
COMES FROM IN LONDON OR ENGLAND, OR ANY CITY AROUND THE WORLD, BY WHAT PAIR OF
SNEAKERS THEY'VE GOT. AND WE CONTACTED YOU BECAUSE YOU'RE A LEGEND. THE FIRST TIME I
HEARD OF YOU WAS ON THAT BLONDIE TRACK "RAPTURE".

(Laughs).

DO YOU REMEMBER YOUR FIRST PAIR OF SNEAKERS?

I don't want to date myself, but I've been around a while. I remember the sneakers I was crazy
for were PF Flyers. Have you ever heard of them?

THERE'S A LOT OF AMERICAN BRANDS WE DON'T KNOW.

Now that I'm thinking about it vividly I know excatly what it was. The advertising. Being a kid and
watching all your favorite TV shows, PF Flyers were advertising that you could run faster and jump
high. In the commercial they'd show kids running down the street, running fast and then a kid would
jump, and they'd freeze the frame and say "run faster, jump higher". And the reason was because PF
Flyers had magic wedges. And the ad would go into an animation, and this magic wedge would come
out of the sneaker. Then it zoomed back into the sneaker and you'd be able to run faster and jump
higher. Of course I begged relentlessly. Typical parents, they would buy the cheapest pair of anything
sneakers they could find. $2.99 rejects, we used to call them, and I wanted to be just like all my little
buddies up and down the block where I grew up in Brooklyn. I eventually got a pair and remember now
that I did something really bad and my mother was really upset with me. I tried to cut out the magic
wedges, cos it was magic. That's my first remembrance of sneakers.

When I became a little more conscience of it all the coolest sneaker was Converse. A canvas sneaker in
white or black high-top, low-top, and it was a sneaker that you had to have. No more, no less, that was
the fucking sneaker. It could be the first sneaker that was endorsed and promoted with the use of the
basketball.

I THINK IT WAS.

The thing I remember was to wear your sneakers fucking until literally the soles where almost gone.
The sneaker would be stinky. The sneakers would smell so fucking bad that parents would make kids
put them out on the fire escape. This thing would literally have fungus growing in it, it was disgusting.
There was an urban New York City ritual, though it wasn't popular in my neighbourhood but we would
do it anyway...once you wore your sneakers until they were unwearable we would tie the laces together
and go out to a lamp-post and throw up the sneakers, 15, 20, 30, however many times it took until the
sneakers landed on top of the pole. It was really big in the Hispanic neighbourhoods, every lamp-post
would have 50 to 100 pairs of sneakers. And they'd been there for years thoughout the seasons, and
they would mould into one ugly clump. Then what happened, which coincided with Hip hop, at the
beginning of the 70s. A new aesthetic creeped in, where being street, and also being fly, was important.
And more and more and more how your sneakers looked spoke about who you were, how you held
yourself and it became the cool thing to do. Converse and Pro-Ked both became cool sneakers,
because they started coming out with different colours. So you would co-ordinate outfits with matching
straight-legged jeans. You'd have red jeans or a red jean jacket or a red Pro-Ked which were cool.
That was the beginning phase of hip hop. And then the suede Pumas came out it went to a whole other
level. Then you had a sneaker which cost a lot of money where it was almost like buying a pair of
shoes, which was something to get to grips with. And you discovered that if you wanted to keep them
like they were fresh out of the box you had to be careful of weather, cos they'd quickly get dogged. In
the early phase of sneakers, when I was a kid, you would wear a pair of new white sneakers, go out of
your house and all your buddies would come and step on them.

ANDY, YOU HIT ON TWO OF MY FAVOURITE

THINGS - THAT AWESOME FRESH EROTIC

SCENT OF NEW SNEAKERS RIGHT OUT OF BOX.

BEFORE I EVEN PUT MY NEWBIES ON.

I SPEND SOME FINE MOMENTS SNIFFING AROUND IN THERE.

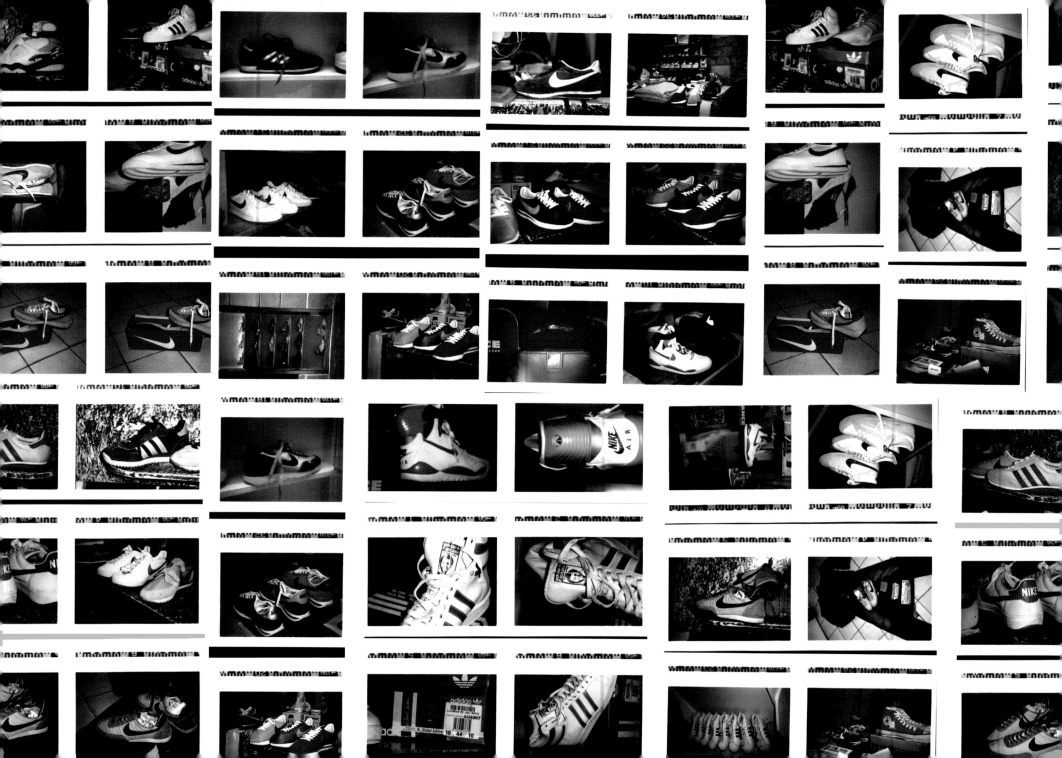

STÉPHANE FROM PREPPY CLOTHING

PARIS, JAN 97

I started to get sneakers since...ohhh...way the fuck back. I still have Nikes LDV, a purple and yellow pair, my pride and joy, Talwin, Pegasus, Elite, a blue and yellow pair from 1982 and Chicago. I usually buy running shoes. I'm bored of basketball shoes. I don't like the look of them. I hate Jordans. They're only good to make money with. I collect Nike rather than any other brand because I can make more money!!!
Hey, check this out!!...Adidas SuperRips, the ancestors of the Superstar. I've got a pair in white leather with black velvet stripes and the SuperRip logo on the back...

Talking about ancestors, I've still got a pair of Robert Haillet from 1965, you know the ones before the Stan Smiths. I love low cut shoes. My clients are Japanese of course, you know, the ones who've just come back from the Gaultier warehouse. They're the only people I can sell my Patricks to!...Then you've got your techno freaks who only want Puma Discs and Nike Air Force 180.
In Paris right now the suburban kids wear Nike Air Max Classics (like London kids wear those ugly white Reebok). But I don't sell them. I still get Nike Wimbledon. So you're really from the hood with those on your feet. I also have a stock of old Adidas

Superstar made in France that I usually sell to rich Japanese or I-want-to-be-rich-but-I-have-to-sell-some-records rappers.
I wear trainers because I've got flat feet and they're good for my feet. I own one pair. Asics is my favourite brand, I own a pair of Asics Bruce Lee. My dream sneaker would be a running shoe, with an old sole, cut at the back, colourful and made with Scotchlite. I never buy trainers related to sports personalities, more likely related to movies or TV..."Starsky and Hutch".
I don't collect boxes but I've got some fucking annoying Japanese clients who hunt for them. But I'm happy when grown-up people

from the suburbs buy my trainers, cause they couldn't buy them when they were kids. They are the ones who brought back the sneaker culture. Never forget.

I'd like to be seen dead in the Nike model 2017.

das

8 (T1)

TRAINER
OPHY
Y
HY

Die Marke mit den

adi

My mum used to call them Bugas, and they used to make your feet stink. but you had to go through different trainers to see what they would do for you.

I remember the days when Adidas Samba were £7.25. and to see those trainers which are now £44...but it's all competition. I am a bit sad that Adidas have not grabbed the market and have let these other pretenders come in. because I am old school...
It's a different era though.
Yeah. don't get me wrong. I don't have no problem with that. But like I say. I'm still old school and still after a pair of Adidas Galaxy. And I'll be an Adidas man through and through.

DO YOU REMEMBER THOSE MITRE MEMPHIS?
Oh yeah them black ones. They didn't look too stylish. you know they were in the league below the Pumas and the Adidas. same thing with Gola.

YOU WEREN'T WEARING GOLA AZTECS...
NO NO NO...It was the Gazelles. the Sambas. the Mambas. you name it. I think I have had just about everything in Adidas.........

YEAH?
Yeah!

DO YOU REMEMBER WHEN VIP CAME OUT, IT WAS ALMOST LIKE A SAMBA....
Yeah. I didn't like them. they was just a gimmick. And when they bought out the Mamba I don't know what the hell they were trying to do there. Maybe they were trying to say that for a pound difference you can have the main one...I suppose it is foolish heart flaunting with whatever is in at the time.

.........in comes Puma freak............

I SEE YOU'RE WEARING PUMA PELE...
I enjoyed Puma because the top stars wore Puma. like Pele.....

YEAH. WHAT YEAR WAS THIS....?
1976.....Pele wore Puma. so did Maradonna.

YOU WERE ONE OF THE FIRST PEOPLE I SAW WEARING PUMA STATES.
I remember that well. and they cost! And I did like Pumas for that reason. All the finest always wore Puma. And the promotional situation they put you in. I felt for it. The bigger the star the greater the reason I wore Puma. Just like encouraging Michael Jordan to wear Nike. Ryan Giggs with Reebok. and Ian Wright with Nike. I went for that. Apparently. the deep down ownership of Troop were Clan members.

REALLY. YOU'RE KIDDING. WHAT. I MEAN. WHY?
I saw it on a documentary on TV. I don't know if it's true. the story could have been warped...and Troops faded. so maybe there is something in it.

イディアしだいで、楽しさが無限に広がる「アディカラー・システム」

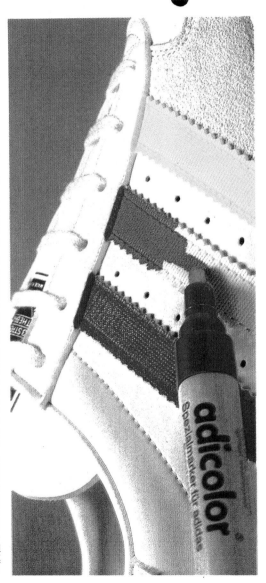

adicolor
Spezialmarker für adidas

●世界初時発売。スポーツシューズに新たなカラーイメージを加えるアディカラー
システム。マーカーを使ってラインを自由にカラーできる画期的なもの。
いまは、世界で1足しかない、あなただけのシューズが創造できる●甲被は、足
どの色も軽やかに人工皮革で汚れても簡単●耐久性の高い自信のソール。

●ライン部分はほぼんどのセールスポイントの多いのがアディ

ラーLIの特徴

ホーム用に楽しむ。 塗ましの言葉を色々に（塗き換えで）

ランジュシューデッカード を演出）

●ラインの色は付属マーカー（別売）で12色までお選びいただけます。

	バイオレット		ブラック	
	ブルー		グリーン	
ホワイト		イエロー		オレンジ
シルバー		ピンク		
ゴールド		レッド		
ブラウン				

●付属マーカーの色は（別売）で12色までお選びいただけます。

cm	22.0	22.5	23.0	23.5	24.0	24.5	25.0	25.5	26.0	26.5	27.0
アディダスサイズ	3½	4	4½	5	5½	6	6½	7	7½	8	8½

MEMORIES OF CHUCK CLONES FROM CHARLIE'S SNEAKER PAGES.

Up until the late 60s, Converse Chuck Taylor All Stars were pretty much the standard sneaker for young boys. There were two basic questions in picking out your sneakers then. 1. High-top or low-top?. 2. Black or white? For those not wanting to spend extra, or, as is still true, whose parents won't spend the extra to get the genuine article, the major department stores and shoe stores produced their Chuck Clones. Around 1970, the genuine article went for around $10, while you could have a pair of Clones for $5. J C Penney produced a sneaker that I always referred to as the J P C Air Cooled. The three large letters on the ankle patch were the unique slanted letters used on Penney store signage in the 50s and 60s. Air Cooled was printed on the ankle patch, and referred to the ventilation eyelets in the arch area. Sears produced a sneaker with the brand name Jeepers. I don't know if Converse actually made Jeepers for Sears, but Jeepers looked more like Chucks than the other Clones. My older brother Bruce had a pair, and I thought they were a dead ringer for Chuck Taylors. Montgomery Ward produced a sneaker called Skips and had been using the brand name back in 1931 and possibly before.

The rubber out-sole around looked nothing like Converse because it wasn't textured. NBAs were another brand of Chuck Clones and a reader of Charlie's Sneaker Pages told me these were sold by the Thom McAn shoe store chain. Mr Sneekers were a brand of sneakers from Mitsubishi and can be seen on Charlie's Sneaker Pages. Converse even had their own Chuck Clone called the Coach. The shoe was very similar to the Converse Chuck Taylor All Star. The major difference was the ankle logo patch which had "COACH" in the center in blue print, with Converse printed on the arc of a circle around the top in red print. The words 'Athletic Shoes' circled around the bottom and the logo patch had four small stars.

SEATTLE ON THE SOLE, FROM FATHER TO SON
BY CYNTHIA ROSE

If any two people embody the "Seattle myth", it's arts entrepreneur Larry Reid and his skateboarder son, Marshall. Pre-grunge Larry ran a series of gallery-venues, which served up a heady concoction of pop, rock and art – and the odd biker convention. The legendary sites had names like Graven Image and Rosco Louie (Northwest slang for "right" and "left"). And they booked entertainment from the likes of Mother Love Bone, Mudhoney and Nirvana. Reid also started Seattle's Centre for Contemporary Art and managed the press for Fantagraphics Comics, publishing heroes like Pete "Hate" Bagge and Daniel "Ghost World" Clowes. Larry Reid's son Marshall grew up skateboarding with members of Pearl Jam and now works part-time in the band's pool hall, The Garage. Marshall was a member of Seattle's seminal Fallout skate team, tied to the record and skate shop of the same name. These days Marshall helps his dad design nightclubs and attends all Seattle Mariners' home games.

HOW DO YOU SAY TRAINERS IN YOUR MOTHER TONGUE?
MR: I call em shoes. That's it, shoes.
LR: Tennis shoes.
MR: In ebonics, it's kicks.

WHAT WERE YOUR FIRST PAIR OF TRAINERS?
MR: TRXX from K-Mart, they got four stripes instead of Adidas three and are made of plastic, hard plastic. They're like $4.99 a pair.
LR: Well I remember my first pair, they were called Red Ball Jets. High-tops.

HOW DO YOU WEAR YOUR LACES?
MR: I prefer untied.
LR: But I'm always coming around, telling him to tie his shoes!

DO YOU KEEP THE BOXES?
MR: All of em, to store the things I carry in my back left pocket when my back left pocket gets too thick with crap.

WHAT'S THE CRAZIEST THING YOU'VE EVER DONE THAT INVOLVED TRAINERS?
MR: Put garden slugs - live ones - in a kid's shoes at YMCA camp. One of a billion...er...pranks.
LR: Bunny-hopped over a set of stairs on my skateboard when I was about 38...I was wearing Vans.

WHAT ABOUT THE BEST SHOES FOR SKATEBOARDING?
MR: The best pair ever were the first run of Air Jordans. The red, black and white ones that are around five hundred bucks now. Because they had ankle support and a gummy sole that stuck to the board, and two layers of leather on the sides of your feet, so you wouldn't wear em out as fast when you did ollies.

EVER TRADE TRAINERS WITH FRIENDS?
MR: I used to, with other skateboarders, because the difference between a goofy-footed skateboarder and a regular-footed skateboarder is your right shoe wears out or your left shoe wears out. So if I found somebody who wore the same size shoes as me, we could trade the one that was wearing out and make the shoes last an extra two weeks or month. It works so long as the shoes are the same brand.

WHO'S YOUR FAVORITE SPORTS PERSONALITY?
LR: Ken Griffey Junior, the world's greatest baseball player, possibly of all time! He was a kid phenomenon. His Dad, Ken Griffey Senior was a member of the Big Red Machine, the Cincinnati Reds, in the late 1970s. They actually played together here, on the Mariners, and hit back-to-back home runs - they used to bat each other in! That was before Dad got into a wreck in his son's Mercedes Benz and moved into coaching. The Mariners drafted Junior right out of high school. His Nike contract started about the first year he came into the league, 1989, and he's always been with Nike.

SO WHEN DID YOU START YOUR SHRINE?
LR: Just this year, in the off-season, because I believed that Junior might need some help in breaking Roger Maris' 1963 record for home runs in a season - that was 61. Junior's now on a pace to hit 65.

SO, MARSHALL, WHO'S YOUR FAVOURITE SPORTS PERSONALITY?
MR: Mark Gonzales, the skateboarder. The Gonz, he's the most insane skateboarder and he wore Nike Air Jordans. He used to paint em different colours. He always got the hooks.
LR: He's also a talented visual artist.
MR: He's a world-famous artist. Like a lot of skaters who remain well-know in their 30s, the Gonz expanded being famous by doing amazing art. And I'd add Jamie Lynn, the pro-snowboarder - those guys go for the biggest shit you could imagine. Jamie is sponsored by Vans, and has done an amazing TV commercial.

WHY IN A TOWN LIKE SEATTLE, WHERE IT RAINS AND IT'S COLD A LOT OF THE TIME, WHY IS THE CONVERSE SNEAKER SO UNIVERSAL? WH IS IT THE GRUNGE SHOE FOR GIRLS AND BOYS OF ALL AGES?
LR: The engine which drove that grunge trend was one of "no economics". By and large these musicians were attempting to survive on meagre incomes and most of the look - like ripped-up jeans - was simply the result of not being able to afford better stuff. Like wearing long underwear under busted jeans was because that kept you warm, but it cost less than buying new jeans. Converse are the cheapest tennis shoes you can buy, hell, they're probably the cheapest shoes you can buy! But I think Joan Jett started that fashion trend here, some people say it was the Ramones in the 1970s, but I think Joan was a little before that.
MR: I do remember I saw her wear red ones. But I also saw pictures of Mark Gonzales wearing Converse. I wore those sneakers way before I skateboarded. I guess the Converse sneaker really is Seattle. If anything is Seattle on a sole, that's it.

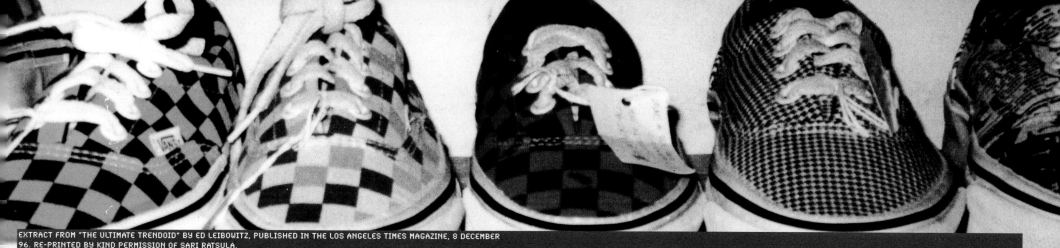

EXTRACT FROM "THE ULTIMATE TRENDOID" BY ED LEIBOWITZ, PUBLISHED IN THE LOS ANGELES TIMES MAGAZINE, 8 DECEMBER 96. RE-PRINTED BY KIND PERMISSION OF SARI RATSULA.

TRICKLING INTO THE COMPANY CONFERENCE ROOM, THE AFTERNOON'S FOCUS GROUP IS GREETED BY ENOUGH IMAGES OF MASS YOUTH CULTURE TO PUT EVEN THE MOST JITTERY TEENAGER AT EASE. STILL HIDDEN BENEATH MISSHAPEN BLACK SHROUDS ARE 200 PROTOTYPES FOR VANS' 1997 FALL WOMEN'S LINE. TWELVE COEDS FROM COSTA MESA AND SANTIAGO HIGH SCHOOLS IN ORANGE COUNTY HAVE BEEN SUMMONED HERE TO HEAP PRAISE, RIDICULE OR INDIFFERENCE UPON THE SNEAKERS. THEIR ENTHUSIASM MAY SIGNAL MASS PRODUCTION; THEIR SCORN, PREMATURE FASHION DEATH. FROM HER PERCH ON A HIGH FORMICA COUNTER, SARI RATSULA HAS WATCHED THE ROOM FILL UP, HER ROYAL-BLUE VANS DANGLING ABOVE THE CARPET. AS IS HER CUSTOM, VANS' 32-YEAR-OLD VICE PRESIDENT OF DESIGN AND PRODUCT DEVELOPMENT IS DRESSED ENTIRELY IN BLACK. SUDDENLY, RATSULA CALLS THE MEETING TO ORDER. BRIMMING WITH SELF-ASSUREDNESS, SHE WOULD SEEM THE VERY APOTHEOSIS OF SOUTHERN CALIFORNIA BEACH CULTURE - AT LEAST UNTIL SHE BEGINS TO SPEAK. "WE BELIEVE THAT YOU ARE THE TYPE OF GIRLS WHO WILL BE WEARING OUR SHOES," RATSULA PROCLAIMS, REVEALING MORE THAN A HINT OF A FINNISH ACCENT. "WE'RE REALLY HAPPY WITH THAT. SO WE WANT YOU TO TAKE A LOOK AT THE PRODUCT BEFORE WE COME OUT WITH IT. AND WE WANT YOUR FEEDBACK. WE DON'T WANT TO HEAR ANY BEAUTIFUL STORIES. WE WANT TO HEAR, 'OH, IT'S HORRIBLE! WE DON'T LIKE IT!' AND BETTER YET, IF YOU CAN TELL US WHY." SHE GESTURES TO THE SIX VANS EMPLOYEES WHO WILL BE JOTTING DOWN OBSERVATIONS IN THEIR NOTEBOOKS. "WE'RE JUST HERE TO TAKE THE INFORMATION. YOU WON'T HURT OUR FEELINGS." TO ANTICIPATE THE VOLATILE DESIRE OF THESE GIRLS, RATSULA HAS FOR THE LAST SIX MONTHS CONFERRED WITH THREE FASHION AND COLOR FORECASTERS, TRAVERSED MUCH OF EUROPE MONITORING TRENDS AND KEPT APPRISED OF THE LATEST RAGES AMONG THE MODISH YOUTH OF TOKYO. AND SHE HAS ALSO DRAWN DEEPLY FROM HER OWN FASHION SENSE. ONCE, HER ECLECTIC TASTES MADE HER A CURIOSITY IN BUSINESS SCHOOL IN HELSINKI. BUT SINCE SHE JOINED THE COMPANY IN 1990, HER SENSIBILITIES HAVE SPAWNED MORE VARIETIES OF VANS THAN WERE CHURNED OUT IN THE 25 YEARS BEFORE HER ARRIVAL. CRAFTING SHOES FOR THE AMERICAN ATHLETIC FOOTWEAR MARKET IS NOW AN $11.4-BILLION INDUSTRY. IT HAS ALSO BECOME A SPECULATIVE - AND SOMEWHAT RIGGED - SCIENCE. IN VANS, RATSULA FOUND A DEFIANT ANOMALY. EVEN THOUGH FOUNDER PAUL

VAN DOREN AND HIS PARTNERS HAD SOLD THE COMPANY BACK IN 1988. ITS "OFF THE WALL" SKATEBOARD SHOE AND CANVAS SLIP-ON HAD SURVIVED A DECADE WITHOUT MUCH ALTERATION; AND THE DESIGN FOR ITS LACE-UP BOAT SHOE WAS AT LEAST TWICE THAT OLD. AS A LINE-BUILDER, RATSULA WAS HAMPERED BY VANS' ENTRENCHED CULTURE. "ALL THE REPS HATED ME." VANS PRODUCTION PROCESS POSED EVEN GREATER OBSTACLES. THE FACTORY WAS ONLY EQUIPPED FOR VULCANIZATION - A 150-YEAR-OLD METHOD IN WHICH THE RUBBER SOLE IS FUSED TO THE UPPER IN A HOT OVEN. UNABLE TO ALTER THE SHAPE OR ERGONOMICS OF THAT SOLE, RATSULA VENTURED AN EXPERIMENT IN EXOTIC UPPERS..."NICE VELVET SNEAKERS", IN GOTHIC PURPLE, NAVY BLUE OR BLACK, WHICH BECAME MASSIVE SELLERS AND THE FOUNDATION OF VANS' WOMEN'S LINE. EACH SEASON, VANS PRODUCES WELL OVER 100 MODELS, IN A PANOPLY OF COLORS AND PATTERNS, SHIPPING OUT NEW PRODUCTS TO RETAILERS EVERY SIX TO EIGHT WEEKS, RANGING FROM $27.99 TO $64.99 A PAIR. BACK IN FEBRUARY OF 1966, WHEN RATSULA WAS BARELY A YEAR OLD, PAUL VAN DOREN LAUNCHED THE VAN DOREN RUBBER COMPANY WITH HIS BOTHER JAMES AND TWO PARTNERS. HIS VAN DOREN SHOE WOULD BE BUILT LIKE A BATTLESHIP - CANVAS THICKER THAN KEDS OR CONVERSE; MASSIVE VULCANIZED GUM RUBBER SOLES THAT REFUSED TO BLOW A HOLE NO MATTER HOW OFTEN THEY WERE DRAGGED ACROSS THE ASPHALT. RELUCTANT TO SEDUCE RETAILERS WITH AN UNKNOWN BRAND OR TO LET A MIDDLE-MAN ERODE HIS MARGINS, HE DECIDED TO SCATTER VAN DOREN RETAIL OUTLETS THROUGHOUT LOS ANGELES, SAN DIEGO AND ORANGE COUNTIES. HIS COMPANY WOULD ALSO BE KNOWN FOR CUSTOMIZED SHOES. "AT ONE POINT IN OUR CAREER, VAN DOREN SAYS, "EVERY SCHOOL IN SOUTHERN CALIFORNIA, THE CHEERLEADERS, THE DRILL TEAM AND THE MARCHING BANDS, WERE WEARING OUR SHOES - BECAUSE THEY COULD GET THE SCHOOL COLORS." SCRAPING TOES AND HEELS ON THE PAVEMENT AS THEY CHARGED DOWN HILLS, SKATEBOARDERS EMERGED AS THE MOST CONSPICUOUS ABUSERS OF VANS DURING THE 1970S AND AN "OFF THE WALL" MODEL WAS GRUDGINGLY CREATED FOR THEIR BENEFIT. BUT NO YOUTH SUBCULTURE COULD PROMOTE VANS AS EXPLOSIVELY AS THE APPEARANCE OF A PAIR OF CHECKERBOARD SLIP-ONS IN 1982'S "FAST TIMES AT RIDGEMONT HIGH". "SEAN PENN HIT HIMSELF ON THE HEAD WITH IT." STEVE VAN DOREN SAYS, "AND NOW EVERYBODY WANTED THESE CHECKERBOARD SHOES." 1995 SIGNALED VANS' TRANSFORMATION FROM A REGIONAL MANUFACTURER TO A GLOBAL EXPORTER OF THE CALIFORNIA ETHOS, AND IN 1996, SALES TO ITS INTERNATIONAL ACCOUNTS REACHED $26.3 MILLION, A 103.5% LEAP FROM THE PREVIOUS FISCAL YEAR...

JO SCOFIELD SIZE 4 | ZANE SIZE 11 | DAVE 7½ | GABBY SIZE 6 | Sas 5½ | SIZE OND | LOU JONES SIZE 6½ | Elliott 9½

Tracey 6 | | ZOE. 7 | Matt BICKLEY 8½ | Ben Size 11 | MAURICE SIZE 11 | ROSS 8½ | Neil 10

Blondeini Size 6 small | THOMAS 8 | Paul 11 | ODIE 10 | Jane - SIZE 39. | PRISCILLA SIZE 5 | LOOLOO 6½ | Chris 8

FABIAN 9 | DEBBIE 6 | JUSTINE si 5. | SIZE 10 | ANDY size 10 | WAX 10 | Dave Sean 9½ | Matt: Size 44

SAM SIZE 4 | MIKE 10·5 | Phil SIZE 13 | GEORGE S: 5 | ED 8" | Janet: SIZE 5 | ZORZA'S 8½ BARCELONA | Helen 6

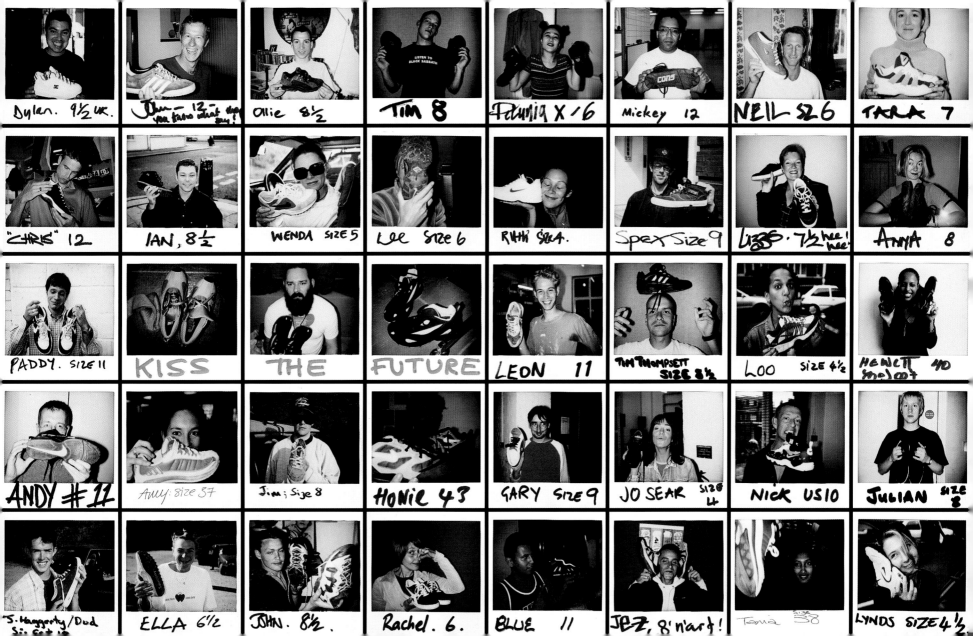

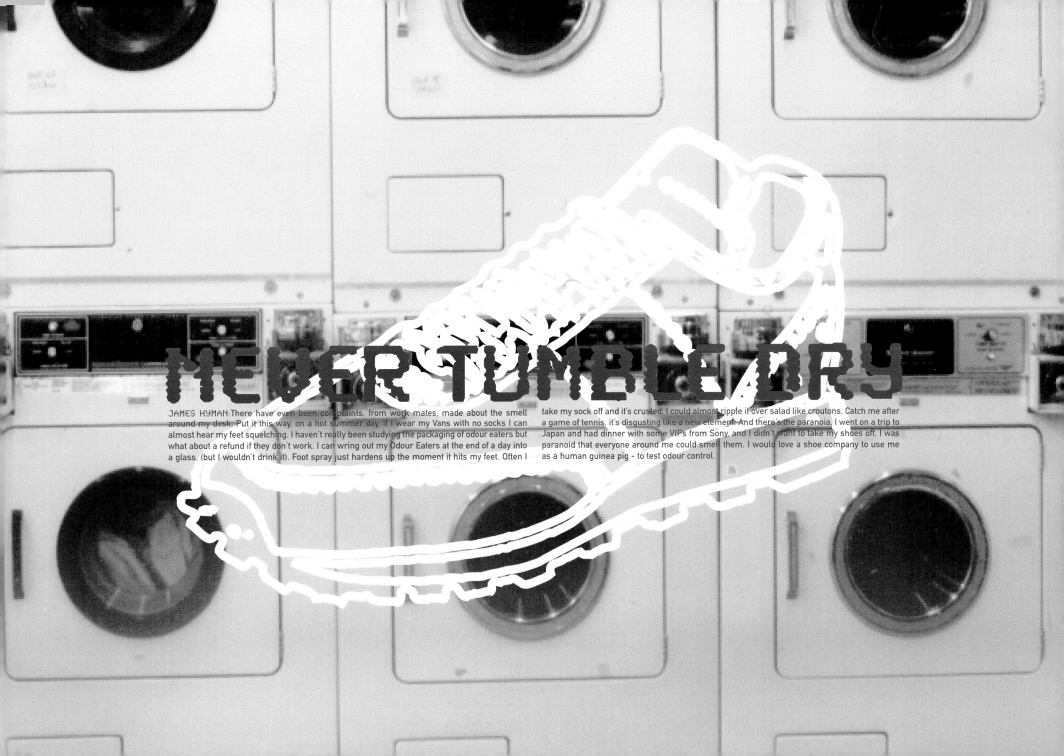

NEVER TUMBLE DRY

JAMES HYMAN: There have even been complaints, from work mates, made about the smell around my desk. Put it this way, on a hot summer day, if I wear my Vans with no socks I can almost hear my feet squelching. I haven't really been studying the packaging of odour eaters but what about a refund if they don't work. I can wring out my Odour Eaters at the end of a day into a glass. (but I wouldn't drink it). Foot spray just hardens up the moment it hits my feet. Often I take my sock off and it's crusted. I could almost ripple it over salad like croutons. Catch me after a game of tennis, it's disgusting like a new element. And there's the paranoia. I went on a trip to Japan and had dinner with some VIPs from Sony, and I didn't want to take my shoes off. I was paranoid that everyone around me could smell them. I would love a shoe company to use me as a human guinea pig - to test odour control.

FASHION, FUNCTION AND FILTH
BY PHILLIP DIPROSE

With a pair of anti-shoes selected for the night out it's looking good for the evening. But a major difficulty can arise from the use of trainers at a club and this stems from the speed with which a new pair can look old. Use, and abuse, in a club can rapidly and premature age your finest footwear.

Imagine the scene: You walk through the door and for a short while feel like the Mack. The semi-lit bar area and cloakroom give just enough light to make all the effort you put into your choice worthwhile. Having decided what would be the most appropriate, and at the same time exclusive footwear selection, this is your time. Looking box-fresh clean and poking artistically from beneath your combat fatigues it all seems fine standing by the bar with the first drink of the night you can happily soak up the atmosphere. Wearing a long-since deleted pair of Adidas lawn-bowls shoes you are content in the fact that you have the most obscure pair of anti-shoes of anyone in your group. The moment is perfect until someone who doesn't care about such 1982 rarities ruins everything. All it takes is one misguided foot on the end of someone else's leg to make the fatal contact. Sliding heavily across the suede toe all that is left to do is mourn. Glancing down, the tell-tale signs are wholly visible. Black marks denote a whole cocktail of horrors. Spilt drink, cigarette ash, dirt and whatever else, all collected on someone's sole, has been given to you. The perpetraitor walks away, ambling off towards the chill-out room unaware of the deep psychological damage s/he has just inflicted.

Stepping back from this horror scenario a number of questions need to be asked to anyone who can empathize with this situation. The first is why is it so important to wear your best trainers to a club? Why is it necessary to try to wear more obscure trainers than your friends? And finally, is it not painfully obvious that in a club-situation this heart-ache is bound to occur? The answer to the lasr question is obviously going to be a resounding yes, but the answers to the other two are less easy to figure out. Maybe it is just a sad trainspotter sense of one-up-manship - the same urge which

drives people to spend endless hours in second-hand record stores looking for the 12" white label remix which was never released on a major. The same obsessives who search for the extra-rare pin-head Star Wars figures and would be at their happiest possessing a signed piece of Baba Fett's script.

Perhaps it is the chance to show your stuff to a select group of like-minded people who in the fractured and splinter 90s make up your very personal gang. Feeling alienated from an increasingly impersonal society there are few chances to impress, or even just to share symbols which our peers relate to. But I have yet to meet a person of the opposite sex who was suitably impressed by my trainer choice, so I'd have to go for the sad trainer-spotter theory.

All of this makes me question the motives of trainer-designers. These days no designer would have their job if they were so naive as to think that trainers are still used for sport. We all know that there are a few social misfits who use them for running, b-ball or whatever else, but they are a tiny minority. For everyone else trainers are an object of character, status and identity.

Bearing in mind that so few trainers get to see a track or pitch you have to think about why they are designed in the way that they are. It doesn't take the world's greatest cynic to see why the trainer companies actually want your box-fresh clean trainers to look old and broken as soon as possible.Because ilt would be more difficult to convince the buying masses to part with cash solely on the basis of a newly discovered piece of air, gel, rubber or plastic that will no doubt revolutionize sport. It is far easier for them to plug products when the trainers on peoples feet are wearing through at the toes and look as if they have been sand-blasted. Is this why they're made of such fragile materials? And this is especially true of the top of the range models. Sold under the guise of perfect performance-enhancing objects they are built with absolutely no compromise to longevity. Designed to be used for sport, trainers provide the following: Wham, Bam, Win the race, Snap. For the non-sporting trainer-spotter this translates into lovely

lightweight, ultra exclusive trainers for the first couple of months and then rapid deterioration. Snapped torsion bars, punctured air, leaking gel...the choice is yours. But after owning such envy-creating objects you can't return to the bottom of the range, hard as nails, cheap trainer. Having worked up from childhood's Green Flash to the beauties paid for by credit card, you are unable to return.

The only way to beat this vicious circle is to keep your slightly soiled trainers in the hope that in a few years time they will become classics. This actually happened, witness the early 90s interest in retro footwear. Market stalls and obscure stores became targets for those in search of the ultimate old skool footwear. Attics and backs of cupboards were plundered for those trainers that hadn't been thrown out since the late 70s.

But having pointed out the ludicrous nature of trainer ownership I have to confess that I covert my neighbours' new trainers. And I will continue the grail-like quest for the perfect pair. They will be found in a small shop on closing down day. They will be cutting edge, but at the same time will only use comfort-enhancing technology. They will be understated and only noticed by those in the know. They will keep their fresh look even when I have bought my next pair. And when I bring them out again in five years time, they will have really come into their own.

JEFF HACKMAN
LEGENDARY SURFER AT HIS BOOK LAUNCH,
"MR SUNSET", WRITTEN BY PHIL JARRAT,
QUICKSILVER STORE, LONDON 97

BACK IN THE 50S AND 60S IN HAWAII, WHAT SORT OF
SNEAKERS WERE YOU WEARING?
In the 50s it was very cool, and there was a brand called Jack
Purcells and they had a little black tip just here...they were blue
and they had a little black stripe right on the toe and you had to
wear them with these Penelton shirts.......
SO HOW LONG HAVE YOU BEEN WEARING VANS THEN, BECAUSE
I SEE YOU WEARING VANS TONIGHT, DID STUART GIVE YOU
THEM?
No I wear Vans because to me, they fit my foot and feel real comfortable
you know, but they um..they don't last that long.
DO YOU SKATEBOARD AT ALL?
A little bit.
VERT OR JUST CARVING ABOUT?
Just on the street. I remember 1965, there was a real trend in
Hawaii for really wild print tennis shoes you know, and they had
flowers like full yellow and red flowers, one shoe would be all red
and the other would be all yellow, and that was the real fad for
about a couple of years.
DO YOU REMEMBER ANY PARTICULAR SURFERS WHO WERE
INTO THAT?
We were all into it, especially Joey Kabel, Jock Sutherland and
Fred Hemmings and all these guys.
I GUESS YOU SPENT MOST OF YOUR TIME IN THE WATER
THOUGH...
Yeah that's right, so we didn't really care too much about shoes!

HARRY HODGE
PRESIDENT OF QUICKSILVER

DOES QUICKSILVER MAKE TRAINERS?
No.
ARE YOU THINKING ABOUT DOING IT?
Not at all, never, as James Bond said,
never say never.

★

R

I would love to smell the Keds of a hot and sweaty FINE looking YOUNG girl. Maybe after a hard day of cheerleader practice

WALL STREET JOURNAL
20/2/97
"REEBOK ISSUES APOLOGY FOR NAMING SHOE INCUBUS"

An "Incubus", according to medieval legend, is a demon that has sex with sleeping women. Reebok stress that those involved in the naming were not aware of its meaning.

THERE'S BEEN A LOT OF DISCUSSION ABOUT MASTURBATING WITH KEDS. AS SOMEONE WITH APPROXIMATELY 35 YEARS EXPERIENCE IN THE FIELD, I FEEL QUALIFIED TO SPEAK ON THE TOPIC. THIS ARTICLE WILL DEAL EXCLUSIVELY WITH USING THE RUBBER SOLES TO MASTURBATE. I WILL LEAVE IT TO ANOTHER AUTHOR TO WRITE ABOUT TECHNIQUES INVOLVING COMING INSIDE THE SNEAKERS. ALL OF THE METHODS DESCRIBED IN THIS ARTICLE WERE DESIGNED FOR GIRLS TO USE ON BOYS; HOWEVER, EXCEPT FOR THE "WALKING THE DOG" METHOD, THEY CAN BE DONE SOLO.

STYLES OF SNEAKERS:
SNEAKERS COME IN MANY STYLES AS EVERYONE IN THIS GROUP KNOWS. ALTHOUGH THIS ARTICLE REFERS TO KEDS, IT INCLUDES ALL KEDS-LIKE SNEAKERS INCLUDING LACE-UP OXFORDS, SLIP ONS, AND T-STRAPS REGARDLESS OF BRAND NAME.

THE SOLE: THE MOST IMPORTANT PART OF THE SOLE IS THE PART THAT CORRESPONDS TO THE BALLS OF THE GIRL'S FEET. THIS PART IS KNOWN AS "THE WORKING RUBBER." ALL MASTURBATION OCCURS HERE SINCE THIS IS THE PART OF THE SNEAKER THAT GETS RUBBED AGAINST THE PENIS (OR VICE-VERSA). EACH MANUFACTURER USES DIFFERENT KINDS OF RUBBER AND MOLDS IT DIFFERENTLY ON THE SOLE. THE MOLDING OF THE RUBBER SOLES IS IMPORTANT TO SNEAKER MASTURBATION. GENERALLY SPEAKING, LESS IS BETTER, BUT COMPLETELY FLAT IS BORING. MOLDING CHANGES AS THE SNEAKERS ARE WORN. EACH WOMAN OR GIRL WALKS DIFFERENTLY, AND SHE WALKS ON DIFFERENT SURFACES.

I DO NOT HAVE A QUANTIFIABLE CLASSIFICATION SCHEME FOR EVALUATING MOLDING SO I WILL DISCUSS A FEW:

CLASSIC KEDS HAVE A CREPE RUBBER SOLE WITH A FAIRLY HIGH RELIEF (THE BUMPS ARE RATHER HIGH). THIS MEANS THAT THEY MUST BE WORN FOR A WHILE TO WEAR DOWN THE ROUGH EDGES.

KINNEY CAPERS ALSO HAVE A CREPE RUBBER SOLE, BUT WITH A LOWER RELIEF. THEY DON'T HAVE TO BE WORN AS LONG TO GET THEM TO A CONDITION SUITABLE FOR MASTURBATION. SOME MANUFACTURER'S RELIEFS ARE SO LOW THAT THEY CAN BE USED RIGHT OUT OF THE BOX. HOWEVER, IT'S ALWAYS WORTH WHILE TO REMOVE THE "GLAZING" THAT SNEAKERS ARE SOMETIMES DELIVERED WITH TO EXPOSE THE FRESH RUBBER. I'VE ALSO SEEN "PEBBLE GRAIN" (VERY SMALL, EVENLY SPACED BUMPS) ABSOLUTELY FLAT AND SMOOTH GROOVED INITIALLED WITH THE MANUFACTURER'S LOGO STAMPED INTO THE SOLE.

SHOE MANUFACTURERS DO NOT MAKE SNEAKERS WITH MASTURBATION IN MIND. THE MOLDING OF THE SOLE IS INTENDED TO PROVIDE TRACTION AS THE GIRL WALKS WHILE WEARING HER SNEAKERS. WHAT WORKS WELL FOR TRACTION, GENERALLY DOESN'T WORK WELL FOR MASTURBATION.

THE BOTTOM LINE IS THAT IF IT'S RELATIVELY FLAT, IT'S PROBABLY USABLE.

THE RUBBER ITSELF HAS INHERENT PROPERTIES. SOME RUBBERS HAVE A NATURAL TEXTURE AND ARE "GUMMY;" THEY TEND TO GRAB AND TICKLE THE PENIS. OTHER RUBBERS ARE SMOOTHER AND HARDER, AND THE PENIS SLIDES OVER THEM MORE EASILY.

ANOTHER FACT TO CONSIDER IS THAT AS RUBBER AGES, THE SURFACE OXIDIZES. IF YOU WANT GOOD PENIS-TO-RUBBER CONTACT, THE SNEAKERS SHOULD BE WORN OCCASIONALLY TO SCUFF OFF THE LAYER OF OXIDATION AND CONSTANTLY EXPOSE FRESH RUBBER.

HOW THE SNEAKER HAS BEEN MOST RECENTLY WORN ALSO AFFECTS THE WAY IT TICKLES THE PENIS. SNEAKERS WORN ON ROUGH CONCRETE PICK UP TEXTURING DIFFERENTLY THAN SNEAKERS WORN ON TILE OR WOOD. ONE OF THE MOST INTERESTING SENSATIONS IS ONE CAUSED BY RUBBER ON THE SOLE OF A SNEAKER WORN BY A GIRL TAKING LONG WALKS ON THE BEACH IN THE SAND. SNEAKERS ALSO FEEL DIFFERENT WHEN THEY FIRST COME OUT OF THE WASH.

LUBRICATION:
SUSTAINED RUBBER-TO-PENIS CONTACT CAN BE ABRASIVE ESPECIALLY IF USING A SNEAKER WITH A HIGHLY-RELIEFED, GUMMY RUBBER SOLE. YOU WILL NEED MORE LUBRICATION WITH NEWER, LESS-WORN SNEAKERS THAN WITH ONES WHERE THE RELIEF IS WORN DOWN.

TECHNIQUE ALSO HAS A BEARING ON THE PENIS-TO-RUBBER CONTACT. SOME METHODS PUT MORE PRESSURE ON THE PENIS, AND OTHERS MAKE A MORE INTENSE CONTACT. IN OTHER WORDS, SOME METHODS ARE MORE TOLERANT OF RELIEF THAN OTHERS. A SUBJECTIVE "TOLERANCE LEVEL" IS GIVEN WITH THE DESCRIPTION OF EACH METHOD.

Answer machine;

MY NAME IS BERT MOSHIER AND I'M UNABLE TO ANSWER THE PHONE RIGHT NOW...BEEB.

IS IT A GOOD TIME FOR YOU? FIRST THINGS FIRST, WHERE DO SNEAKERS FIT IN YOUR LIFE?

Well sneakers are sneakers. I hate to say it in some ways, but they're a major aspect of my life, both from a G-rated and a non-G-rated perspective.

WHAT'S G-RATED FOR THOSE WHO DON'T KNOW.

Non-sexual. For me sneakers are as much a utility as they are fashion...If I have to choose between utility and fashion I usually choose fashion over utility.

OK, SO HOW MANY SNEAKERS HAVE YOU GOT?

Uhhh 450. Probably given away almost 200 over the years.

WHAT'S THE CONNECTION WITH SNEAKERS AND YOUR WEB SITE?

My website...you have the sexual and the non-sexual aspects of sneakers and with the non-sexual I've got photographs and news of what's coming out. You can get notification by e-mail and go find what's brand new. That's one advantage. The other thing is that I'm trying to get a sneaker FAQ. I'm finding it difficult to get help from sneaker manufacturers, they're always asking, what's in it for you? They're very suspicious of somebody trying to do them a favor and basically I'm a third party. Right now Converse love the idea and say, we'll send the questions to our corporate lawyers and our factory people. And I've been waiting two months to hear back, and if every set of questions I send in takes this long it's not going to work, right?

MOVING ON, SO WHAT ABOUT THE OTHER SIDE OF YOUR WEBSITE...

Oh, you mean the sexual aspect? Well that started many years ago for me. When they're real young guys sometimes come without even trying and that's what happened to me. I was wearing a pair of sneakers, playing on the chin-up bar and all of a sudden I came. My toes were digging into the sneakers, and I don't wear socks, it was really cool and, for me I was hooked on sneakers from that point on. Some guys are very much into jerking off with their sneakers, or using the sneakers in place of sexual anatomy, so therefore they're fucking.

For me it's not that. I find getting my feet sweaty after a long day to be very exciting, and it's sort of sweaty and grimy. And it feels really cool recognising that I might not be alone. When I first started my own internet domain, which would have been many, many years ago, before the web was even thought of, I decided to start a mailing list. The first thing I started talking about was dark clothing and dark sneakers, and the internet Gods said, we don't think there's enough of an interest. So I started the mailing list and the topic turned to sex. Then I went back to the internet Gods and said, hey I've got 50 to 100 people all talking about sneakers, and they said, well there must be enough of an interest. I always tried to keep it G-rated by running the non-G-rated or sexual aspect for those who are 18 and above. We're pan-sexual basically, we support everybody regardless of their sexual orientation, and it's password protected. You don't get the password unless you join the group and you're over 18.

PEOPLE HAVE FETISHES FOR BOOTS OR STILETTOS, SO WHY NOT SNEAKERS? IT SEEMS LIKE SUCH A NATURAL THING. I THINK MORE AND MORE PEOPLE WILL BECOME SNEAKER FETISHISTS AND IT WOULD-

N'T SURPRISE ME IF YOUR NUMBERS GREW TEN-FOLD WHEN THIS BOOK COMES OUT.

I've helped a lot of people. When they join the list they say, I thought I was the only one in the world.

HOW DO YOU FEEL ABOUT THE POSSIBILITY THAT ONE DAY YOU MIGHT HAVE TO STOP YOUR WEBSITE BECAUSE OF CENSORSHIP AND THE MORAL MAJORITY?

I think that's a violation of our US Constitution. As a parent I'm well aware of wanting to protect my child from discussing things over the internet that she doesn't need to know about until she is old enough to handle it. At the same time, I want to be able to read what is mature and I want her, when she reaches the age of maturity, also to be able to read mature stuff. It's her right as far as I'm concerned.

WOULD YOU EVER CENSOR ANY OF THE MATERIAL THAT'S SENT TO YOU?

Absolutelypositivelybeyondashadowofadoubt. I do not allow any kiddie porn. There may be some there but it's purely by accident. If I ever sense that there's any kiddie porn, it's gone. I'm sorry but that's gone. Or bestiality, there's no place for that.

TWO CONSENTING ADULTS?

In other words do I allow gay and lesbian stuff out there? Yes, or heterosexual, and it can be three guys and four girls, basically an orgy and I have no problems with that. I've got penetration out there.

CONSUMER AWARENESS

HOW MUCH CONSUMER AWARENESS IS THERE ABOUT NIKE'S MANUFACTURING POLICY, AND DOES IT EFFECT OUR DESIRE TO PURCHASE TRAINERS? WITH A PURCHASE OF A NEW PAIR OF TRAINERS, WHAT IS RUNNING THROUGH THE MIND OF THE CONSUMER? AS ONE TAKES THE LID OFF THE CARDBOARD BOX, REVEALING A PRISTINE PAIR OF TRAINERS, ARE THERE ANY THOUGHTS OF WHO HAS MADE THEM? IN INTERVIEWS CONDUCTED WITH FELLOW CONSUMERS OF TRAINERS, NOT ONE OF MY TEN INTERVIEWEES CONSIDERED THIS AT THE TIME OF PURCHASE. ALTHOUGH THREE PEOPLE WERE AWARE THAT TRAINERS WERE MADE IN DEVELOPING COUNTRIES, THEY DIDN'T CONSIDER THE WORKERS. ONE PERSON HAD PREVIOUSLY SERIOUSLY CONSIDERED WHERE CONSUMER PRODUCTS CAME FROM, BUT CONCLUDED, "EXPLOITATION HAPPENS WITH EVERYTHING. JEANS, TRAINERS AND COMPUTERS. THAT IS THE NATURE OF CAPITALISM." IN RELATING THE CONSUMPTION OF TRAINERS TO MARX'S VIEWS ON THE COMMODITY AND CAPITALISM. IT'S EVIDENT THAT HIS THEORIES ARE STILL APPLICABLE TO THE CONSUMER MARKET TODAY. "COMMODITY FETISHISM" IS WHEN THERE IS NO AWARENESS OF THE SOCIAL LABOUR OF AN OBJECT'S PRODUCTION. AS A PAIR OF TRAINER APPEARS UNTARNISHED, "... BUTTERFLY LIKE FROM THE GRUBBY CHRYSALIS OF PRODUCTION". IN A CONTAINED PACKAGE, IT SPEAKS NOTHING OF THE EXPLOITATION OF LABOUR WHICH HAS PRODUCED THESE SHOES. (LEE 1993.15)...AS MARX STATES IN "CAPITAL", THERE IS A DEFINITE SOCIAL RELATION BETWEEN MEN, THAT ASSUMES, IN THEIR EYES THE FANTASTIC FORM OF A RELATION BETWEEN THINGS...THIS I CALL THE FETISHISM WHICH ATTRACTS ITSELF TO THE PRODUCTS OF LABOUR AS SOON AS THEY ARE PRODUCED AS COMMODITIES. (1920.43) COMMODITY FETISHISM IS THEREFORE INSEPARABLE FROM THE PRODUCTION OF COMMODITIES. LABOUR WITHIN THE CAPITALIST TRAINER MARKET HAS LITTLE, IF ANY, POWERS, BUT WHAT OF FROM THE SPHERE OF PRODUCTION AND THE WORKER. THERE IS LITTLE TO ASSOCIATE THE ACT OF PURCHASING A PAIR OF TRAINERS FROM A RETAILER IN LONDON, FOR EXAMPLE, WITH THE CONDITIONS OF A WORKER IN INDONESIA. LABOUR WITHIN THE CAPITALIST TRAINER MARKET HAS LITTLE, IF ANY, POWERS, BUT WHAT OF THE POWERS, NEEDS AND DESIRES OF THE CONSUMER? IN THE RESPONSE OF THE INTERVIEWEE WHO SUGGESTED ONE CANNOT GET AWAY FROM EXPLOITATION, SURELY THIS EXTENDS AND FURTHER REITERATES THE LEVEL AND INTENSITY OF COMMODITY FETISHISM OCCURRING HERE.

"TRAINING" THE CONSUMER

CONTINUING WITH MARXIST THEORY AND COMMODITY FETISHISM, HOW DOES IT ACCOUNT FOR THE DESIRE OF THE CONSUMER TO BUY COMMODITIES? IN CONSIDERING THE AMOUNT CONSUMERS SPEND ON TRAINERS, IN RELATION TO OTHER GOODS, THE DESIRE TO PURCHASE TRAINERS APPEARS VERY STRONG. THE CONCEPTS OF "USE AND EXCHANGE VALUE" AND MARCUSE'S "FALSE NEEDS" ARE USEFUL IN RELATION TO CONSUMER DESIRES. (STRINATI 1995.60) THE DOMINATION OF EXCHANGE-VALUE OVER USE-VALUE IS A KEY CHARACTERISTIC OF CAPITALISM. (LEE 1993.7-8) EXCHANGE-VALUE IS EXPLAINED THROUGH THE LABOUR THEORY OF VALUE. AS ALL COMMODITIES ARE PRODUCED BY LABOUR. IT IS THE LABOUR TIME EXPENDED IN THEIR PRODUCTION THAT DETERMINES EXCHANGE-VALUE. (ABERCROMBIE 1984.135) EXCHANGE-VALUE REFERS TO THE MONEY GOODS CAN COMMAND IN THE MARKET, THE PRICE THEY CAN BE BOUGHT AND SOLD FOR. WHILE USE-VALUE REFERS TO THE USEFULNESS OF THE GOODS FOR THE CONSUMER, ITS PRACTICAL VALUE OR ITS UTILITY AS A COMMODITY. (STRINATI 1995.57)... ADVERTISING IS CREDITED WITH PROVIDING COMMODITIES WITH A PARTICULAR CONTENT OF USE-VALUE, AND IS OFTEN CRITICISED FOR INSTALLING "FALSE NEEDS" IN THE CONSUMER. (STRINATI 1995.60) "FALSE NEEDS" ARE DEFINED IN RELATION TO TRUE NEEDS WHICH CANNOT BE "... REALISED IN MODERN CAPITALISM BECAUSE THE FALSE NEEDS. WHICH THIS SYSTEM HAS TO FOSTER IN ORDER TO SURVIVE COME TO BE SUPERIMPOSED OR LAID OVER THEM". (IBID) IN APPLYING THIS TO TRAINERS. IN THIS CONTEXT. FALSE NEEDS ARE ACHIEVED THROUGH THE FETISHISATION OF THE DESIRED BODY. AND THE DESIRE TO BUY A BRAND FOR THE STATUS WITH WHICH IT HOLDS WITHIN A SUBCULTURE. FOR AS DAN FIELD STATES, "WEARING A PAIR OF ADIDAS...BECAME A STATUS SYMBOL - TELLING EVERYONE THAT YOU COULD AFFORD THE BEST WITHOUT SAYING A WORD" (1995.101) IN A SERIES OF RECENT ADVERTS FOR NIKE TRAINERS, THE USE VALUE OF THE TRAINERS IS NOT IMPLIED. THESE ADVERTS RELISH IN THE TRAINER AS AN OBJECT OF AESTHETIC FETISHISM... THE ADVERT DEPENDS ON THE AUDIENCE'S PRIOR KNOWLEDGE OF NIKE THROUGH THE SYMBOL OF THE "SWOOSH", THE TRAINER IS DISPLAYED PURELY AS AN OBJECT TO BE DESIRED.

...THE REAL NEEDS AND USES OF THE CONSUMER ARE FURTHER COMPLICATED THROUGH THE HISTORY OF ASSOCIATED IMAGES WHICH THE CONSUMER LINKS WITH THE COMMODITY. TONY MARCUS WRITES IN "I-D": IF YOU WEAR ADIDAS, IS THE BUZZ THE REALITY OF THE SHOES AT THE BOTTOM OF YOUR LEGS OR THEIR ECHOES OF B BOY STYLE. BRITPOP. JESSE OWENS OR THE QUANTUM LEAP INTO TECHNO-FUTURISM SUGGESTED BY THE CURRENT SCI-FI DESIGN? (1997.118)AS THIS QUOTE SUGGESTS THERE ARE MULTIPLE ASSOCIATIONS AND CONTEXTUALISATIONS WHICH CAN BE READ INTO A PAIR OF TRAINERS.

...CELEBRITY ENDORSEMENT PURVEYS THE "SPIRIT" AND ATTITUDE WHICH BRANDS LIKE NIKE WISH TO PROMOTE. SPORTS STARS SUCH AS JOHN MCENROE AND ERIC CANTONA ARE CHARACTERS KNOWN FOR THEIR OUTS POKENNESS AND ANTI-ESTABLISHMENT ATTITUDES, THE APPEAL...SEEMS TO BE ABOUT BREAKING WITH THE IDEOLOGICAL AND DOMINANT VALUES IN SOCIETY. SO, ARE CONSUMERS MANIPULATED TO PURCHASE THROUGH THESE MULTIPLE ASSOCIATIONS, AND DOES THIS MASK THE EXPLOITATION WHICH IS ACTUALLY OCCURRING IN THEIR CONSUMER CHOICE?

JUST BUY IT: DESIRING AND CONSUMING TRAINERS
EXTRACTS FROM A BA DISSERTATION SUBMITTED BY
NAOMI BERESFORD-WEBB AT UNIVERSITY OF SUSSEX. SUMMER 97

1. THE US ANNUAL SPEND ON RUNNING SHOES IS $7BN (£4.3BN), WHICH IS EQUIVALENT TO THE COST OF RELIEVING THE THIRD WORLD'S DEBT BURDEN. ("THE INDEPENDENT" 1997)

"A LOT OF PARENTS ARE UNDER A LOT OF PRESSURE TO BUY EXPENSIVE TRAINERS. ESPECIALLY WITH LITTLE GIRLS, BECAUSE THE SPICE GIRLS ARE WEARING AIR MAX. ALL THESE LITTLE GIRLS WON'T HAVE ANYTHING LESS THAN AIR MAX, WHICH IS ABOUT £65. WHEREAS ONCE YOU COULD GET A TRAINER FOR £35 NOW YOU HAVE TO SPEND OUT...NOW EVERYBODY AT SCHOOL HAS GOT TO HAVE AIR MAX." (NEVILLE AYRE, FATHER OF GIRLS AGED 7 AND 10, LONDON, FEBRUARY 98)

FANTASY TRAINERS DRAWN IN FRIDAY AFTERNOON DOUBLE ART

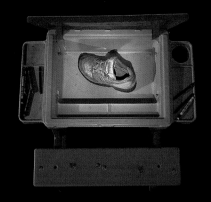

SUBJECT: SNEAKERS THE BOOK
DATE: FRI 9 MAY 97 22.33
FROM: STAFF MARTINEZGALLERY.COM

It's like going through the different grades in school..different sneakers represented points in my life.

As a young kid growing up in Brooklyn, my first pair of sneakers were traditional Keds, which after a while became played out and eventually were considered a sissy sneaker - kids would goof on you calling the sneakers in Spanish, "Pro Hojos". I graduated to Pro-Keds in my adolescent years, when I was really into tagging, and as I matured, I started wearing Converse's Chuck Taylors, when I could afford to.

As I grew older and my art and styles started changing, I painted my sneakers and used a more stylized sneaker. That's when I wore the Pumas and the Adidas, as hip hop became integrated into the urban New York scene. It was all a part of the street vibe and wildstyle.

As I've matured and analysed all the newer sneakers the one that, I believe, prevails overall is the energetic Nike. And as far as creative new styles go I find the Fila sneaker to be one of the best. So, both of them represent me and all I represent...the fresh and new urban image.

When I was at school...I had this exercise book, and me and my friend used to spend our time you know writing in all the labels.

FLINT 707

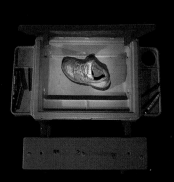

HE WEARS THOSE CUTTIES IN BE

RIPPED FROM SHEETS AND LACE

S SMILED MY BODY IS

Hello officer, I was just breaking in my trainers

Why Nike's the runaway leader among burglars

CHRISTIAN SCIENCE MONITOR
DATE: OCTOBER 9 96
ARTICLE: JUST DON'T DO IT: JAPANESE
CRAVE A SHOE.

Nike Air Max sneakers are a coveted commodity in Japan, one salesman sold a used pair for $900. The underside of the trend causes the street crime that has made brand name clothing controversial in the US. Thieves have
burgled two high school athletic clubs and police have
arrested traders for importing fake Air Max or defrauding customers trying to buy real ones.

NEW YORK TIMES
ARTICLE:
5 ARE KILLED BY GUNMAN IN BRONX
SHOE STORE
20 DECEMBER 95

"Mr Vernon had been in the store before apparently
casing it, on the pretence of looking for a particular type of sneaker.
Chief K. said he asked for a particular sneaker and when they said they didn't have it,
he just began shooting...
A police investigator said before opening fire the man said 'you should have given me those sneakers'."

FROM: IAN C ROGERS
IROGERS BIGGUN.COM
MON 16 DEC 96 10:03:52 -
0800

That's amazing....Sneaker fetish? I was at the Pasadena swap-meet a
couple of weekends ago and found an amazing pair of old green Nikes.
I asked the guy how much they were and he said "one fifty". I said
"OK, I'll take em", handed him two dollars and said, "keep the change".
He informed me that the shoes were one hundred and fifty dollars, not
one dollar and fifty cents which is the point in the story where I fall on
the ground and hold my stomach laughing and laughing and laughing
at the fat old bastard who wants to sell me a pair of dirty old Nikes for
one hundred and fifty fucking dollars. I thought about trying to make a
deal with him, but stood up and beat his old ass with my fists and stole
them from him instead. They look fucking amazing on me.

FIT TO KILL

My first "proper" trainers
...one's that I chose myself, were a pair of royal blue Hi-Tech Runaways. They were wicked. At the time they meant so much, back then £26 seemed like loads for a pair of trainers, well it did for my parents. I fitted some red and white "electro" laces, real fat and told my friends that was the hip hop way, it was a proud thing. I remember running up and down my road just to feel the new springy soles. A couple of days later I was playing with my mates out on the street, resplendent in my new Hi-Techs, things were cool 'till I got hit on the head with a stone someone threw in the air. Things got all messed up. I couldn't really see as there was blood all down my face, in my eyes and on my new shoes. I was OK but that was it for the shoes, I scrubbed them up but there were these blood stains on the toes and front part I never got rid of them and they were never the same again.

Adidas Stan Smith
I've had a pair of Stan Smiths for about six months and I haven't worn them out of the house yet, I'm waiting for the perfect summer day, winter is a bad time for sneakers and I'm going to keep these kicks in top nick. I've laced them up though with a wicked pair of red and white check phats but I'm kinda thinking that I'm going to need another pair of insoles to get a decent width on those laces, damn, I think my feet are too narrow. I just love that purist look, you know, stripped down, this is a classic shoe, minimalist. The way they're even stripped of the stripes, just punched holes, wicked.

Reebok Fury Pump
Now this is THE technology shoe, check out the detail; Insta-Pump, Hexa-Lite, Scotchlite...top stuff! They've got that look, that wicked hi-tech styling, they're shoes that draw stares. People are always trying to figure out the pump, you can't help but dig that a bit. I've had them for a while now and they're looking kinda broke, which is a pity as they're deleted now. I was conscious of the whole inflatable thing when I bought them, like...they're going to get ripped or punctured or something. I got them so they still fitted me deflated! I saw some bloke wearing them the other day and his big toe had worn a hole through at the front, please...have some respect for yourself, that's sorry, they're nice shoes but is it worth looking like a tramp to show off those kicks!

Nike Air Hurrache
The styling is spot on, a real techno look years ahead their time. They've got all the detailing you need. Ni Air, wicked neoprene "sock" rubber heel support, th laces are redundant. I remember Nike doing them i some wack colours, black and white were the only w to sport them. I remember the look of joy on my brothe face as he opened the box and pulled back the tissue paper to reveal those Huraches, box fresh and bright white. I bought them for my brother, they're the best trainers I never had.

'CORTEZ THE KILLER'

HE CAME DANCING ACROSS THE WATER
WITH HIS GALLEONS AND GUNS
LOOKING FOR THE NEW WORLD
IN THAT PALACE IN THE SUN

ON THE SHORE LAY MONTEZUMA
WITH HIS COCA LEAVES AND PEARLS
IN HIS HAIR HE OFTEN WANDERED
WITH THE SECRETS OF THE WORLDS

AND HIS SUBJECTS GATHERED 'ROUND HIM
LIKE THE LEAVES AROUND A TREE
IN THEIR CLOTHES OF MANY COLORS
FOR THE ANGRY GODS TO SEE

AND THE WOMEN ALL WERE BEAUTIFUL
AND THE MEN STOOD STRAIGHT AND STRONG
THEY OFFERED LIFE IN SACRIFICE
SO THAT OTHERS COULD GO ON

HATE WAS JUST A LEGEND
AND WAR WAS NEVER KNOWN
THE PEOPLE WORKED TOGETHER
AND THEY LIFTED MANY STONES

THEY CARRIED THEM TO THE FLATLANDS
AND THEY DIED ALONG THE WAY
BUT THEY BUILT UP WITH THEIR BARE HANDS
WHAT WE STILL CAN'T DO TODAY

AND I KNOW SHE'S LIVING THERE
AND SHE LOVES ME TO THIS DAY
I STILL CAN'T REMEMBER WHEN
OR HOW I LOST MY WAY

HE CAME DANCING ACROSS THE WATER
CORTEZ, CORTEZ
WHAT A KILLER

THE ROOTS

Where are we from?.....from the Illadelph side. Philadelphia. USA

SO WHAT WERE YOU WEARING BACK IN PHILADELPHIA BACK IN THE DAY?

I mean I was wearing things from CONVERSE to PUMAS to ADIDAS to you know what I mean. NIKES all a dat. and even when times was hard I even wore what we call back in the states. BOBOs...mainly PUMAS and ADIDAS and NIKES though. and that was like the hottest joints. that you know what I mean I wanted to rock at that time.

Like everybody was rockin the shell-tops the hottest thing at the time... "MY ADIDAS"...especially if you was a hip hop lover...and everybody wanted to be like Ra DMC at that time and and so ADIDAS was the shit.

Now I'm rockin whatever I think is different you know what I'm sayin. and since my man Alan Averson. the basketball player for the Philadelphia I'm definitely gonna be sporting them things to support my man. But I rock whatever and just imagine my clothes for the day. We've been given things by ADIDAS and NIKE but not as far as a heavy endorsement or heavy money.

ON ANOTHER TIP. IN LA THE COLOUR OF YOUR SNEAKERS HAD IMPLICATIONS WITH THE GANG THING....

No there is no gang thing in New York or on the East coast. everybody is just out for self. and as far as you wearing a colour. from where I'm from you can wear any colour you want.

RIGHT. BUT DJ MUGGS FROM CYPRESS HILL SAID THAT A LOT OF THE STICK UP KIDS WORE BLUE NIKE CORTEZ OR......

Na. that ain't true. I mean stick up kids might wear black. black is the mediating line between gangs. You can walk anywhere in LA wearing black and you won't be recognised as a gangster. Now where I'm from you might wear black at night time cause you can't be seen. you know what I'm sayin and that's how you go about your stick up missions.......

ANNIE. AGE 74. CAMDEN TOWN. LONDON

NIKE CORTEZ. DICKIES. AND BEN DAVIS. HELL YEAH NIGGA. THIS IS EASTSIDE NIGGAZ SOUTH COMPTON. <187 1964IMPALA>

>>Nike cortez. they're comfortable. and cheap too. all the gangsters wear Cortez so if you have them and a bald head and baggy trousers all the cops are gonna think you are a gang member. no matter what. i still wear them though cause they are firmE shoes. they've been around for a long time. HUMPTY LA '97. via sneaker-nation.com

it Don't Matter   Whut Cha Wearing Cuz...YOU UGLY   <tru@nuff.com>

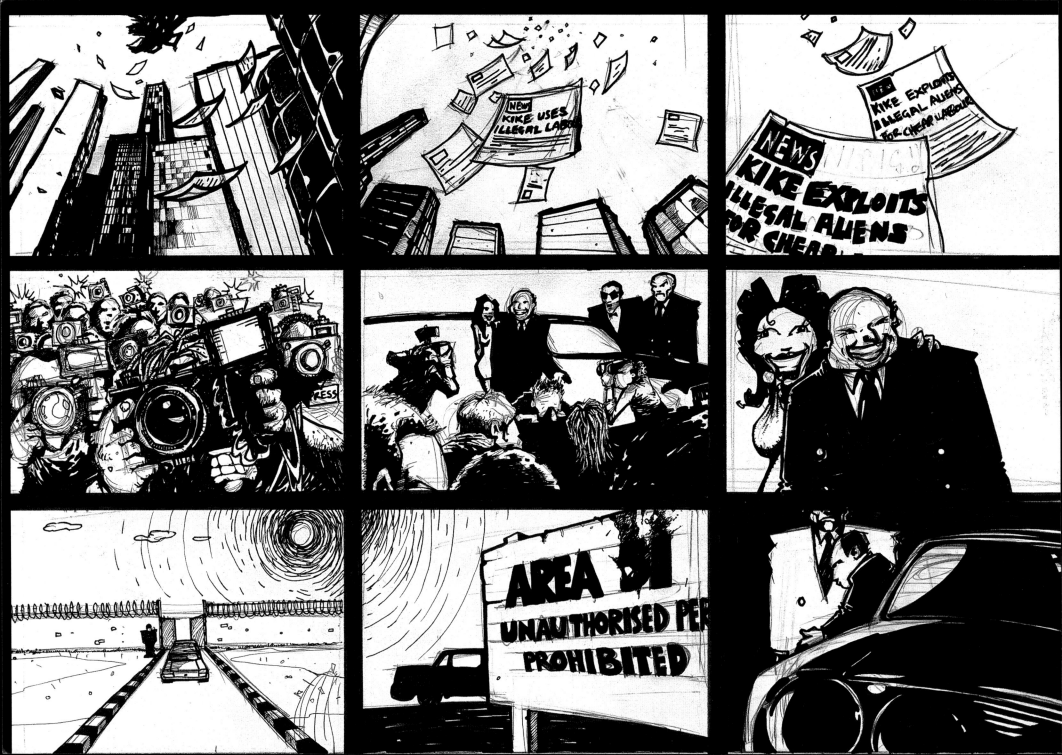

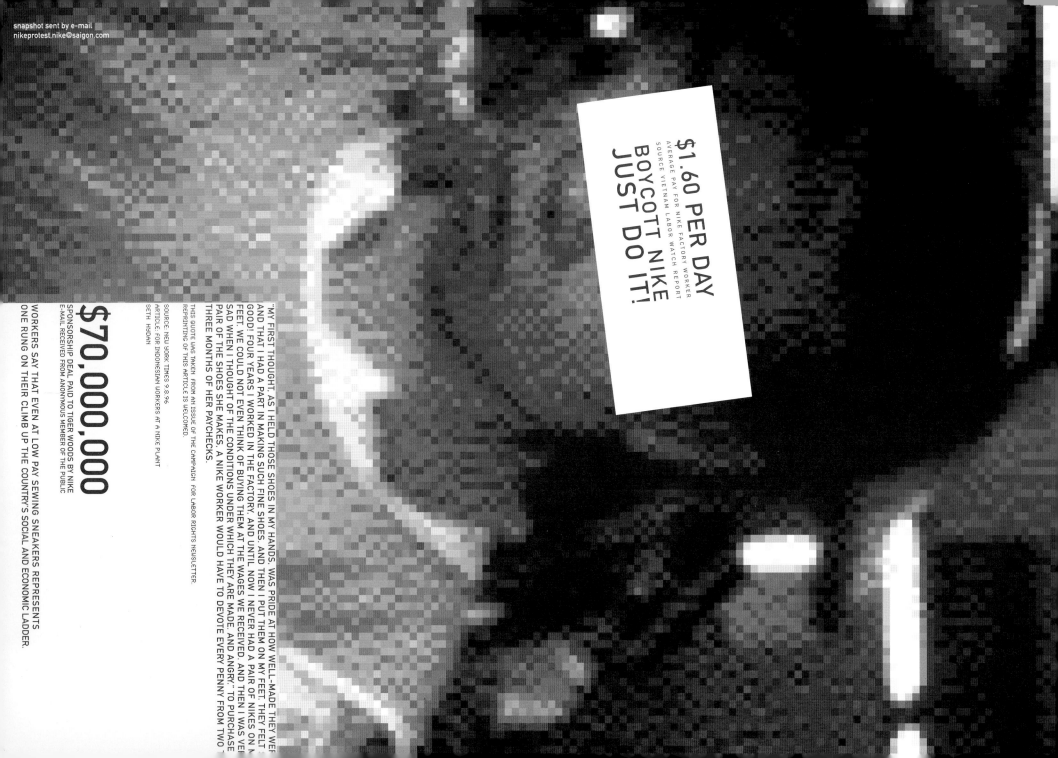

$1.60 PER DAY
AVERAGE PAY FOR NIKE FACTORY WORKER
SOURCE VIETNAM LABOR WATCH REPORT

BOYCOTT NIKE
JUST DO IT!

$70,000,000

SPONSORSHIP DEAL PAID TO TIGER WOODS BY NIKE
E-MAIL RECEIVED FROM ANONYMOUS MEMBER OF THE PUBLIC

WORKERS SAY THAT EVEN AT LOW PAY SEWING SNEAKERS REPRESENTS
ONE RUNG ON THEIR CLIMB UP THE COUNTRY'S SOCIAL AND ECONOMIC LADDER.

SOURCE: NEW YORK TIMES 9.8.96
ARTICLE: FOR INDONESIAN WORKERS AT A NIKE PLANT
SETH HYDAN

THIS QUOTE WAS TAKEN FROM AN ISSUE OF THE CAMPAIGN FOR LABOR RIGHTS NEWSLETTER.
REPRINTING OF THIS ARTICLE IS WELCOMED.

"MY FIRST THOUGHT, AS I HELD THOSE SHOES IN MY HANDS, WAS PRIDE AT HOW WELL-MADE THEY WE
AND THAT I HAD A PART IN MAKING SUCH FINE SHOES. AND THEN I PUT THEM ON MY FEET. THEY FELT
GOOD! FOUR YEARS I WORKED IN THE FACTORY. AND UNTIL NOW I NEVER HAD A PAIR OF NIKES ON M
FEET. WE COULD NOT EVEN THINK OF BUYING THEM AT THE WAGES WE RECEIVED. AND THEN I WAS VE
SAD WHEN I THOUGHT OF THE CONDITIONS UNDER WHICH THEY ARE MADE. AND ANGRY.' TO PURCHASE
PAIR OF THE SHOES SHE MAKES, A NIKE WORKER WOULD HAVE TO DEVOTE EVERY PENNY FROM TWO
THREE MONTHS OF HER PAYCHECKS.

SUBJECT: INTERVIEW
DATE: 14 JUL 97 09:34:33 0000
FROM: "CONNELLY ME" <EJ254 CITY.AC.UK>
TO: VISION@CYBERIACAFE.NET

In May 1997, Elizabeth Connelly, a student of footwear design from Cordwainers College, met with Christian Aid's Policy Officer, Bethan Brookes, at the agency's London office to discuss Christian Aid's view on the manufacture of sports shoes by the world's leading companies, in Third World factories. Christian Aid was set up in 1945 to help refugees after World War II, principally in Eastern Europe, and now works to alleviate poverty around the world. Christian Aid is the official overseas arm of forty British and Irish churches, but it isn't a missionary organisation. The agency works through the programmes of local churches and organisations with people of all religions and none, wherever the need is greatest and currently in sixty countries. Christian Aid helps communities to help themselves. The adage, "Give a man a fish and he'll eat for a day; teach a man to fish and you'll feed him for life", sums up their philosophy of strengthening the poor towards self-sufficiency. Since this interview there have been a number of significant developments in the on-going debate regarding sports shoe manufacture. Most notable were the worker strikes at Nike-producing factories in Indonesia, and former UN Ambassador Andrew Young's fifteen-day trip to Asian factories to evaluate Nike's overseas labour practises. He was sent by Nike. The absence of their mention in the following interview, therefore, has to do with timing.

WHEN DID CHRISTIAN AID BEGIN ITS SPORTS-SHOE PRODUCTION CAMPAIGN?
BB: In 1992 the People's Plan for the 21st Century - a meeting of non-governmental organisations (NGOs) - was held in Bangkok. One of the decisions taken was to study the manufacturing strategies of leading sports-shoe companies, and to look at their impact on workers across Asia.

Three of Christian Aid's partners in Asia took this process forward, carrying out research and campaigning for improvements in working practises and conditions. Christian Aid's report was an attempt to raise these issues in the UK. We commissioned further research in the summer of 1995 in the Philippines and Thailand, and the report came out in December 1995, which was just a part of campaigning work by Christian Aid to encourage better practices by transnational corporations operating in the Third World.

WHAT COMPANIES HAVE YOU LOOKED AT IN YOUR WORK ON SPORTS-SHOE PRODUCTION?
Nike, Reebok and Adidas. Almost without exception, the major companies now produce most of their sports-shoes in Third World countries - many in the same factories, with shoes coming off conveyor belts side-by-side with those of their main competitors.

WHY ARE POOR LABOUR PRACTISES CONTINUING, AND HOW DO THESE COMPANIES GET AWAY WITH IT, ESPECIALLY IN LIGHT OF INCREASED PUBLIC AWARENESS?
I'm not sure there was much public awareness around these issues, until they were raised relatively recently through campaigning efforts around the world. The responses from these companies have varied over the years. For example, Nike used to claim that as the workers were not directly employed by them, the company bore no responsibility for their working conditions or their wages. Now, however, there is a recognition that consumers and campaigners are not willing to accept such a shunning of responsibility.

Obviously, the bottom line is, it's profitable for these companies to produce in countries where labour costs are so low. Paying higher wages to workers will have a cost impact in terms of reduced profits. Organisations working on this issue, such as Christian Aid, are trying to motivate consumers to show that they are interested in buying goods with a clean conscience, so that, if for no other reason, it will make economic sense for companies to ensure a fair deal for workers producing their shoes. Christian Aid wants to be sure, however, that any such moves by these companies are truly effective, and not simply marketing or public relations stunts without substance.

IS IT DIFFICULT TO DISTINGUISH A SINCERE POLICY?
It can be. For example, Nike and Reebok both have codes of conduct, which govern their relationships with the factories and their workers, covering aspects of health and safety, wages and working hours. This is a good start, but, the problem is these companies monitor themselves - Nike and Reebok have sent their own people round to the factories to check up on things, to act as their own watchdogs. There has been no really independent monitoring of these codes. So, while on paper they can be congratulated for establishing and "enforcing" a code of conduct, in reality without independent monitoring, such a code means nothing. The goal is to hold them accountable, and ensure that their big moves are actually meaningful moves, not just words on paper.

HOW IS THAT GOING TO HAPPEN? ARE THERE INDEPENDENT MONITORS WORKING ON THIS NOW?
That's one of the big problems. Nike employ Ernst and Young, who are financial auditors, as so-called "independent monitors". Christian Aid questions whether this is good enough as Ernst and Young are not "social" auditors and don't have any expertise in that aspect of the industry. Actually, the whole issue of monitoring is very difficult. There has been much debate and everyone is pushing for independent monitoring, but the question of how it will work is a difficult one.

AND WHO IS GOING TO PAY FOR IT?
One thing is certain: the workers shouldn't pay for it - either financially or in other ways. It has been suggested that any monitoring body should be a coalition including NGOs, community-organisations and trade unions. But such a coalition may not be able to handle the work load or have the expertise to undertake such monitoring. With some trepidation, NGOs are recognising the likelihood of a whole new industry of social auditing companies springing up to monitor transnational companies. And this has already begun to happen. Some NGOs don't rest easy with this, because they see the risk that these social auditors may view the situation as an opportunity to make a bit of fast money, now they've spotted a hole in the market.

There is a coalition of groups in the UK, which includes Christian Aid, who are working on the issue of verification of company codes of conduct. It has suggested a number of base-line criteria that any verification system should adhere to. For example, there must be input from all sectors involved in the production process, including employers, employees, consumers and impacted communities. Any system adopted must be transparent, and its findings must be released to all those involved in every stage of production. And most importantly, the body which carries out the verification must be fully independent.

EC: WHERE DOES THE UNITED STATES GOVERNMENT STAND IN ALL OF THIS?
BB: Last summer there was uproar following allegations that clothes worn by Kathy Lee Gifford (US chat show hostess) were made in exploitative conditions. Following that, a number of companies, including Nike, came in for a lot of criticism on their working record in the Third World, and a new level of awareness was raised about the operations of American companies producing abroad.

Last autumn, President Clinton set up a task force called the Apparel Industry Partnership, to look at the issue of monitoring and regulating the operations of US companies producing overseas, especially in the Third World. Members of the task force include labour unions, religious leaders, human rights groups and companies. Ten manufacturers are involved including Nike and Reebok. In April of this year, a new code of conduct, the Workplace Code of Conduct, was introduced. It's a voluntary code but it's suggested that US companies sign up and use it in their relationships with suppliers. The code covers wages, trade unions, health and safety and outlaws child labour and forced labour

EC: WHAT'S IN IT FOR THE COMPANIES? IS IT IN THEIR INTEREST TO COMPLY WITH THE CODE?
BB: Nike and Reebok have both signed up to it. The fact is, it's seen as a very strong marketing tool and they've realised that they have to sign because people do care. Not addressing the issue could effect sales.The code is quite strong on independent monitoring. The companies are required to do their own monitoring, but in addition an external social audit must be done. The companies who sign will qualify for a new label which they can put on their products - the "No Sweat" label - which is supposed to guarantee that the product hasn't been made in a sweatshop.

A number of criticisms can be made against the Workplace Code of Conduct, but it's a step in the right direction. The main criticism of the code concerns wages. It suggests that companies should pay the national minimum wage, or the industry average, whichever is the highest. In many of the countries where these companies operate, however, the minimum wage is set purposefully low, in order to attract foreign businesses. A company can pay the legal minimum wage which is still below subsistence level wage. So, pressure groups are pushing for a "living wage", which means a commitment by the company to pay their employees a realistic, fair wage, not just the least they can get away with.

EC: IT'S LIKELY THAT THE OWNERS AND MANAGERS OF THESE FACTORIES SEE THE CURRENT SITUATION AS A GOLDEN OPPORTUNITY FOR THEIR COUNTRY'S ECONOMIES. WHO ARE WE TO TRY TO CONTROL THE DEVELOPMENT OF THEIR ECONOMIES?
BB: Many of the factories in the countries where Christian Aid have researched aren't actually owned by nationals of those countries, but are Taiwanese or Korean-owned. It is likely that money made by these factories goes straight out of the country, and is not helping it's development.

There is an element of truth in the argument put forward by some of the sports-shoe companies that they are doing good in developing countries by providing jobs. For example, conditions in the sports-shoe factories aren't the worst in these countries. If you went to a factory producing solely for the domestic market, conditions are likely to be considerably worse and less safe. The companies are providing valuable jobs. But, having said that, workers aren't being paid living wages, in many cases they still can't get by, and they're often working in hazardous environments.

Christian Aid thinks that, as leaders in their fields, companies like Nike and Reebok have a responsibility not to employ people in exploitative conditions, but rather, to assess what a living wage is. And that's one of the reasons that we haven't called for a boycott. What came through strongly from the research was this: Although the workers often didn't like what they were doing, working very long hours, with compulsory overtime, in inadequate working conditions, the workers were saying, "Yes, we do feel exploited, but if you boycott these goods, orders go down, and we lose our jobs".

Although calling for a boycott is seen as a better way of getting the companies' attention by many people, Christian Aid's responsibility is to work for what the workers want, and they've repeatedly stressed that they want better pay and better working conditions, but they don't want to lose their jobs.

EC: LOOKING AT IT FROM A DIFFERENT PERSPECTIVE. IF THE SHOE COMPANIES WERE MANUFACTURING IN ENGLAND, THEY'D PAY SOMETHING LIKE A BASIC WAGE OF £5 PER HOUR. YET IN COUNTRIES LIKE CHINA, THE PHILIPPINES, AND THAILAND, WORKERS ARE EARNING ONLY A FRACTION OF THAT - ABOUT 23P, 37P AND 46P, RESPECTIVELY. HOW CAN THE SAME SET OF SKILLS BE VALUED THAT MUCH MORE IN THE FIRST WORLD? IS THE THIRD WORLD WAGE COMPARABLE TO THE FIRST WORLD WAGE - DOES IT HAVE THE SAME PURCHASING POWER? WHAT, BEYOND ECONOMICS, IS OPERATING HERE? COLONIALISM, RACIAL AND SEXUAL DISCRIMINATION APPEAR TO BE FIGURING IN THE SITUATION, AS THE FACTORY WORKERS IN THE THIRD WORLD ARE PRIMARILY NON-CAUCASIAN, YOUNG WOMEN. A FEW MONTHS BACK THE BBC AIRED A DOCUMENTARY SERIES, "BRANDED", EXAMINING THE GLOBAL SUCCESS OF THREE VERY POWERFUL BRANDS: NIKE, HEINZ AND LEVI'S. AND THERE WAS A STATEMENT FROM PHIL KNIGHT, NIKE'S FOUNDER, WHICH WAS BOTH FASCINATING AND EXTREMELY TELLING: "BUSINESS IS WAR WITHOUT BULLETS".
BB: Nike tend to be very aggressive.

EC: PERHAPS SOME OF THAT AGGRESSION HAS TO DO WITH THE FACT THAT PHIL KNIGHT WAS A SECOND-PLACED RUNNER.

BB: He certainly seems to have an uncontainable urge to be first in everything. That came over forcibly in their adverts at the time of the Atlanta Olympics, suggesting that winning is everything and to come second is nothing... you may as well not even take part. Nike got into trouble with the International Olympic Committee for those adverts. The IOC accused them of cutting starkly across the ideal of the Olympic Spirit.

EC: HOW DOES CHRISTIAN AID RESPOND TO PEOPLE WHO SAY, "HEY, THAT'S THE GREAT AMERICAN WAY. THAT'S CAPITALISM"?

BB: We're never going to completely change the system. Christian Aid does hope, though, to bring some sort of ethical bearing to it, and believes that a concern for social and environmental issues needs to be integrated into the system. It shouldn't be an excuse for exploitation. From a capitalist point of view, manufacturing sports-shoes ethically can be a way of winning support and custom. That's why we're trying to motivate people to make their voices heard.

EC: DOES CHRISTIAN AID THINK THAT THE POWER IS IN THE CONSUMER'S HANDS AND THAT IT'S A MATTER OF EDUCATING CONSUMERS TO DISTINGUISH BETWEEN ETHICAL AND UNETHICAL MANUFACTURERS?

BB: Consumers should be made aware that the most important thing for a company is how many people are buying their trainers. If consumers make the companies aware that a substantial proportion of the people who buy their trainers are actually concerned about their shoes being made in exploitative conditions, that has a big impact on the company. It's not the only way of putting pressure on, but certainly it's a very important and powerful way.

EC: WHAT'S THE CURRENT LEVEL OF AWARENESS AMONG CONSUMERS?

BB: I'm sure it's gone up. The fact there's been an article saying that Nike's sales have gone down, and that some people are now going into shops and saying that they won't buy Nike on principle, is an indication.

EC: WITHOUT ADVOCATING A BOYCOTT, WHAT DOES CHRISTIAN AID RECOMMEND TO CONCERNED CONSUMERS?

BB: Writing to companies saying, "We've heard about these issues. Is it true?" Rather than saying, "I'm not going to buy the product", saying, "I'm going to be buying trainers, and I will base my decision on which of the companies can convince me that they are producing the most ethical trainers". This is a more positive way of working and gives the companies an incentive to work in the right direction, and not get aggressive about it.

EC: WHAT OTHER ACTIONS DOES CHRISTIAN AID ADVOCATE?

BB: As well as consumers writing letters, shareholders can raise issues. It's happened with Nike. Issues were raised by the Methodist Church at the last annual general meeting. It was brushed over by Phil Knight, I believe, fairly quickly, but it raised the issue in front of other shareholders and the media.

Also, lobbying at high levels by organisations like Christian Aid is really important. So is constantly monitoring what the companies are up to. One thing that we've done with Reebok is that when an issue comes up, or when we've heard about a situation concerning manufacturing in Thailand, for example, we've written to Reebok and asked to know what's happening. The companies need to be made aware that they're being watched.

EC: I'VE HEARD THAT THERE HAVE BEEN DEMONSTRATIONS IN THE STATES. DO YOU KNOW HOW SUCESSFUL THEY'VE BEEN?

BB: When a new Niketown shop opens there have been protest demonstrations outside. These aren't necessarily going to change the company's attitudes, but they do raise public awareness of the issues. It will get in the papers. People will see the protest on their way to work.

EC: HOW ARE THE CEOS AT MAJOR SPORTS-SHOE COMPANIES RESPONDING?

BB: Recent response from Phil Knight to criticism about Nike has been incomprehension on his part as to why Nike is being singled out.

EC: IT'S OBVIOUS WHY. THEY'RE THE MARKET LEADER IN TERMS OF IMAGE POWER AND BRAND POWER.

BB: Actually, Christian Aid has tried not to target just one company. But most campaigns have focused on Nike, and they don't think it's fair. Reebok tend to be more approachable and give the impression that they're taking the issues more seriously and are open to criticism. Perhaps that's easier to do if you're not in the spotlight as much as Nike.

EC: WHAT'S TYPICAL DAILY LIFE LIKE FOR A MAN OR WOMAN, BOY OR GIRL, WORKING IN A SPORTS-SHOE FACTORY IN THAILAND OR INDONESIA?

BB: Firstly, it's mainly women and most of them were working excessively long hours. Often twelve- to fourteen-hour days.

EC: HOW DOES CHRISTIAN AID DEFINE CHILDREN?

BB: The definition may differ from national law to law and international convention, but we define a child as under fourteen. There have been some confused messages in press articles and as a result, many people are under the impression that Nike and Reebok are employing children in the production of trainers. As far as Christian Aid is aware, this has never been the case. The production of trainers takes place in factories and it's not the sort of industry in which we'd expect to find children. Children are most commonly found in home-working situations, for example, employed stitching footballs.

EC: HOW MANY BREAKS DO WOMEN WORKING IN FACTORIES HAVE THROUGHOUT THE DAY?

BB: They're given very little time off. Recent press reports from Vietnam claim instances of workers not being allowed to leave their posts, to go to the toilet or drink water, more than once or twice a day. There's also the very important issue of overtime. Christian Aid found that in almost every case, workers are required to do overtime, especially in busy periods. It's compulsory. Thousands of workers are exceeding national laws on working hours. There have been cases of people being taken off the production line, to clean toilets or perform other menial tasks, if they protest. And as workers are paid a piece-rate for their work, this means lost earnings. Some of the worst conditions in terms of harassment and low wages have been in Vietnam. In the eighteen months in which Nike's been in Vietnam, there has allegedly been one factory manager convicted for abusing workers while another is under indictment, and another has left the country following a police investigation on sexual abuse.

EC: DO THE WORKERS HAVE ANY FREE TIME?
BB: How much free time can you realistically have when you are regularly working a fourteen-hour day. six days a week? In many of these factories. in China for example. workers come from rural areas to work in the factories and they're often housed in dormitories. In Chinese factories visited by Christian Aid researchers, twelve workers share one room, with no storage space for their personal belongings.

EC: CAN THE WORKERS READ?
BB: I would imagine many of the women aren't literate - especially if they have come from remote rural areas. One of the issues regarding codes of conduct is whether or not workers are aware that the codes exist. A recent study showed that the majority of workers in Nike-producing factories knew nothing of the code. Often companies say. "They do know. It's up on the wall". But many of the workers can't read.

EC: How many years do people stay to work in these situations?
BB: A few years.

EC: BECAUSE THEY'RE BURNED OUT SO QUICKLY?
BB: Perhaps. But also because working in the factories is seen as a way for workers, especially women. to move away from rural areas where there are very few opportunities. They'll often work from their late teens to their mid-twenties, four or five. six or seven years.

EC: AND PROBABLY WITH NO EDUCATIONAL OPPORTUNITIES.
BB: ...especially for girls. It can't be denied that many of the workers come to the factories as a way out of a situation with few opportunities. Others see it as a way of earning money for a few years. and will then return to their villages.

EC: SO IT'S SEEN AS A TEMPORARY SITUATION BY MANY OF THE WORKERS, WHICH MUST MAKE THE CONDITIONS EASIER TO ENDURE.
BB: Yes, if you know it's not forever. If people are keen to earn as much as they can in a certain amount of time. or are supporting families back home. it's good to have the opportunity to do overtime. But not everyone wants to stay at work for fourteen or sixteen hours a day.

The problem is that overtime is compulsory. and if workers refuse to do it they're likely to be punished. or even loose their jobs. And. if they are doing overtime. they should be paid a higher rate.

EC: AND GIVE THEM DAYS OFF, AS WELL.
BB: In many of the countries in which companies such as Nike and Reebok produce. a six-day week is fairly standard. Christian Aid's model code of conduct stipulates that all workers should have at least twenty-four consecutive hours of rest a week. and at least three weeks of paid holiday a year.

EC: TO ME, IT SEEMS THAT THIS WAY OF DOING BUSINESS IS ANOTHER FORM OF COLONIALISM.
BB: Many of the transnational corporations who are producing in the Third World have annual incomes higher than the GDPs (gross domestic product) of some countries. The power which they wield is incredible. and their operations certainly can be compared to a new form of colonialism. What mustn't be lost. though. is the fact that the jobs they provide are valuable to the countries in which they produce. They provide money and in some cases. new skills.

Christian Aid's concern is that these jobs are not exploitative. that workers should be given a fairer deal. As well as companies having a responsibility in these situations. the national governments do. or should. as well. It's a difficult situation. Obviously. countries with under-developed economies want to encourage foreign investment. So they've created free-trade zones, where in many cases. labour laws are weaker and companies can more or less do what they want.

EC: THAT'S CHINA'S SITUATION, ISN'T IT?
BB: Yes. And it happens in other places.

EC: HAS CHRISTIAN AID EVER SPOKEN WITH PHIL KNIGHT ABOUT ANY OF THESE ISSUES?
BB: No.

EC: HERE'S ANOTHER INTERESTING QUOTE FROM PHIL KNIGHT IN "BRANDED": " ...ESSENTIALLY THERE ARE MARKETS THAT DICTATE WHAT GETS PAID AND WHAT DOESN'T GET PAID. I MEAN...IF I WERE TO...AVERAGE MICHAEL JORDAN'S SALARY WITH A SHOEMAKER IN INDONESIA, MICHAEL JORDAN WOULDN'T LIKE THAT TOO GOOD, AND WE WOULDN'T HAVE MICHAEL JORDAN AS AN ENDORSEMENT. IN THE SAME TOKEN, A SHOEMAKER IN INDONESIA IS PAID 50% MORE AT ENTRY-LEVEL THAN WHAT HE GETS PAID AT MINIMUM WAGE IN OTHER INDUSTRIES IN INDONESIA, SO WHAT WE TRY TO BE IS GOOD CITIZENS IN THE COUNTRY THAT WE'RE WORKING IN".

IF ANYONE, PHIL KNIGHT HAS THE POWER TO SEE THAT FACTORY WORKERS ARE PAID A LIVEABLE WAGE IN ADEQUATE WORKING CONDITIONS! HE COULD PAY MICHAEL JORDAN $18 MILLION RATHER THAN THE $20 MILLION HE CURRENTLY GETS, AND CUT THE ADVERTISING BUDGET. THERE ARE PLENTY OF WAYS TO SOLVE THE PROBLEM. HAS CHRISTIAN AID EVER SPOKEN WITH MICHAEL JORDAN OR ANDRE AGASSI OR ANY CELEBRITY ATHLETE ENDORSERS ABOUT THESE ISSUES?

BB: No. but American campaigners may have. Back to Phil Knight's quote from "Branded" for a minute... I would like to query Phil Knight's claim that a trainee shoemaker in Indonesia is paid 50% more than the minimum wage. In April. 10,000 Indonesian workers allegedly went on strike because the Nike-producing factory refused to pay the 20-cent per day increase in the national minimum wage. The factory owners said it would cause them financial hardship. I'd also like to challenge another comment. "We try to be good citizens in the country we're working in", which reminds me of a line in Nike's code of conduct.

The code says: "We seek always to be a leader in our quest to enhance people's lives through sports and fitness. That means at every opportunity - whether in the design. manufacturing or marketing of products: in the environment. in the areas of human rights and equal opportunity. or in our relationships with the communities in which we do business - we seek to do not only what is required. but wherever possible. what is expected of a leader."

That's exactly what Christian Aid is asking Nike to do. To be a leader in their field in giving a fair deal to the workers who make their shoes.

© M. ELIZABETH CONNELLY 1997

PLACE
DESIRED
SHOE
HERE

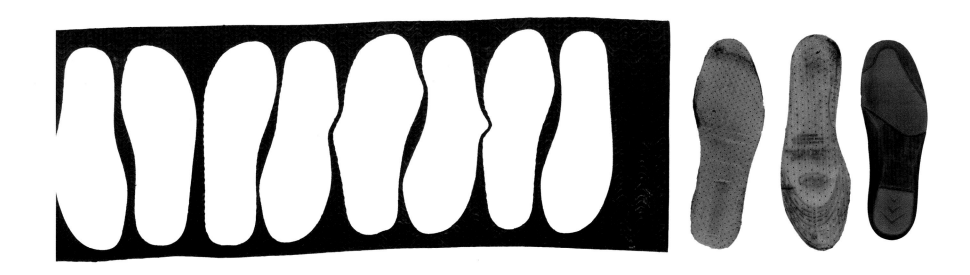

dogs. Dogs shit
on trainers

Worship the lords
bought breakfast
we shall pray

the choice
I want
that one
buy now

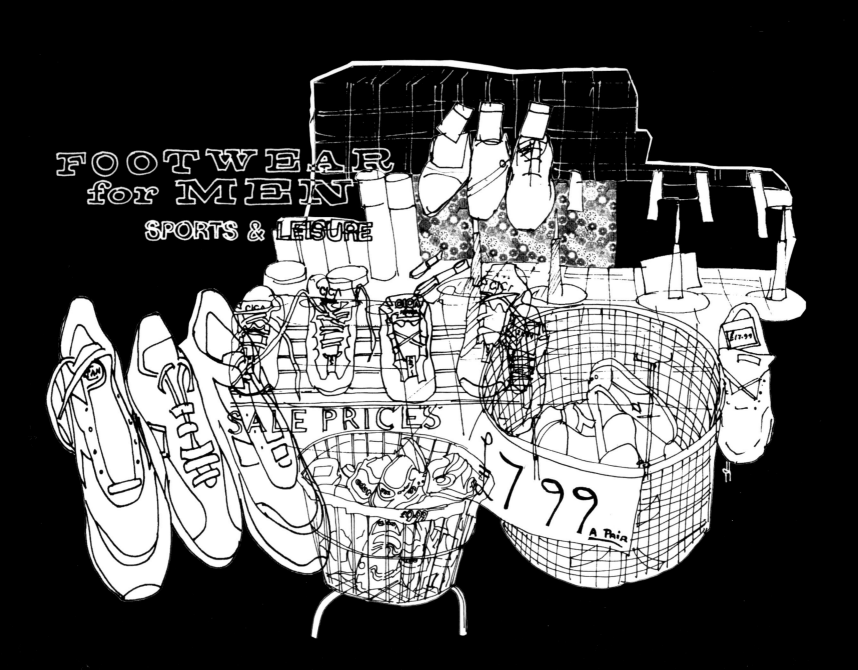

SACRED SNEAKERS BY ADAM CHODZKO

ILLUSTRATED AND HAND-WRITTEN BOOK WAS SENT TO ME BY CHAN SINH MAY THE SISTER OF CHAN SINH CHEUNG, A WORKER IN A CHINESE TRAINER FACTORY.* HE HAD BEEN WORKING ON THE PRODUCTION LINE AS PART OF A TEAM OF FOUR WHO WOULD CHECK THE TREADS OF THE SOULS ON THE TRAINERS BEFORE THEY WERE STUCK ONTO THE UPPERS. DEFORMED TREADS WERE REMOVED FROM THE CONVEYOR BELT AND PARTICULARLY MUTANT VARIATIONS WERE PINNED UP ON THE WALL OF THE STAFF CANTEEN AS A JOKE. THE DEFECTS IN THE COMPOSITION OF THE TREAD HAD BECOME INCREASINGLY PREVALENT BECAUSE THE FACTORY, IN AN INDUSTRIAL ESTATE JUST OUTSIDE LAOYANG, STILL USED AN OUTMODED MOULDING PROCESS WHICH WAS BEING SUPERCEDED BY OTHER PLANTS IN THE REGION WHICH HAD ADOPTED A SILICON INJECTION TECHNIQUE.

Chan Sinh Cheung and the rest of the factory conveyor-belt staff were allowed to keep some of the rejected trainers at a discount; being unable to afford the perfect finished products. But it made them walk badly. So, most soon went back to their blue flip-flops and cheap canvas sneakers. Cheung for some reason continued to wear the distorted factory pairs. He seemed to like the way that he had to adapt to their strangeness.

Furthermore Cheung had begun to believe that "defective" was the wrong way to think about these unwanted trainer souls. They were beautiful by virtue of the fact that, comparatively, there were so few of them. It was as though the deformed had dared to stray from the notion of perfection and the regularity of the mass produced. Fascinated by the uniqueness and complexity of the flaws he would stare at these strange formations and think of his grandmother gazing at the lines on the palm of a hand or the patterns made by tea leaves at the bottom of a cup. He had even seen her contemplating the light patterns dappling the ceiling, reflected from a puddle in the yard outside. She was able to read these traces as glimpses into the future and was respected locally as a remarkably accurate (although often enigmatic) fortune teller. This was a talent that Cheung seems to have inherited.

By creating a series of nodules and indentations in random combination on the rubber souls there was the capacity for thousands of variations. Cheung began to develop a manual over the next few years which painstakingly catalogued all of these possible treads and attributed to them meanings which revealed both the strengths and weaknesses of the wearer. (for example: "I am quick to understand the world, but my troubles will arise from being too suspicious of it".) Each pair of trainers would carry a different sacred meaning. He believed that the wearer would always coincidentally choose the trainers that carried meaning that would be relevant to them. The sneakers would reveal the truth! The manual would be published very cheaply in every language and would be given away free with every pair of trainers. That way, the wearer could contemplate

the meaning of their own souls if walking alone. On meeting another person both parties could show their treads, consult their manuals and know more about themselves and each other than a verbal greeting could ever achieve. If a group of people were arguing and a fight was brewing then all they had to do was to find out what the combination of all their treads meant in order to find a solution to their conflict.

Sport would develop a sacred aspect if the meaning of the winning and losing sneakers was announced publicly so that the audience could check the personal relevance of the result with their own shoes.

When the ground was wet the impressions from the treads of many pairs of trainers would be left. This would supply enough texts to provide meaning for many more difficult problems. A history of recent paths inscribed into the ground could construct whole parables. Cheung imagined that in times of trouble crowds of people would head towards parks after rainfall in their trainers. All Cheung had to do was to convince his boss that all this would be possible with a few minor alterations to the existing machinery at the factory, and the publication of his manual.

He spent some months trying to gain permission to speak to his boss. The secretary eventually relented and offered him a ten minute meeting. According to his sister, Cheung looked forward to this encounter with consummate enthusiasm. Nothing would deter him from believing that his boss would realise the importance of the idea. He was absolutely confident, and besides, the flawed sneakers that Cheung wore carried a meaning that meant that everything would work out.

However on the day of the meeting Cheung disappeared and has not been seen since, despite the extensive efforts of his sister. May, The boss claims that the meeting never took place and the manual was found hidden in some bushes near to the factory. But, May discovered that one of the pages from the book had been torn out and is sure (but cannot prove) that this page was the one that gave meaning to Cheung's own treads.

*all names have been altered to protect the anonymity of those involved.

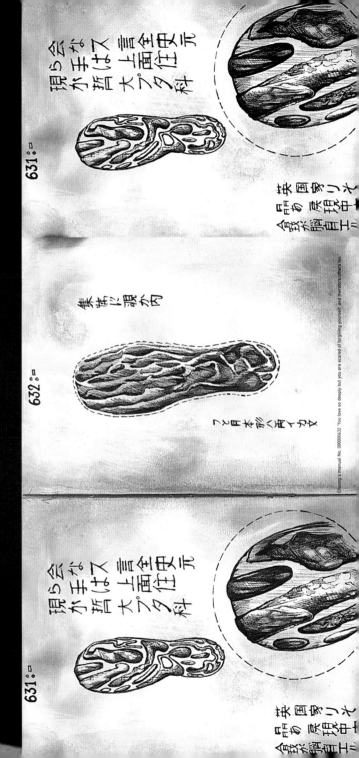